The Fairytale Of America's Butterfly

By:

Andre L. Simmons

I got a fairytale to tell…

Thank you. I Love You.

Dedication

I dedicate this book to the prince; my son Jamari Ondrej Simmons. I dedicate this book to the princess; my daughter J'Adora Krismas Simmons. I dedicate this book to the broken 16-year-old girl, don't worry your pieces will mend again. I dedicate this book to the lost 17-year-old boy that's still searching, don't you dare give up, and you'll find your way. I dedicate this book to the single parent, I'm proud of you. I dedicate this book to the strong independent woman, you're a queen. I dedicate this book to the man that lead and provides for his family, I salute you. Above all I dedicate this book to the society that we are all a part of. Though class may divide us, and religion may separate us, equality is the key, and we are one.

Prologue

The caterpillar stays in its cocoon imprisoned without food for weeks. Sometimes the caterpillar remains in the cocoon for a month. Inside the cocoon, its body is broken and completely reshaped. Maintaining just a little of its original form. Caterpillars go through many stages of transformations: *egg, larva, pupa, and adult.* The wings start to emerge, and when it finally breaks the walls of its prison, a beautiful butterfly arises. That ugly insect will never crawl again because now it has wings, and it's going to fly. Jesus resembles the shape of a butterfly, after going through the pain on the cross.

There is a caterpillar in each one of us. With each day of our lives we're faced with many challenges and temptations. Each day that God blesses me to see, I continue to evolve as a stronger and wiser man. Great men throughout history were like butterflies. They transmitted their wisdom, from person to person, helping them blossom. I know who I am today and that's the greatest feeling of all. Once upon a time I was an imprisoned caterpillar, and today I am a shackle free butterfly flying high.

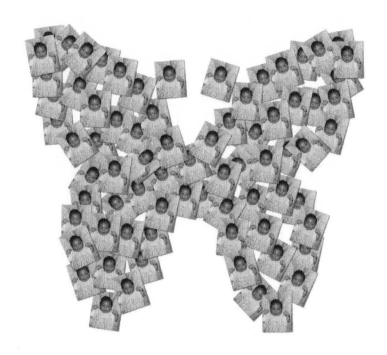

Larva: Andre. *November 29th, 1983.*

1: Larva

My 29-year-old mother drove herself to Columbia Hospital for Women in Washington D.C. on November 29th, 1983. My father was in Georgia at the time due to military duty. I came onto the scene after my mother had a caesarean section. I was 8lbs and 10oz. Silence is what the ears of everyone heard in the delivery room. I didn't cry as of result of swallowing some of the afterbirth. Immediately, I was taken into the intensive care unit. I remained there for the next 7 days. My mother and I didn't leave the hospital until 10 days later.

Even though my mother had a government job, she struggled for a year to make ends meet. She was a single parent, and the cost of living was high. So, at age 30 she decided to leave the life she wanted to live and moved back home to North Carolina. When we arrived, she did not receive the warmest welcome from her mother. She joined five out of seven of her siblings and their children: Iris and son Corey, Celestine and daughter Kanika, Allan, Vonice, and Janelle all in one home.

My mother started working in Sunny Point, North Carolina and soon after, she purchased her very own home in 1986. It was a 3-bedroom Mobile Home. My mother's master bedroom was on one end, my room was in the middle which I rarely slept in, and aunt Janelle's room was next to mine.

Shortly after moving into our new home, aunt Janelle gave birth to Kendrell on August 30th, 1987. The next year she gave birth to Gregory on August 16th, 1988. This was the beginning of *"The Simmons 5"* and our journey together. I also had a Golden Retriever named Jack. I remember the one time he pooped in the corner. Jack didn't live long; he was hit by a car. One day my mother received a call from the Department of State located in Washington, D.C. for a job. She didn't want to move. She had just purchased her very first home. She later had a change of heart after having a conversation with an older co-worker by the name of Fannie Allen. "That house is material Joyce. God has something better in store for you." She confirmed. Those words encouraged my mother to move back to Washington D.C. the summer of 1990. Aunt Janelle, Kendrell, and Gregory later moved in with us the winter of 1990. Then we moved to 11318 Kettering Lane, Upper Marlboro Maryland. I don't recall ever having much because when we moved there, the 5 of us slept in the master bedroom on the floor. It didn't matter because a house isn't a home without a loving family, and that's exactly what we had. Although we were living in Maryland, I never missed spending a summer in North Carolina.

"I remember his eyes. They are just like mine. Every time I look in the mirror, I see him. I try not to look at myself too much." - Ida Lokas

2: P.S. Daddy I Love You *(Part One)*

Every summer when I saw Sandra Massey, my mother's first cousin and my father's brother's wife, she would always ask me the same Question.

"You talk to ya daddy?" She'd say.

That repetitive question became extremely annoying after a while. However, she could cook some good food. She would always cook for Kendrell, Gregory, and I. If it weren't for her cooking, I probably would have cursed her nosey ass out; and gotten an ass beating by my grandmother, even still it would've been worth it. I often wondered if she had a thing for my father. I didn't know what was so special about him. Family members made him out to be some sort of celebrity. I didn't know him well enough to acknowledge him as such, because he wasn't a big part of my life. I remember my father bought me a brown 15-speed bike. He personally dropped it off to me. I was so happy. I thought it was the most beautiful bike I had ever seen. He didn't stay long and that was the only time I saw him that summer of 1992. He lived in Wilmington, North Carolina which was only forty-five minutes from my grandmother's home.

3: **Team Player** *(Part One)*

There were enough male relatives in my family to make a football team. Every so often we would all get together and play in a family member's vast yard. We usually played football or kickball. I hated playing football. I could never throw the ball as well as the rest of the boys. I was teased relentlessly because of it. Instead of getting upset, I would laugh right along with them.

My grandmother kept a lot of glass jars around her home. She would use them to put vegetables and fruits in. I had another use for them. I would take the jars and use them to catch different things that crawled or hopped. I caught three different species of ants, crickets, frogs, grasshoppers, and spiders. I hated lizards. I was terrified of them. There were always different types of snakes crawling around, but I don't recollect anyone ever being bitten.

When I was a kid, I was fearless. Or at least I thought I was. My cousin Delvin, who I would also see every summer lived in Bolivia, North Carolina. She lived fifteen minutes away from my grandmother's home. We were very close in age. Exactly one year and twenty-eight days apart. I loved Delvin, and she loved me. There were two things that highlighted my visits to aunt Dollie's *(Delvin's mom home)*. I was going to eat a lot and I would get the chance to play with Delvin's doll babies. I enjoyed styling their long luscious locks and I was fascinated with their different wardrobes.

"Faggot" was a name I was often called by my male cousins. The girls would always talk about how big my butt

was. They would also talk about the way I switched when I walked. I had rhinoceros' skin. Words back then were just that, words.

It was the summer of 1993, and it started off with different relatives and their friends touching my butt here and there. I would always say "No!" or "Stop!" Yet on the inside something was really saying "Yes." and "Please don't stop." There was a time while playing football, I was tackled, and someone pulled my pants down. When I got up my penis was erect, and my bare ass was showing. Everyone started to laugh. I pulled my pants up and ran back to my grandmother's home.

One night I asked my grandmother if I could spend the night at Player 1's house. She said yes, but only if it was ok with his mother. She also said to make sure I returned the first thing in the morning. I told her I would, left the home, and headed up the road to stay for the night. Kendrell, Gregory, and I were not permitted to go up the road. It was a no-zone for us kids *(aka The Maryland Crew)* because we weren't from there. I always got a little pissed because I was older than they were. I felt I should at least have a little more privilege. When I got to his house, we spoke, and we wound up going to his room. As we were lying on the bed, I felt him reach over and pull my pants down. I already knew what was about to happen. I backed up on him, and his penis was already hard. He carefully slid his penis between my butt cheeks. Every time someone would walk past his door, he would take it out. After he was finished, we fell asleep. That following morning, I went back to my grandmother's. It was my last time ever entering that house.

We were all playing hide and seek one day, and the rule was that no one could hide in my grandmother's home. While the seeker was counting, everyone scattered off to hide. I went into my grandmother's house to use the bathroom. Player 2 decided to follow me inside.

"Where are you going?" He asked.

"I'm going to use the bathroom. Where are you going? Why are you following me?" I quickly asked him.

"Come on, you know. Let's do it." He said with a sly grin.

"Where? There are too many people around." I said nervously.

Before I went into the bathroom, he pushed the middle room door open and said we could do it in there. I was hesitant because I was afraid that someone could walk in catching us at any moment.

"What about the closet?" He asked noticing my hesitation.

"Alright." I agreed.

He walked in the room as I went into the bathroom. Once I was finished, I walked into the bedroom. There he was sitting in the closet with his shorts pulled down to his ankles and his penis standing at attention. I sat down on top of him.

"Is it in?" I asked.

"No. Stand up." He said.

I stood up and then he told me to come down on it slow. I felt the pressure of his head trying to go inside, but it never made it all the way in. I just sat there on his dick.

"Move on it." He said.

I started to move in a circular motion. He began making noises.

"Hush before someone hears us." I whispered.

We did it for a couple of minutes before we decided to go back outside to join everyone else.

Not only was Player 3 nice to me, but he was also very attractive. I didn't see him that often during the summer because he would be off visiting other family members. One hot summer day I was outside playing with my cousins and I saw him walking. His face lit up when he saw me. He didn't know I was down for the summer and he was very excited to see me. When we hung out, he'd always touch my butt and laugh when no one was looking. One day while his mother was working, he invited me to come to his house to play video games. He insisted that I come alone. I accepted his invitation. When I got there, I knocked on the door; however, no one answered. I knocked again and still no answer. I opened the door and called his name.

"Andre, come back here!" He shouted.

I walked to the back and there he was lying on the bed in the nude. I just stopped at the door in shock.

"I thought we were going to play video games." I said dumbfounded.

"We will later. Come touch it." He demanded.

I walked towards him and touched his dick. I watched it grow right before for my eyes.

"Come here Andre." He whispered.

I took off my clothes and got into bed with him. I was lying flat on my back. He leaned over and kissed me on my cheek.

"Turn over." He whispered.

I turned over and I could tell he was having difficulties sticking it inside of me, because he instantly became soft again. He then told me to get on all fours and bend over.

"You have an ass like a woman Andre." He said admiring my body.

Again, he tried to go inside. Once he got the tip in, he began moving in a back and forth motion. But he was never quite all the way inside of me. I guess once he was tired of dry humping me, he got up and put his clothes back on. I looked at him and did the same.

"Are we about to play video games now?" I asked breaking the silence.

"No. Come over tomorrow so we can play video games." He suggested.

Player 4 was the tallest and the darkest of them all. He was also the least attractive. I was stunned when I found out that his dick didn't measure up with his height. He was very rough with me. It would hurt; however, we continued to do it a few times over the summer.

It felt so weird doing things with Player 5 because we were like brothers. I disliked doing things with him, however he would often do things with Player 6. Player 6 was the biggest bully that I have ever encountered. He teased me unremittingly and for some odd reason I never hated him for it. Another time while I was in my grandmother's yard, I noticed him walking towards me. As I turned around, he grabbed me by my waist and started air humping me from behind. I was trying to remove his hands from my waist, but he wouldn't let go.

"Let me go!" I shouted.

"Shut up faggot." He said and pushed me to the ground and walked away.

One-night Player 5 stayed at my grandmother's and he mentioned to me that Player 6 wanted to have sex with me.

"Player 6 said he's going to rape you." He revealed.

I never believed that for one second. Nothing ever happened between us.

4: **Trinidad & Tobago** *(Island Life)*

August 27th, 1994

Aunt Janelle, Kendrell, Gregory, and 27-day-old Audrekia dropped my mother and I off at Regan National Airport in Washington D.C. I wasn't sad to leave my baby brothers behind, because I knew I would see them again real soon. The fact that I was moving to another part of the world never crossed my mind. I was just ecstatic to get on an airplane. I was even more excited to have a window seat. I saw the *(Fasten Seatbelt)* light flash.

"Mom, can I raise this?" I asked pointing to the shade.

"Yeah, sure." She said.

The sight was nothing like I had seen before. There were so many lights as far as my eyes could see. It reminded me of Christmas.

"Mom, is this our new home?" I asked my eyes gleaming.

"Yes, that's Trinidad and we're about to land." She answered.

After we landed, the seatbelt light went off. We gathered our belongings and exited the plane. There was a long line of people.

"Welcome to Trinidad Mr. and Miss Simmons." A lady greeted us, leading us to the short line. "I think I'm going to like it here." I said to myself. When we got our luggage and walked outside the airport, I noticed that there was something off and different about the car we were getting into. Then I realized that the steering wheel was on the opposite side, unlike the ones in America.

"Mom, do you see that?" I asked her giggling.

"I've never seen that before." My mother said.

I noticed that they also drove on the opposite side of the road. They should have called this place *"The Opposite Island."* We pulled up to this tall building known as Regent Towers. We walked into the building and entered our new home. At that moment I began to really miss Maryland. I suddenly realized that this was my new life, and that I had to make the best of it.

There was food in the refrigerator when we got there. We had barbeque chicken and potato salad. It was a little spicy, but so good. I slept in my mother's room for the night. When I awoke the next morning, I looked outside the window. My eyes followed the road up until I spotted the ocean. The water was a different color than what I was used to seeing. I couldn't wait to go outside.

"Today they are taking us sight-seeing." My mother said to me when she noticed I was up.

I was thrilled. I took a shower and quickly got dressed.

When we hit the road, things didn't look as different as I thought they did, until we turned down a road and the scenery began to change. The next thing I knew we were driving up a mountain. I'd never been on a mountain before. I felt like my life was in danger. I was that afraid because I thought we may fall off.

"Where are we going?" I blurted out nervously.

Everyone laughed.

"We are going to Maracas Beach. This is the way to get there." The lady who picked us up from the airport explained.

"Is this the only way to get there?" I asked looking around terrified.

I was so over that sightseeing trip. The roads seemed to shrink; and the fact that we were on a one lane highway, driving up a mountain to what seemed like our deaths, made me uncomfortable. When we finally arrived, the scenery was unlike anything I'd ever seen before. The water was a dark blue, depending on the sunlight. When the sun hit it, it appeared to be a little lighter. The water was different than what I was accustomed to seeing on the beaches like Chesapeake, Holden, and Myrtle. The trees were different as well; some had fruits on them.

"What is those round light green melons?" I asked.

"That's a coconut tree." Mrs. McGaffie enlightened me.

"I thought all coconuts were brown and a lot smaller." I said confused.

The grocery stores in the United States sell brown coconuts. I saw a few guys with truckloads of coconuts on the side of the road selling them. My mother wanted to try one, so a guy took a machete and started hacking away at the coconut until a liquid started to gush out. He made a hole so that we could drink the water. My mother tasted it.

"It's really good. Here Andre you try it." She said handing it to me.

I gave her a look hoping she would understand that it meant no thank you. However, she insisted that I try it, so I finally took the coconut. It tasted like flavored water; however, it reminded me of orange juice with pulp. I made a face and handed the coconut back to her. After my mother finished drinking her coconut water, she handed the coconut back to the guy. Once again, he started hacking at the coconut until he cut it in half. He handed the coconut back to my mother along with a chip.

"What's that?" My mother asked giggling.

"It's the coconut jelly." The man responded in his Trinidadian accent.

The correct way to savage a coconut is to drink it dry and then eat the jelly on the inside of the walls. My mother thought it was ok. I didn't care for the slimy jelly not one bit. The next thing we tried was Bake And Shark. It's fried shark and it's served in homemade sweet bread. It was so delicious.

After our eventful Sunday, I had to go to bed early that night because I had my first day of school the following day. That was the first time that I had ever worn uniforms. I wore a white short sleeved shirt and navy-blue shorts. I didn't know what to expect. We pulled up to a huge house and the sign read The International School of Port-of-Spain.

"That's it? That's my school?" I asked looking disappointed.

I wasn't expecting my school to look like someone's house.

"Yes, that's it." My mother said.

"They can't be serious." I thought to myself after walking into my classroom. My first day as a 5th grader, and I only had 7 people in my class. The 5th and 6th graders were combined. Once I got settled in, we were asked to introduce ourselves. Everyone was from places that I'd never heard of, and their father's jobs were what brought them to the Island. I was the only odd one from the U.S. and my mother's job was what brought me to the Island.

"I am Andre LeDale Simmons. I was born in Washington D.C. and I lived in North Carolina and Maryland. My mother is Joyce Simmons and she is the first black secretary ever to work at the U.S. Embassy as the Ambassador's Secretary." I said proudly and didn't stutter a single word.

There was one other black student in my class besides me. She was a girl from Africa and she had an older brother. There were only three blacks in the entire school, and I was the only black American.

The International School of Port-of-Spain

The International School of Port-of-Spain officially opened September 1994. At this time the school realized its dream of parents and corporate citizens that had been articulated since 1990.

The International School is a private corporation registered in Trinidad, and its corporate shareholders are the Embassy of the United States of America, EOG Resources Trinidad Limited, British Petroleum Trinidad and Tobago and British Gas Trinidad and Tobago Limited. It is also registered with the Ministry of Education in Trinidad & Tobago and represents a special effort on behalf of parents and businesses to provide a college preparatory, holistic education for students aged 4 - 18. Mr. and Mrs. Thomas Tunny were the founding teachers and they started out at 18 Victoria Avenue with 50 students. During the past 15 years, the school has provided educational services for hundreds of students from 40 different nations around the world.

The teaching faculty, supported by a strong spirit of parent activism, led the way in promoting and establishing quality educational programs. By 1996, the school completed an accreditation process with the Southern Association of Colleges and Schools in the United States. With this recognition, The International School of Port-of-Spain joined a unique group of schools located around the globe that served the growing needs of students from the local community and expatriate families of the business and diplomatic community. The student population began to expand by 50% every six months and was soon located at three separate sites.

5: Raggedy-Ann Doll

Sista Sista

Being the only child had its perks. I got any and everything I wanted, but nothing could substitute a sibling. I didn't have Kendrell and Gregory with me, and I became extremely lonely. I never thought I would or could feel that way. There was a man named Winston Garcia and he was Ambassador Donnelly's personal driver. He had several daughters and they all lived with their mothers, except Lyndyann. Her mother didn't want to keep her, so he was left raising her alone. Due to his schedule he was unable to care for his daughter the way she needed to be cared for. Winston asked my mother if she could watch her. My mother agreed, and she came to stay with us for a while. The first time I saw her, my thoughts weren't positive at all. She looked raggedy and she had an odor. I didn't want her to be my sister. Sadly, Winston died in a car crash and Lyndyann went to stay with her Grandmother. Given the news and seeing her walk out of the door; I cried like a baby when she left. I wanted my sister back.

6: **Mommy's Heels**

With my mother being the Ambassador's secretary, there were always fancy events or dinner functions to attend. I would love watching my mother get all dolled up like a Hollywood star. I would just lie on the bed staring at her as she got ready. Watching her put on her makeup and smelling the scent of her perfume was just heavenly. She had a walk-in closet with plenty of clothes and shoes to choose from. Thinking back, whether it was matching pants suits or gorgeous sequin gowns, I don't remember my mother ever wearing the same outfit twice. That night Winston was attending a function with her.

"How do I look?" She turned to ask me.

"Mom you look so good." I replied grinning from ear to ear.

She just smiled, and then the doorbell rang.

"It's Winston." She said.

"I'll go let him in." I volunteered getting up from the bed.

I walked downstairs, and I opened the door.

"Good evening Andre, how are you doing?" Winston said and reached out to hug me.

"I'm good. Mom will be down in a few minutes." I said.

My mother came down the stairs. I watched Winston and the way he looked at my mother. I was in awe with him and the way he treated her. I could tell at an early age that he had a lot of respect for my mother. My mother blushed like a teenage girl. I was happy for her. When my mother was happy, so was I. My mother kissed me goodnight and, on her way, out I looked at the shoes she was wearing. I smiled to myself because she wasn't wearing my favorite heels. I looked out the peephole and watched them drive away. I went back upstairs and made a right to enter my mother's bedroom. I went straight into the closet. There they were black leather open toed clear bottoms, with straps that wrapped around the ankle. I grabbed the shoes and headed back into my bedroom. I took my clothes off until I was completely nude. I unplugged my portable CD player that was on my dresser and took it in the bathroom, plugged it in, and pressed play. I bent over to look in the cabinet and grabbed the baby oil. I squeezed a little bit of the oil in my hand and started rubbing my body down.

"This is my song!" I said aloud.

I started whining my hips and shaking my ass to the beat. I walked into my room and sat on my bed. I grabbed the first shoe and slid my foot in the left one. It fit perfectly. I wrapped the straps around my ankle to the middle of my leg and I did the same one with the right. I walked back into the bathroom. I stood there just staring at my body and questioning God why he didn't make me a woman.

"Yasss! Look at these legs!" I said aloud in admiration.

I just loved the way my legs looked in those heels. I tucked my dick between my legs where it appeared that I had a vagina. While I was trying to dance, my penis was tucked in under my butt. It caused me to get a hard-on. I continued to dance to song after song. By then I worked up a nice sweat. I never went over an hour dancing in her heels. The last thing I needed was for her to catch me dirty dancing in her shoes. Afterward I made sure I returned the heels the exact way I found them. Then I went back to my room and played video games until I fell asleep.

7: **P.S. Daddy I Love You** *(Part Two)*

December 25th, 1997

My father shipped his love all the way from North Carolina to the Island of Trinidad under my Christmas tree. My mother revealed to me that the PlayStation video games Final Fantasy VII and Alien Trilogy, and a Cowboy's blanket all came from him. Clearly my father was clueless about the son he had, because I have never been a fan of football. I loved baseball and the New York Yankees were my favorite team. My father didn't know me, and I didn't know him.

My mother and Winston at party in Trinidad. *1997.*

8: Ocean Of Tears

One of my mother's good friends Georgette and her daughter Materra, came over for dinner. Materra and I attended the same school. When the four of us got together we would always have a great time. Unfortunately, it was Sunday, which meant our fun wouldn't last long because we had school the following day. After dinner Materra and I were upstairs in my room playing video games. I walked downstairs to the kitchen to fix Materra and myself something to drink. As I was tiptoeing down the steps their voices were faint. I could barely hear them; my mother and Georgette whispering. I was about to scare them until I heard two words. These two words stopped me dead in my tracks. I heard them say two words: *"Andre"* and *"Gay"* in the same sentence, and I was mortified. I eased body quietly backup upstairs to my room.

"Where are the drinks?" Materra asked.

"I'm not thirsty." I said without giving eye contact.

"Boy I am." She laughed. "Why didn't you make mine?" She asked.

I just sat there on the bed staring, with the controller in my hand.

"Dre?" She said turning to look at me.

I said nothing. I was in a daze.

"Dre, are you alright?" She asked pushing my shoulder.

My eyes filled with water as tears streamed down my face. I wanted to tell her what I overheard; however, the words wouldn't come out right. I put the controller on the bed and walked back downstairs. Instead of walking out of the front double doors, I walked through the living room and walked out of the side door to escape. I didn't get a chance to grab my keys because they were in the kitchen. Before I could even close the door, I heard Materra coming down the steps behind me.

"Dre what's wrong?! Where are you going?!" She yelled.

I hopped the gate and quickly paced less than two minutes to the shore. I sat there and cried my eyes out. She followed me, and before I knew it, she was sitting directly beside me.

"What's wrong with you?" She asked concerned.

I tried to get the words out, but I kept crying.

"My mom, she thinks I'm gay." I said tearfully.

"Boy, your mother doesn't think that." She said reassuringly.

"I heard her; my mother and your mother were talking about me. I heard them Materra!" I said crying with tears pissing down my face.

"Come back into the house." She said grabbing me by the arm.

"I don't want to stay in that house with that woman!" I said snatching away.

Materra gave up, and eventually went back to the house. Neither my mother nor Georgette came outside to check on me. I stayed outside and watched the sunset. My pride wouldn't let me get up and go in the house. So many thoughts were running through my head. After being eaten alive by mosquitoes, I finally went back into the house the same way I left. I was hoping not to run into my mother. I walked upstairs and got straight into bed fully dressed. My mother knocked on my door.

"Andre, open the door." She ordered.

I wanted to open the door; however, I felt so ashamed and embarrassed. What was I going to say? Did my mother really say those words? Did my mother really think I was gay? After standing on the other side of my door for so long, and because I was reluctant to open it; my mother finally left. That night before going to sleep, I prayed:

"Dear God, please don't wake me up in the morning."

The next morning, I awoke to my alarm clock going off. I couldn't move. I was so drained. I dragged myself into the bathroom to take a shower. I didn't reach for my rag or the soap. I just let the water run on my body. I didn't brush my teeth or my hair. I didn't even care to iron my uniform. I grabbed my book bag and went outside to wait for Mr. Geoffrey. That morning I felt like my mother knew what type of son she really had. All these years I was able to hide my true nature. But the night before the makeup finally came off. My actions revealed who and what I was. I felt like my mother didn't love me anymore. I was waiting for her to call my name, rush to my rescue and say, "Andre I know, and it's ok." That never happened. When Mr. Geoffrey pulled up, he knew something was off with me because I would always greet him with a smile. That day there was no Joker's grin *(Mr. Geoffrey would always say in reference to my smile every morning)*. I got on the bus and went straight to the back to find a seat. We weren't even out of Westmoorings neighborhood yet, before my mother was in her car waiting at the next stop.

"Good morning Mr. Geoffrey. Andre, come with me." My mother said standing at the front of the bus.

I got up out of my seat and got off the bus.

"I can't have you go to school looking like that." My mother said once we were in the car.

I couldn't bear to look her way. She drove us back to our home. I went upstairs to my room, closed the door, and fell asleep. My mother and I never had a conversation about what happened the day before.

9: Friends

One of my best friends named Arthur, *(aka Krusty)* was a white boy from Houston, Texas. I loved him like a brother. He had blonde hair, freckles, and light brown eyes. He was a year younger than I was. If I wasn't at his house, he was at mine. His mother was the first white woman's food that I had ever tasted. She loved to cook, and I loved eating her food. Arthur's mother was the only woman I knew who would cut the edges of the bread. She was famous for her mayo spread, deli sliced, honey turkey sandwiches. I didn't see Arthur's dad that often; however, they looked just alike. I loved that woman and she considered me to be her son.

Callie *(aka Lil Sis)* was a white girl from Canada, and a good friend of mine. She had long blond hair with grey eyes. I must say she truly loved me. She called me her Big Bro and I was just that.

Another good friend of mine named Kelly *(aka Boobs)* was a white girl. Kelly's family didn't care that much for black people, but her mother fell in love with me before I moved back to Maryland. Kelly's mother was famous for her giant Oreo cream stuffed cookies.

Brandon *(aka Oreo)* was biracial. He was the star basketball player at our school. His dad worked at the U.S. Embassy with my mother. I had never been around such a group of kids that were so nice to me, and we weren't even blood related. I was treated as an equal. They made me feel special when I was with them. The movies didn't lie; white people were perfect and the happiest people on earth.

The age to have access to drugs or alcohol was nonexistent. If money was presented, drugs were available. Weed was something that Arthur and Callie loved. I tried sipping some alcohol at a party once, and it felt like my insides were melting. I told myself never again would I ever drink alcohol on that island. I just loved going to the parties to dance, hang out with my friends, and most importantly eat the catered food. All my friend's parents had big houses and fancy cars. The fathers worked, while the mothers were housewives. My mother was the only working female out of all my mother's friends. I was the only one whose father wasn't present.

10: **Trini Gyal**

It was just like any other Sunday at Jesus Is The Answer
(J.I.T.A.). I was ready to leave the moment my mother
made me get up to go there. Fiola was a girl that went to
the same church as my mother. She became good friends
with Materra. When church was over my mother was
fellowshipping with other members of the church. Me,
trying my best grin and waving at people, I spotted her. She
was tall and slender. She wore an all-black dress suit. Her
hair was in a bun and she was the prettiest dark-skinned
girl that I had ever laid eyes on in person. I never had the
courage to say anything to her. Every now and then, we'd
frequently make awkward eye contact.

I told Materra that I thought Fiola was so pretty. She then
took it upon herself to tell Fiola behind my back. This
caused them to start teasing me. A lot of times they'd look
at me, whisper to each other, then point and laugh. I didn't
know what that meant. The only places that I would often
see Fiola were at church when I attended or every birthday
party that Materra had at the Roxy Pizza Hut. It wasn't until
my 9th grade year, the same year that I was leaving, that I
asked Fiola out. She said yes. I was so happy that she had
given me a chance. The only problem was that we would
hardly see each other. When I would see her at church, I
never said anything to her. One weekend I went to
Materra's, and to my surprise Fiola was there. Fiola kept
acting funny towards me. She then asked me to come
upstairs with her. I already knew what the deal was, and I
didn't want to go. She literally begged me, so I eventually
caved in and decided to go.

Once we were upstairs, we went into Materra's bedroom and she closed the door behind us. Fiola told me to lie down on my back, and I did. I was extremely uncomfortable. She unbuckled my belt and unzipped my pants. Then she got on top of me and kissed my lips. She looked at me and I looked at her. I tried kissing her and I stuck my tongue in her mouth and moved it around the best way I knew how. My dick still wasn't hard. I was hoping someone would save me.

"What are you two doing?" Materra shouted coming into the room.

Fiola started laughing. "Thank you, God!" I was more than happy to see Materra come through the door; she saved me from pure embarrassment.

**Miss Universe/Miss Trinidad and Tobago 1998,
children from school and myself at the U.S. Embassy in
Trinidad.** *1998.*

Miss Universe/Miss Botswana 1999 and myself at the U.S. Embassy in Trinidad. *1999.*

11: Caribbean Boy

The first play I starred in was a play that my 5th grade class came up with titled: Trini Christmas. Instead of 8 reindeer, we had 8 dolphins. Of course, I played Santa Claus. I wore a swimsuit and scuba diving gear. It was an amazing play.

Four years later, I was in the 9th grade and I starred in another play called You're a Good Man Charlie Brown! I played Schroder. Another classmate of mine was cast as Schroder as well. He was a white boy by the name of Jimmy Denzell. He made the yearbook; however, I didn't. I was extremely pissed. I truly disliked my drama teacher Ms. Barnes. I couldn't stand her.

The Tri-Island Exchange was an annual completion held among the International schools of Curacao, Aruba, and Trinidad. The sports included were basketball, football *(soccer)*, softball, and volleyball. I participated in the games in 1997 and 1998. In 1999 they were canceled due to a tropical storm.

When it came to the Spanish Club, I was hesitant to join at first. I was glad that I did because that year we took a trip to Puerto Rico. Visiting Puerto Rico probably had to be my favorite island out of all the islands because it was so Americanized. The mall's food court had the best Chinese food. Everywhere you looked there were beautiful people. The water there was so blue, and the people were friendly. It's unfortunate that I missed out on the trips to Spain and Venezuela previously. I hope to one day get the chance to visit them.

My overall experience in Trinidad was amazing. I met so many wonderful people that were from all over the world. I got the opportunity to meet two Miss Universe who happens to have been women of color Wendy Fitzwilliam of Trinidad and Tobago 1998, and Mpule Kwelagobe of Botswana 1999. I especially loved the drive to Grande Riviere Beach; and getting the opportunity to see the leatherback turtles lay their eggs was an amazing and unforgettable experience. I was so fascinated by the beautiful scenery and the fact that I was able to watch nature take its course up close and personal. I had such a wonderful time.

The fat boy in me terribly misses the jerk chicken and pork on St. James Street and the Bake And Shark on Marcus Beach. I will never forget this part of my life. There are so many great memories that I will cherish forever.

12: Largo High School

Flashback:

When I was a kid going to Kettering Elementary, in Kettering, Maryland the high school I never wanted to attend was Largo High. Reason being, one day my cousin's brother stayed for the weekend and we were walking to my favorite Chinese carryout called Peter's. As we neared, I heard all this noise. When Lynn and I reached the corner there were so many people fighting. I hid behind Lynn and kept walking to Peter's, making our way through the crowd. There was blood everywhere. I couldn't believe what I was seeing. I later found out that it was the Largo High School students. I later told my mother that I never wanted to go there when I got older.

Fast Forward:

August 23rd, 1999

I entered the building with my mother by my side. There were students everywhere. We walked in the office and there was a boy sitting in the office with a bloody nose. "On the first day? Why did I have to leave Trinidad?" I thought to myself. I didn't start school on my first day. It didn't bother me at all. After leaving school, my mother treated me to Peter's Chinese food.

On my second day, I was sitting in class and the students were staring at me like I was some creature from outer space. While sitting in my 2nd period class this kid was staring me up and down, from head to toe.

"I like your Nike TNs." He said.

"Thank you." I said never looking his way.

'Where are you from?" He asked.

"I'm from Maryland." I stated.

"No, you're not. Not dress like that." He said making a face.

"How am I dressed?" I wondered.

"Like a white boy." He said.

"My clothes are from Old Navy." I defended.

"Exactly! White boy." He argued.

I turned to look out the window ignoring his last remark. I noticed that some of the students were leaving.

"Hey where are they going?" I asked him.

"Skipping school. They're probably going somewhere to fuck." He said flat out.

"Oh." I responded.

I looked back up at the teacher and I could still feel his eyes on me.

"Hey!" He shouted.

"What?" I answered annoyed.

"Do you get down?" He wondered.

"I don't understand what you're asking me." I explained.

"Never mind. What's your name?" He wondered.

"White Boy." I said directly.

"You're a funny dude." He said laughing.

I went back to my work; however, I couldn't help to think about the kids I'd seen skipping school. Why would anyone want to skip school? I would never do that. That was dumb. Throughout the rest of my first week I counted a total of 17 fights. I was told about the rainbow club and how it consisted of gays and lesbians. There was a total 180 from The International School of Port-of-Spain.

The first day that I decided to skip school wasn't until the following week on Friday, September 3rd, 1999.

13: **American Beauty**

August 15th, 2001

"That's her over there." Phil said.

She was cute, slim, and her smile was to die for.

"What's her name?" I wondered.

"It's Jai." He said.

When Jai started working at Shoppers, she was immediately recruited by Sherelle and India. Jai also made another list. The list of a pack of grown immature scavengers betting on which one of them would fuck her first. Deep down inside I felt offended. I had never even spoken to her and I wanted to defend her. Every time a new cute girl started working at Shoppers it was the same old thing. I believed depending on the type of girl that she appeared to be, if anybody had a chance with her, it was Phil. He was dark skinned, clean cut, smooth dude, and worked as a bookkeeper. He always dressed nice, he was in shape, and drove a grey Tahoe. He was in his mid - 20's. I on the other hand was in the 12th grade; I was fat, pimple faced, and car less. I didn't have my driver's license and I was pushing shopping carts. I had no chance and never thought twice about it.

August 20th, 2001

I didn't see Jai again until I was waiting at the bus stop to catch the A-12 to get my hair cut. I looked up and there she was.

"Hi, where are you going?" She asked and smiled. She had such a lovely smile.

"I'm going to get my hair cut. Where are you headed?" I asked her.

"Work." She said.

The conversation was brief: but even so, I felt good about myself that day. I had on a red Matt Giraud shirt, Old Navy jeans, and a fresh pair of Timberlands. As she turned around to get on the bus, I checked her out. She had on boots, black fitted pants, and a white collared shirt. Her soft jet-black hair was wrapped up in a high bun on top of her head. I gazed at her while she strutted to the back of the bus and sat down in a seat on the side that was closer to me. She never looked my way, but I know she knew I was staring at her. "Damn, that girl is sexy." I thought to myself. One day I'm going to make her mine.

14: 9-Eleven

September 11^{th,} 2001

The sounds of running water woke me up. I glanced over to check the time. It was a few minutes past 6:00AM. I already had my mind set that I wasn't going to school that day. The water stopped. I got up out of bed to use the bathroom hoping that my mother believed I was going to school. I got back into bed, rolled over, and dozed off. I woke up once again to a door closing. I got up to peek through the blinds. I saw my mother taking her daily stroll to the bus stop. The feeling of disappointment came over me, but I got back into bed anyway. It didn't matter; I didn't care anymore. "Fuck Largo High School!" I closed my eyes and went back to sleep.

I woke again and glanced over at the time once more. It was now past 9:00AM. "Why the fuck am I up so early? I seriously could have gone to school today." My guilt was getting the best of me. I shook it off and went downstairs. I turned on the TV and I couldn't believe what I was seeing. *Breaking News* flashed across the TV screen. I saw two burning buildings. I changed the channel to Fox, and it was on there too. What I was seeing wasn't registering. I flipped the channel to CNN. It was on every news station. The words I kept hearing: New York, Washington D.C., World Trade Center, Pentagon, airplanes, and terrorist attack. Then it dawned on me. My mother had a job interview at the Pentagon. I knew I had to leave because I knew my mother was on her way back home. I didn't have time to wash my ass or brush my teeth. I ran back upstairs, grabbed some clothes and quickly got dressed. As I was headed downstairs, I heard the jingling of keys at the front door.

"Oh shit!" I thought to myself. "She's back!" I said aloud as I ran back upstairs to hide in my closet.

Settled in the closet, I sat as still and as quiet as a church mouse. I heard the door open. I heard her footsteps walking up the steps. I just knew she was headed straight to my bedroom. I just knew I was caught. "Why oh lord of all the days did I choose to stay home? Never again." I told myself. I waited for her to enter my room, but she walked into her room and closed the door. It was silent for a few seconds, and suddenly I heard an outburst. My mother was crying. I never heard my mother cry like that before. I could tell she was on the phone; however, I didn't know with whom. All the hollering and shouting she was doing was making it hard for me to understand what she was saying. My heart got full. I wanted to run and hold her, but I was supposed to be at school. I didn't know what to do. My mind was telling me to run and console her, but my feet wouldn't move because of the ass whooping I would receive if she knew I stayed home from school again.

"I have to go pick up Andre from school!" She cried out.

She got off the phone and I heard her enter the bathroom. She went back downstairs, and I heard the jingling of the keys once more, the door opened, and then closed. I walked into her room and peeped through the blinds. My watery eyes saw her drive away. I dropped my head and walked back to my room to grab the rest of my things to head out. I walked about a quarter of a mile from the house and turned straight back around. I was hoping that on her way back she would see me walking from the direction of my school. As I was walking past the mailbox, she pulled into the driveway. She got out the car and her eyes were a little puffy from crying.

"I went to your school to pick you up." She said. I didn't respond.

September 14th, 2011

After what happened on Tuesday, September 11th, I told myself that I was going to go to school every day from that point on. That Friday morning when I was on the floor eating leftovers, I slid the fork from my teeth quickly and continued eating. I bit down on something hard; and what I thought was a piece of the food. I stuck my fingers in my mouth and pulled out something white. "What the hell?" I thought to myself. There wasn't anything on my dinner plate that was white. I ran to the bathroom. I looked in the mirror and smiled, and there it was. I realized that I chipped my tooth.

"That's what the fuck I get. Damnit man." I snapped.

15: **Prom Date**

April 22nd, 2002

I never had any intentions of going to prom. Besides who was going to go with someone like me? If I couldn't go with the person that I really wanted to go with, then I wasn't going. My two choices were between two people, and that was India or Jai. Both Jai and India said I was a nice guy; however, I knew India wasn't feeling me at all. One day they were both working, and Jai was sitting down on her lunch break. As I finished organizing the shopping carts, I walked inside and sat down beside her.

"You're sweating." She said.

Talk about an awkward moment. Here I am about to ask this girl to go to prom with me, and that's the first thing she says to me.

"Do I smell or something?" I asked her timidly.

"No, you don't." She said and continued eating her salad.

"Can I ask you a question?" I finally said breaking the silence.

She looked at me, and I looked back at her.

"Yes?" She said with a smirk on her face.

"Will you go to prom with me?" I wondered.

She looked away, then back down at her salad.

"Andre you're a nice guy. Why don't you ask India?" She said trying to let me down easy.

"I would love to go with India, but she isn't dependable. I don't want her standing me up on my night." I quickly returned.

"I don't know Andre. I already went to my prom." She said toying with her salad.

"Ok, no problem Jai. I just thought I would ask you." I said as I got up to go continue my work. "Fuck it. I didn't really want to go to prom anyway." I said to myself.

Quite frankly I was just tired of my family asking me about it.

Can you spot 18-year-old me? Graduation photo. *2002.*

16: **P.S. Daddy I Love You** *(Part Three)*

May 3rd, 2002

I saw my father again for the first time since the early part of the previous decade. This was the same month as prom. Our encounter was brief, but I did talk to him about the girl I was interested in. I thought maybe he would show interest in me if I spoke about something he could relate to like women for instance.

"Her name is Jai, and she works at Shoppers with me. She's cute. She doesn't mind that I don't have a car; and she said I was a nice guy." I told him elatedly.

"That's good, that's real good son." He responded with a smile.

"Dad, can you come to my graduation next month; if you're not too busy?" I asked.

"Yeah son I can come." He said.

I was so excited; however, I was trying my best to be cool about it. I just knew this would be a new beginning for us.

"Dad, I have a brother, right?" I suddenly asked.

Even though I felt awfully uncomfortable asking him about his other son, I often wondered if he thought my mother was putting me up to it.

"Yeah you have a brother, his name is Adron." He replied.

"Oh, ok cool; you both have the same name." I said. "Of course, they do Andre, duh." I instantly thought.

"Yeah, his mother named him after me." He explained.

There were so many questions I wanted answered. It was unjust. It was now becoming clear to me that this was the reason my father wasn't a part of my life. Out of all the siblings I had, Adron was the only boy besides me. In that moment, I knew Adron was the favorite son. I'd never seen a picture of him or heard his voice; however, I was envious and jealous because I felt he was the chosen one. My mother just had to fuck everything up. Here I am, 18 years old and being raised by my mother. No wonder why I'm so fucked up and confused. I was being raised by a woman who had no idea how to raise a man. I had to meet this Adron someway, somehow.

"Dad, where is Adron now?" I asked him.

"He's in Wilmington and he works at the mall. Footlocker, I think it is." He said.

I didn't want my father to leave me again, but I knew he had to. However, I was still excited because he told me that he was going to be at my graduation, and it was only a month away on June 5th, 2002. I mentioned it to my mother that he was going to be there, and she was happy for me.

June 5th, 2002

Since my father didn't show up the day before my graduation, I figured he'd be there the following day. The next morning my father was still a no show. I wanted to ask my mother if she'd heard from him; however, I decided not to. Trying to think positive, I thought he'd surprise me. Later that morning my mother, aunt Patricia, aunt Celestine, aunt Janelle, and cousins Kanika, Keisha, Kendrell, Gregory, Audrekia, Djuan, Dayvon, Ayana, and Pastor Rowe attended my big day. After I graduated, everyone met back up at my mother's home. I knew he wasn't there. I knew he wasn't in the state of Maryland. I thought just maybe I was going to get a call from him to explain his absence; but that never happened. I tried my best to look on the bright side of things. I told myself that I made it through 13 years of school. I can finally put that behind me, including my father.

17: **Good Girl**

Flashback:

JVaughn and I both attended Largo High School, but he never knew I existed. I was aware of his bad boy reputation because his name was very popular when it came to a school fight. He drove a green Ford Crown Victoria. JVaughn started working at Shoppers shortly after I did. He worked in the meat department. In the beginning we never spoke to one another, but he would often catch me staring at him when he was outside on his smoke break. One day he spoke.

Fast Forward:

"What's up Andre? You went to Largo right?" He said.

"Ye- yeah. I was th… there from 10th through 12th grade." I stuttered.

"I remember you. You kept to yourself. Where were you 9th grade?" He asked.

"I was in Trinidad with my mother. She worked at the U.S. Embassy she was the Ambassador's Secretary." I said proudly.

JVaughn and I became cool. I liked him because he wasn't afraid to acknowledge me in front of his friends or co-workers who would often talk behind my back. They'd swear that I was gay or said disrespectful things about me. JVaughn was the first guy that I ever smoked weed with. He was a wild card, but I trusted him.

September 13th, 2002

Jai had on a floral brown dress with knee high boots with a folded flap. I was skeptical from the start. I was seriously hoping Jai was going to change her mind about going to this cabaret. JVaughn picked me up. I had a little to drink. When I saw Jai at the cabaret, I could tell she had a few drinks. The music was so loud. JVaughn, Dwight, Aaron, his cousin, Jai, and I were all sitting at the table, and all eyes were on Jai. She kept trying to force herself on me in front of them. I just smiled and played it off.

"Jai, can you please calm down?" I whispered in her ear.

Ignoring what I said, she took my head and pushed it down between her legs.

"She is a fucking freak!" Dwight shouted out.

I was humiliated. I felt disrespected. I wanted to beat her ass. "The first thing come tomorrow morning I am going to dump Jai." I plotted silently. I didn't sign up for this and I never knew this girl was so loose. Thank God it was dark, because my eyes were filled with water. I was heartbroken. If I had a car I would have left; however, I was riding with JVaughn and I planned to stay the night at his place. I was high from the weed that JVaughn had me smoke earlier, and I was tipsy. Jai wanted to dance, so she took my hand and led me on the dance floor. Jai was *"White Girl"* drunk, and all eyes were on her while we were on the dance floor. Whiles she moved to the beat her dress kept riding up. At that point I was numb. I just turned all the voices off around me while they gawked at my Jai. After we went back to the table, JVaughn told me that they were going to the car to hit a joint and they wanted me to come. I wanted Jai to stay, but she followed. JVaughn and Aaron were sitting in the front seat. I was sitting in the back on the right side, Jai was in the middle, and Aaron's cousin was sitting on the left. We were passing the joint around in rotation, and Jai didn't smoke.

"Andre, I want to get out." She said.

The weed was making her nauseous, along with all the alcohol she consumed. That night was a bust, and I just wanted to go home.

"Never again will I go to a club with this girl." I said disgustedly.

While leaving the venue to head to our cars I heard someone hollering in our direction.

"Hey man, that's not your girl!" A guy shouted out.

"What?!" Jai responded with her drunken ass.

"Hey, my man, that is his girl." Dwight said back to the guy.

At that point I didn't even care whose girl she was. I was utterly disgusted with her.

"Hey Dre, you're going to go stay with Dwight for a while, and I'll pick you up later from his house." JVaughn whispered to me.

"Why? JVaughn the only reason I agreed to come out was because Jai wanted to come to this thing, and because you said that I could stay with you." I said with frustration.

"I promise I'll pick you up in a few hours." He said.

I wasn't feeling Dwight. I never trusted him I didn't know what these dudes had planned, but I knew some way somehow, I had to make it back home. "Even if I have to fucking walk, I'll be damned if I go anywhere with Dwight." I thought. I made sure Janice gave Jai a ride home, and asked Carl if he could take me. When I finally made it home, I walked into the bathroom and my eyes were bloodshot red. I was still hurt. Where was the girl I once loved so much? I wanted her back. I wanted to dump her so badly for humiliating me like that, but I knew Jai needed me in her life and I wasn't going anywhere.

18: **Brother** *(Part One)*

December 24th, 2002

The family that lived in Maryland all traveled to North Carolina for Christmas. I had my own hidden agenda, and that was to meet my brother. I never told anyone, not even my mother. I had Delvin take me to Independence mall in Wilmington. I went looking for my brother to see if I could find him. I remembered my father telling me that he worked at Footlocker, and I hoped that he still did. I walked in and started checking out a few of the shoes. I glanced at a couple of guys working there. Never seeing my brother before, I was hoping one of the guys resembled me. Unfortunately, none of them did. I walked over to them looking at their name tags.

"Excuse me does Adron Massey work here?" I asked one of the guys.

"No, we don't have anyone by that name here." The guy responded.

"Ok, thank you." I said turning to leave.

19: The Lord Of The Rings

Flashback:

My mother and aunt Janelle had traveled down to North Carolina to visit their mother for a couple of days. Jai was off that night and once I got off work from Shoppers, I went to go scoop her up. Before heading to Target, I had picked up my sister Lyndyann, and my two cousins Kendrell and Gregory as well from my home. Of course, I went straight to the DVD section of the store so we could have movie night even though Lyndyann, Kendrell, and Gregory all had school the following morning. Nothing really caught my eye however; I did come across a movie called The Lord Of The Rings: The Fellowship Of The Rings. I read the back of the DVD cover and it sound interesting. "Damn this movie is almost 3 hours long." I had thought to myself. After leaving Target we headed to Giant. I had found a recipe online to make chicken and broccoli alfredo. I hate shopping at Giant, it's so expensive I should have just picked up the food while I was at work.

Within the first couple of minutes of watching the movie I had thought what the fuck is this? By the time the movie had ended my sister and I were the only ones up. We were instant fans. The story fulfilled and inspired me in such a magical way but left me wanting more especially with the ending for a possible continuation. Peter Jackson was now my favorite movie director of all time just like that. Jai, Kendrell, and Gregory had all fallen asleep. I googled to see if it was a follow up and turned out not only was part II titled: The Lord Of The Rings: Two Towers which came out in the theaters last year on December 18th, 2002, part III

The Lord Of The Rings: The Return Of The King was headed to theaters later on in the year December 17th. Unfortunately, The Lord Of The Rings: Two Towers wasn't going to be released on DVD until August 26th, 2003.

August 26th, 2003

Instead of me waiting until 8:00AM for Target to open up near me, I had drove to the Walmart in Bowie, Maryland instead since they opened up at 6:00AM. Soon as I got home, I had watched the movie from beginning to end. Another brilliant masterpiece. My sister ended up watching it once she had arrived back from school.

Fast Forward:

December 18th, 2003.

My sister and I went to see the movie in theaters the next night after the opening day due to it being sold out and a conflict with our schedules. Oh boy oh boy I did my hardest to prevent my sister from seeing my eyes water up during the ending. 10 out of 10 would be my score for the Lord Of The Rings trilogy. Even though no movie would ever replace my number 1 movie of all time The Neverending Story, The Lord Of The Rings trilogy was now in 2nd place, The Color Purple 3rd, The River Wild 4th, The Long Kiss Goodnight 5th, The Notebook 6th, Howl's Moving Castle 7th, Beauty and the Beast 8th, Double Impact 9th, and Pretty In Pink 10th.

20: **Mother's Lingerie**

February 11th, 2004

The closer it got to Valentine's Day, the redder Shoppers became. The only time of year that Shoppers was filled with men was on Valentine's Day. That year I wanted to do something special for Jai; however, I had no clue of exactly what I wanted to do. It was finally lunch time, so I decided to go to McDonald's. As I was crossing the street a guy stopped me and asked if he could show me something. He opened a large black suitcase and he had all types of lingerie that he probably stole from either Victoria's Secret or Frederick's of Hollywood.

"No thank you." I said as I continued walking.

"My brotha?" He uttered.

I turned and answered, "Yes man?"

"How much are you trying to spend?" He anxiously asked.

"This twenty-dollar bill I have in my hand is to buy lunch sir." I stated.

"All right brotha, I give it to you for $10.00. That's the lowest I went all day brotha." He offered.

"Sir, if you're still here when I come out of McDonald's I'll purchase it." I said and continued to my destination.

While walking I started to think that if I purchased that garment, the message to Jai would be evident. We were both turning 21 that year but I still wasn't ready to be intimate with her. Maybe if I purchased it, we could save it for when the time was right. After ordering my food and coming out of McDonald's, I noticed the guy was still waiting. I kept my word, bought it and took it to my car.

Valentine's Day

February 14th, 2004

When the day finally arrived, I was scheduled to work from 10:00AM - 2:00PM. I hated working those shifts because I'm not a morning person. Little did I know that Mrs. Tina, the head cashier was going to beg me to stay late, so I ended up working until 3:30PM. Jai wasn't at work that day because she was getting her hair, nails, and feet done for our date.

Later that evening I went to pick her up. Her sister Jamie opened the door.

"Hi Andre." Jamie said with a smile.

"Hi Jamie." I said returning the smile.

"Jai, Andre's here!" She yelled upstairs.

Her sisters Minnie and Ayana came downstairs as well. I looked up as Jai turned the corner. She had a huge smile on her face, and she looked beautiful as usual. She had a fresh roller wrap and her thick beautiful curls stopped a little past her neck. She was dressed in a black skirt that stopped below her knee, a red shirt that matched her Mary Jean pumps, topped with a black peacoat. Jai handed me a small red gift bag and inside were a pair of boxers. I gift wrapped the red and white lace lingerie in a red and white box, with red and white paper. I also purchased her a teddy bear, 1 dozen roses, and a box of chocolate. She gave me a hug and quickly started opening the box like it was Christmas morning. When she saw what was inside her face lit up and we both smiled at each other. Following the gift exchanges, we left the house and headed to Olive Garden for dinner. The wait was tremendously long; however, the conversation between Jai and I made the time fly by. During that time in our relationship I was able to talk to Jai about any and everything. Yes, she was my girlfriend but more importantly she was like my best friend; and above all she didn't judge me. It was nothing that I wouldn't do for her.

Of course, Jai didn't wear the lingerie that evening; however, it was later brought to my attention three days afterwards, that Jai's mother went into her room that she shared with her sister Ava; she rambled through her personal belongings and tried on the red and white lingerie that I purchased her daughter. I thought the saying was *(Like mother, Like daughter)* in this case it seemed as if the mother wanted to be her daughter. That was creepy and nasty at the same time.

21: **Birthday Sex**

Flashback:

September 12th, 2004

"It's time Andre, and we are getting older." Jai said.

"The only reason why you want to have sex is because your nosey ass girlfriends are questioning you about our sex life. Felicia has two babies, April is in a stable relationship, and Wendy's still a virgin. Besides we have plenty of time for that. What's the rush? I told you before I don't want to have sex until I'm 25 years old." I told Jai hoping she'd back off and change her mind.

"I'm not waiting that long to have sex. I'm a woman and I have needs." She snapped back.

I looked at her and that's when I realized that the teenage girl, I met on August 15th, 2001 was now a young woman. There was not one person that I was able to talk to about this. I knew something had to be done. Dating a girl like Jai was a blessing and curse at the same time. I got the girl that the boys lusted after. The gay rumors that haunted me didn't stop just because I was dating the hottest virgin at Shoppers.

From that moment on, we would often try to have sex. I wasn't into kissing, foreplay, or touching her sexually. I just wanted to get this thing over with. We tried for a couple of months and nothing. Neither one of us knew what the hell we were doing. It was fucking frustrating. I didn't want to have sex. Things like going to the mall, movies, and restaurants were no longer on the top of the list. If Jai got me alone her goal was for us to attempt to fuck. After trying for months to have sex, there was only one explanation; something was off, and it was all becoming so clear to me. My dick wasn't compatible with Jai's vagina. Every time I would try to penetrate her, my dick would just bend. I didn't understand why my dick was so soft; and yet any other morning I'd literally wake up with a hard-on. I wound up nicknaming her vagina. I called it *"Brick Wall."*

Every time Jai hit the scene with her girlfriends she would always come back and update me with the topics that were on hand. We were still the hottest topic of their discussion. I found out that Felicia didn't like that fact that I nicknamed Jai *"Brick Wall."* That was the thing about Jai; certain things were never kept between us. She would often reveal what was going on in our relationship to the outside world.

My birthday was coming up, and I convinced myself that it would happen then. Dinner was a must for my birthday, so I was looking forward to that.

Fast Forward:

My 21st Birthday

November 29th, 2004

After days of planning, I picked her up to bring her back to my mother's home. We went downstairs to my room, which was in the basement. As she was taking her clothes off, I went into the storage area which was right outside my room to press play. I had a small boom box on top of the deep freezer. The song that I chose was Janet Jackson's "Anytime Anyplace." When I walked back into my room, I noticed she was wearing the red laced Victoria Secret lingerie that her mother tried on when I purchased it a year ago. She looked at me, and she was smiling. I walked over to her, and she put her hands behind my head to pull me in closer for a kiss. She started off by pecking me on the lips. She then began licking my lips as she slowly stuck her tongue in my mouth. I pulled back slowly.

"What?" She asked concerned.

"Nothing lay down on the bed." I said.

She lied down on the bed and spread her legs. I got on top of her. "Why can't I get hard? Maybe I'm over thinking it." I bent over to kiss her. While kissing her I played with my dick, trying to make myself hard. "Come on dick, work damn it!" I thought to myself. I got up off the bed and lubricated my dick. I started to feel a tingling sensation. I looked down and I was getting hard. "Ok Andre, it's now or never." I got up off the bed once more to get a condom. I tore it open and put it on. Then I put more lube on. I unsnapped the bottom piece of the lingerie, grabbed my dick, and positioned myself to enter her.

"Wait!" She yelled pushing me back.

"What's wrong?" I asked.

"That hurt. You're not sticking it in the right place." She informed me as she repositioned herself.

"Where am I sticking it?" I asked alarmed.

"My butt!" She screamed. "Let me show you." She said as she grabbed my dick and put it in her vagina.

"Wait." I said trying to play with my dick some more to make myself semi hard once more.

I then put more lube on. She took it in her hand once more.

"Ok." She said.

"Is it in?" I asked.

"Yes." She replied.

The minute I was inside Jai, I felt empty. My best friend disappeared right in front of my eyes. I was finally fulfilling her longing desire to have sex. We were now like everyone else. Sliding it in and out; I could feel my dick growing with each stroke. She gripped my back tighter. I couldn't believe I was fucking. She moaned as I went deeper. I started going faster and faster, and then suddenly I felt an intense rush at the head of my dick. Without warning I thrust my hips forward and I started to cum. Once I was done, I tried to pull out.

"Don't stop." She begged.

"I'm done. I'm soft again." I said disapprovingly.

I leaned over and kissed her on the lips.

"How did I do?" I asked.

"It was amazing. I have to pee." She said smiling.

She got up and went upstairs to use the bathroom. I followed her. Once she finished, she reached for a tissue to wipe. Instead of dropping the tissue in the toilet, she showed me that there was some light blood.

"I'm sorry, was I too rough?" I asked her with a worried look.

"No Andre, my hymen broke. You were gentle." She assured me.

"Have you decided where you want to eat at for your birthday?" She asked changing the subject.

"There's a Chinese buffet in Virginia that I would love to try. We should hurry up and get ready to go before my mother comes home." I said opening the bathroom door.

The whole experience was just awful to me, and extremely forced. However, the most awkward moment of the evening was seeing her wear the lingerie that her mother tried on. Jai never wore the lingerie for me again.

22: **Happy & Nappy** *(Part One)*

February 19th, 2005

It was a weekly routine to get my hair cut. Every Friday morning, I would go to Largo One Barbershop before school. It wasn't until I was 21 that I heard one of man's greatest nightmares, coming to a reality.

"Hey Dre, it happens to the best of us dawg." Carl said.

"What are you talking about?" I asked.

"It's starting to happen." He said.

"What are you talking about?" I repeated.

"Your hair is starting to thin on top, and it started a couple of months back." He said.

I quickly lifted my head up to see what he was talking about. I looked to the left and looked to the right. I bent down to see the top of my head.

"Carl, I don't see anything." I said nervously.

"It's a slow process. You don't see what I see. I've been cutting your hair since you were a teen. I can see the difference." Carl added then asked, "Is your father a thin top?"

"Yes, he is. My mother has thin hair too. I guess it was going to happen sooner than later." I said shrugging it off.

23: We're Pregnant!

March 29th, 2006

Jai and I decided not to find out the sex of the baby until he or she was born. That didn't sit well with our families and friends. Everyone was anxious to know the sex of the baby. When it came to baby names, we decided that the baby's name would either start with an A or a J.

"We should name him Andre Jr." She suggested.

"I don't know about that. What if he is a boy and we name him Andre, and God blesses us with another boy? I don't think that would be fair to him." I said.

"Ok, calm down. Let's have this baby first, and then see if there will be a baby number two." She said and laughed.

"I know, I'm just saying." I quickly said.

"Ok how about this; we come up with three boys' names that start with the letters A and J, and three girl names that start with the letters A and J. Within a week we will come back together and share the list with each other and decide on the name for either a boy or a girl, deal?" I suggested.

"Ok, deal." She agreed.

April 2nd, 2006

That Sunday evening at dinner, I told my family what Jai and I decided to do about the baby names. They weren't too pleased, but they finally agreed to let us have our way; or so I thought.

"I do have a name that I love if we are having a boy." I mentioned.

"What is it?" My cousin Kanika asked.

"I love Jeremiah." I responded.

"I don't like that." She said shaking her head.

"Damn!" I thought. In that moment I made a promise to myself that I wouldn't reveal any more names to my family.

April 5th, 2006

The following week Jai and I got together to discuss baby names. We hit the jack pot when we realized that we each had the name Jamari on our lists. We instantly knew that that was the perfect name for a boy. For the girl, we decided on Aquarius. I didn't like that name, but it was cute. I decided to take Jai's suggestion to name him after me into strong consideration. I love my name; however, I wanted it spelled differently. I came across the German spelling which is Ondrej and we both loved it. There was no second guessing the last name. It was obviously going to be Simmons.

24: Hollywood

March 25th, 2006

With a new baby on the way, I felt it was time for us to start planning our move to L.A. I had a month to plan for her birthday, and there was no place better than a trip to L.A. I felt that it would be about business, yet pleasurable. I was so excited to be with Jai and the idea of traveling such a long distance with her. We had taken a trip previously to North Carolina to get my driver's license when I was nineteen. We also went to see Trina in concert. That trip was a bust. Everything went wrong. The Greyhound ride was ridiculously long, I failed my driver's test, and Trina basically was a no show. We later learned that the show was reported a scam.

April 23rd, 2006

We arrived at the airport early that morning, and we flew from Reagan National Airport to Chicago O'Hare International Airport. We then flew from Chicago O'Hare International Airport to LAX. That had to be the longest flight of my life. From my view, I could only see land and more land. At least if something was to go wrong, and we were flying over water we would have a better chance of survival; Cast Away anyone? "Wilson!" Once we landed Jai and I were on our star watch. The only celebrity we saw was Adrianne Curry. She's best known for being the first winner of America's Next Top Model. We got our luggage and caught a taxi to The Westin Bonaventure Hotel & Suites. L.A. itself wasn't a pretty city but we were still excited to be there. Once we arrived at the hotel, we went to the customer service desk only to find out that we were unable to get our room right away. Once again, I had to call my mother all the way from the west coast to the east coast to save the day. After that was settled, I was able to take in the view of the beautiful hotel. When we entered the elevator, there was a plaque on the wall stating that the movie True Lies was shot there.

"That's so cool. The movie True Lies filmed a scene here. Have you seen that before?" I asked Jai reading the plaque.

"No." She simply said.

"We will watch it when we return back to Maryland." I said.

The room was nice, and the bed looked so comfortable. As tired as I was, there was no time for sleep. Jai was pregnant, and I wanted to make sure she was ok.

"How are you feeling?" I asked her.

"I'm ready to go and look around." She said ignoring my question.

"Ok." I responded.

I took a quick shower, got dressed, and we headed out. The city was somewhat dead. After all it was a Sunday.

April 24th, 2006

We woke up around 8:00AM the next morning. We had breakfast, and it was the best breakfast ever. We caught the metro from red line Wilshire/Vermont to

Hollywood/Highland. The street was literally paved with Hollywood stars' names. I wanted to see if I could find Janet Jackson and Marilyn Monroe's stars. Unfortunately, I was unable to find them. Somehow, we wound up getting free tickets to a taping of Jimmy Kimmel LIVE! The taping was scheduled for later that evening. We went to see the movie Silent Hill at the famous TCL Chinese Theatre to kill some time. It was so empty inside. There were only four other couples besides Jai and me, but it was the first showing of the day.

After the movie, Jai and I had lunch at the Inner Courtyard of Hollywood and Highland. We had such a blast. We were taking turns interviewing one another, as if we were already superstars.

"Miss Jai, what brings you to Hollywood?" I asked leaning my hand towards her as if I were holding a microphone.

"I'm on break from filming my latest blockbuster darling." She responded flipping her hair back and forth, looking fly as ever wearing her dark shades.

"How's that going Miss Jai?" I asked with a smile.

"Just marvelous darling. Just marvelous." She said laughing.

We looked at each other and started cracking up laughing. I really wanted this to happen. I always dreamt of being famous. It felt great being away and enjoying life as I felt it should be.

We went back to the hotel to rest up because we knew we had to return to the show later that night. While we were walking back to the taping of Jimmy Kimmel Live! There were three guys staring at us. I reached out and grabbed her hand, holding it tight. When we made it to the line, I was able to relax. Natasha Henstridge was the main guest of the night. She was the lead actress in films Species and Species II. It was cool seeing how everything worked at these types of shows. We later caught ourselves on TV which was a great moment. I had called the east coast to remind my mother to watch, but she had fallen asleep.

April 25th, 2006

The Aquarium of the Pacific was at the end of the blue line. We spent a few hours there however, the only thing that was on my mind was where we were going to eat for her birthday dinner. L.A. had so much to offer. I mentioned a restaurant to her that was in Trinidad that rotated, with a beautiful view of the city and ocean. The view was absolutely breath taking. The hotel we were staying in had the exact same thing. I just wanted her to be happy. Wherever we decided to eat I wanted it to be special. She loved the idea and suggested that we eat at the restaurant on top of the hotel. After we rested up for a bit, I took my shower and got dressed for dinner. When Jai walked out of the bathroom, she had her crinkled hair in a bun, wearing dark red lip stick, a short black dress that stopped above her knee, with a lace dress over it.

"Jai you look so beautiful tonight, and the best you've ever looked." I said smiling.

"Thank you, Andre." She said smiling back.

She wasn't a woman who needed to wear a lot of makeup, but when she did, she was stunning. I didn't know if it was because we were in L.A. or if it was her pregnant glow. Everything became clear to me that I was going to spend the rest of my life with that woman. I was determined to fight my inner self and keep that part of me buried deep down inside. If I couldn't do it for myself, I was going to do it for Jai and my unborn child. It was my past, and I kissed that sin goodnight. Jai and I had a quickie after dinner, and she seemed very pleased with my 6 minutes and 17 seconds performance.

April 26th, 2006

We caught the metro back to LAX; which was what we should have done before. The ride was longer; however, much cheaper. Once we arrived back in Maryland, I just knew it was a new beginning for us and more than anything I couldn't wait to return to L.A. just us 3.

Didn't you know

I was waiting on you

Waiting on a dream

That'll never come true

Didn't you know

I was waiting on you

My face turned to stone

When I heard the news

Kanye West Lyrics Bad News

25: **Bad News**

Flashback:

The Three Musketeers. We had an unbreakable bond and love for one another that can never be broken. I couldn't wait until Gregory turned twenty-one on the 16th of August. I've always wanted to take him and Kendrell to Trinidad for a carnival. As fate would have it you can't always plan as much as you like. Sometimes God will intervene that plan for his own. Kendrell announced in the fall of 2005 and that he was going into the Navy. His basic training started in the spring of 2006. During the fall of 2005 Gregory and I were coming up with ideas to start our own T-Shirt line; however, I started working at HEW Federal Credit Union on December 19th, 2005 instead. Jai and I were also planning on moving to L.A. in the summer of

2006. Gregory felt that Kendrell and I were moving on with our lives, and he no longer wanted to stay in the state of Maryland. He didn't want to be the only boy. We began noticing how Gregory started to withdraw from everyone, which led him to start skipping school. When he got word that he wasn't going to graduate from high school, he decided he wanted to go to North Carolina to finish school. The family that lived in Maryland all laughed it off because they heard it from me before as well. I didn't like school, but I still graduated. Lyndyann and Kendrell graduated in 2005. Gregory was the last of us to graduate. Audrekia had many years to go because she wasn't going to graduate until 2012. We all felt if he just held on just a little while longer, he would be alright. He decided to go to North Carolina anyway and he got himself a one-way ticket to Supply, North Carolina.

Fast Forward:

May 27th, 2006

Jai, Ava, and I were on our way to see X-Men: The Last Stand. Five minutes away from the theatre my phone rung.

"Greg shot Alfred!" Delvin shouted.

"What do you mean?!" I cried out.

"Greg shot Alfred!" She repeated.

I squeezed my phone, pushed my body back into the driver's seat, and closed my eyes. I almost forgot that I was driving. I quickly came back to reality.

"Andre what happened?" Jai asked.

"Greg shot Alfred. I knew some shit like this was going to happen. We all said he was going to start selling drugs, get killed, or kill somebody." I said.

I got back on the phone.

"Where is he at?" I asked.

"They are looking for him. Andre, please don't tell your mom." She said.

"I'm about to turn around and go back home. My night is fucked." I said.

"No. Don't go back home. Just keep doing what you're doing. I'll call you and update you." She said.

My body was numb, and that five-minute drive felt like ten hours. My spirit was heavy. We finally arrived and entered the packed theatre. There were loads of people when I got in line to purchase our tickets. I didn't feel like eating popcorn or anything. As soon as we took our seats my mother called.

"Hello?" I said.

"Greg shot Alfred!" She cried out.

"I know mom. I know." I said.

"Where are you? Come home, come home. No one can reach Janelle. Her phone is going straight to voicemail." She cried.

"I'll be there after we leave the movies." I said.

"Alright." She sobbed and hung up the phone.

As the movie continued to watch me, my phone vibrated. Delvin was calling again.

"Yeah?" I asked.

"Greg didn't do it, and he's here with me." She said.

"Thank God. Where are you guys at?" I asked.

"We're at grandmas." She said.

"I don't want to talk to him, but I'm calling off from work tomorrow and I'm coming down there to get him myself. I'll call you later." I said.

We hung up.

"Greg didn't do it." I whispered to Jai.

What a sigh of relief. I knew what had to be done. I had hope that this was a warning to Gregory. I hoped he figured out that he didn't belong down there. I was finally able to get into the movie, and it wasn't bad. It was the best one I'd seen.

After the movie, I dropped Ava off. Then I called Delvin again.

"Hello what's new?" I said.

"Alfred is dead. Greg did do it. They took him away Andre. They took him away." Delvin confirmed.

"Damn! I thought you said he didn't do it! I'm almost home! I'll call you in a little bit!" I yelled.

I pulled into the driveway. Jai and I headed inside. The house was dark. I walked upstairs and entered my mother's room. Audrekia was sitting on the bed. Even though it was dark I could tell that she'd been crying as well. She got up off the bed, walked into the bathroom, and closed the door. My mom was sitting up looking at me.

"Andre, I didn't know that boy was is so much pain." She sobbed.

Even though Gregory was locked up for allegedly killing Alfred, he was the pick out of the three of us. He wasn't the only one in pain. I was in pain too. My mother didn't know her own son was in a prison within himself.

"Were you all able to reach aunt Janelle?" I asked.

"Yeah Janelle knows." She said.

May 28st, 2006

The next morning came so soon. I was sitting in the living room when aunt Celestine walked in. She suddenly started to break down. I had to get out of there. That day was India's daughter, my goddaughter's birthday party, and I promised her that I would be there. I got ready to go. Before leaving I called India.

"India I'm on the way. Something bad happen last night. I will tell you about it when I see you. Is it ok if I bring a few kids with me to your daughter's birthday party?" I asked.

"Awwww Dre, I hope everything is ok. I'll see you when you get here." She said.

I took Jai, Lyndyann, Audrekia, Djuan, Dayvon, and Ayana with me to the party. I couldn't enjoy myself because home was where I needed to be.

When we all got back home, they were getting ready for prayer. I didn't want to be a part of it. We joined in a circle holding hands. The minute sister Rowe started to pray, I busted out crying. I put my hands to my face. Seeing me break down caused everyone else to do so. The tears flowed endlessly down our faces. I regretted ever saying anything about wanting to become a star. If it weren't for me, Gregory wouldn't have ever left. Fuck that dream. I just wanted my little brother back.

26: **Brother** *(Part Two)*

June 29th, 2006

When I joined Myspace, the first person I wanted to search for was my brother Adron. I saw a few people with the name Adron Massey. I didn't know his name was that common? I came across a page without a picture, and it was an Adron Massey from Wilmington, North Carolina. This was very close to my hometown Supply. This person had not signed on in a couple of months. Could that be him? I crossed my fingers and prayed to God that this Adron Massey was indeed my brother.

I sent the person a personal message that read: *"I'm Andre Simmons from Maryland. My father name is Adron Massey. I think we are brothers. If this is in fact you, I would love to meet you. God bless you and have a great day."* I waited hours for a response, which turned into days, which turned into weeks. I totally forgot about it. Until one day I was signed on and I noticed that I had a new message. I opened it and it was from the same Adron Massey.

It read: *"OMG are you serious? I was always told that I had a brother. I would love to meet you too."* I was overwhelmed with joy. I told my mother and Jai that I found my brother over the internet. He eventually uploaded a picture of himself. Adron was very good looking. I didn't see my father in him, so I assumed he looked more like his mother. Adron revealed to me that he had two children as well; a boy a year older than Jamari and a girl a year older than J'Adora. I originally wanted to meet him to see who turned out the best; but that was no longer in my mind. I was now blessed that I found him. The best part of it all was the genuine interest in him wanting to meet me as much as I wanted to meet him. My brother and I kept in contact via phone and text messages.

27: Tug-Of-War

Flashback:

Since November 29ᵗʰ, 2004 was long behind me now. Jai wanted to fuck every chance we were together; in my car, her car, parking lots, on the grass, in the rain, all over my home, and her room. It was all about pleasing her sexual desire. Jai didn't want to just have sexual intercourse; she wanted oral sex as well. However, the vagina didn't taste like "Peaches And Cream" as 112's song said. It was sour and tart. I never wanted her to suck my dick either. That's something she wanted to do, and she would always use too much teeth for me to truly enjoy it. I would always tell her she didn't have to; however, she always insisted. Not one time did she get me off that way. As months and years went on, into 2005 and early 2006 all the sex we were having, condoms were no longer a priority in our relationship. Was I ready to become a father? Fuck no, but I had been cumming in Jai's vagina for months. I knew Jai was pregnant before she did. When she told me her period was late, it was unusual. Her period was never late. When Jai and I found out that we were pregnant, we kept it quiet until her first doctor's visit. Even though Jai had already taken two pregnancy tests prior, we still wanted confirmation. When it was confirmed, I knew the news would be a surprise to my mother because Jai and I had always kept our business very private. Not only was Jai pregnant, but my sister was too. Moving to L.A. and becoming an actor was still at the top of my list. Nothing was going to prevent that from happening. Not even a baby was going to stop me. Jai and I were a team and we would always have each other's back. My mother was the first to know, then Delvin, Kendrell, Gregory, and Lyndyann. My family was very supportive. Jai's family on the other hand felt indifferent about the situation. Even though Jai and I no longer worked at Shoppers, they got the news that Jai and I were having our first child together. A friend of mine named Red; also, an employee at Shoppers informed me that Jai's mother was saying all kinds of things about me to other employees who knew of Jai and me. I never confronted her mother about it because I knew what type of father I was determined to be. It didn't matter what she thought, or how she felt about the situation. I refused to be the type of father she assumed I would be.

Fast Forward:

July 12th, 2006

I was curious to find out for myself, so I decided to go to Shoppers. Kim, who worked as a bookkeeper was telling me everything that Jai's family said. From that day forth, I never went back to Shoppers. Curiosity killed the cat "Ha-ha!" I decided I'd confront Jai about her mother. However, I decided not to stress the issue too much because she was pregnant.

"Andre doesn't seem like the type of guy that would take care of kids Jai." - Jai's father.

I felt that Jai's father's opinion, concerning the type of father he assumed I'd be was unnecessary. This is coming from a man who didn't intervene or stand up for his daughter when she was kicked out into the streets at twenty-one by her mother. Reason being;

"There will only be one wife in this house." - Jai's mother.

She was only jealous of the fact that Jai had gotten her first car. Any sane mother would be happy that their daughter was doing something positive; however, not her. This was the same woman who accused her husband of sexually molesting Jai and her younger sister Minnie when they were little girls. That was a damn lie. What sane mother would stay with a man if he was sexually molesting her children? Only a weak-minded individual would stay, unless it was a damn lie. Since I have known the family, Jai's mother constantly dragged that man's name in the mud. Through it all he's always done his part and provided for his family. I go on record to say that she's crazy. Jai's mother has always been, and probably always will be crazy.

There's this whole perspective of *"First comes love, then comes marriage, then comes the baby in a baby carriage."* I realized that I had to make a choice. I concluded that I was going to join the military and make something of myself. I wanted to prove that I could be the best father ever. I was determined to prove the doubters wrong.

When I talked to the Air Force recruiter Sgt. Smith on July 26th, 2006, he explained that I if I were to join the military, I wouldn't be allowed to bring my girlfriend and new baby unless I was married. After receiving the information, I went straight home to discuss it with Jai.

"Jai, I'm joining the military. The only way you and the baby can travel with me is if we get married." I said.

"We should get married then." She responded.

I was ok with the idea of getting married, because it meant my family would be together while I was making a better life for us. On the contrary, I never wanted to get married. I was just determined to be a better father than her father, as well as mine.

When the time came for me to take the ASVAB, I failed it purposely. I sat there, glanced at the questions, and marked any answer without thinking twice about. I never took it again. Honestly, my heart wasn't in the military. I only investigated it as my last resort. I didn't feel I was there just yet. Be that as it may, that still didn't change the fact that a baby was on the way. Whatever the future held, and if Jai and I didn't work out; I still believed that we would be great responsible parents. I also believed that no matter the outcome, we'd both equally do our part for our unborn child.

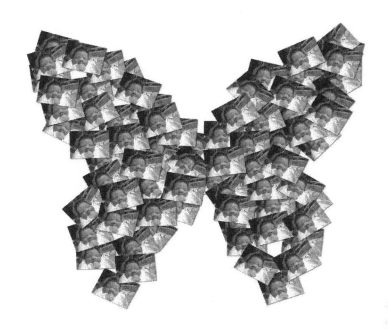

Larva: Jamari. *October 18ᵗʰ, 2006.*

28: **Jamari Ondrej Simmons**

Sex: Male

Weight: 7lbs. 11oz.

Time: 20:18PM

Mother's Age: 23

Father's Age: 22

In French, the name Jamari means - warrior. The name Jamari originated as a French name.

Ondrej is a Czechoslovakian boy name. Meaning - courageous.

October 18th, 2006

That afternoon Jai returned home from her final doctor visit. She was due to give birth any day now. She was in the bathroom when she called for me.

"Andre, I think my water broke." She said sitting on the toilet.

"Are you in any pain?" I wondered.

"No." She responded.

Right away I called my mother to tell her the news.

"You guys should go to the hospital." She told me.

I quickly got up and hopped in the shower. After gathering everything we needed, we headed over to Prince George's Hospital Center. We checked in and were asked to wait in a small room. They told us a nurse had to verify that her water broke.

"How are you feeling?" I comforted her.

"I feel mild contractions." She said with a slight smile.

The nurse finally came in to examine Jai.

"Yes, your water broke." The nurse confirmed.

She then told us to wait while they got us a room. I called my job to inform that I was at the hospital with my girlfriend, and that I wouldn't be coming into work. Afterwards we watched TV for a while.

"Is there anything you need? Anything I can get you?" I comforted.

"No, I'm okay." She replied.

A couple of hours passed. Then there was a knock at the door, and Jai's mother walked in. Neither of us wanted her there. However, after seeing her, I had a slight change of heart. I felt like she should be there to share the moment. Our whole demeanor changed, but it wasn't about her that day; it was about the birth of our child. Her mother wasn't even there for thirty minutes, before she needed a favor.

"Andre, can you do me a huge favor and go pick up Minnie from school?" She asked.

I couldn't believe she was asking me to do this. I was the one who called her to share this moment with us, and now here she was asking me to go pick up her daughter from school. I felt bad for all her daughters because they had her for a mother. I was torn. I didn't know what to do. Where was Jai's father? By that time Jai's contractions were back to back. My mother wasn't there yet; however, she called to let me know that she was on the way. If I did leave, I didn't want to leave Jai alone with her mother. I was waiting for Jai to tell her mother no, but that never happened.

"What's the name of the school?" I sighed and asked.

She gave me the address and I left the room. Before I left the hospital, the nurse let me know that I had time before she would deliver. What I thought would be a straight trip back and forth, turned out to be several. Since I had time, I stopped by the house to get my check, so I could cash it. I rushed to the Share Branch Credit Union. After standing in line for about 15 minutes, the teller told me that they couldn't cash a postdated check. I was so upset, but it was my fault. I should have checked the date on the check. I left to pick Minnie up from school. When I arrived she was nowhere to be found. I later found out that her friend's parent dropped her off at home. What a total waste. I should have stayed. It was after 8:00PM when I called my mother to get an update.

"Andre, where are you?! Jai's pushing!" She said excitedly.

I started speeding down highway 202. I was rushing to get back to see the birth of my first born. Then I heard it, it was the sounds of his/her cry on the other end of the line. My heart fell to bottom of my stomach. I was absolutely shattered.

"It's a boy! Andre you have a boy!" My mother cried out.

I was about to break down over the phone.

"Hurry up Andre, and take your time getting here." My mother said.

I could only blame myself. I was there however, I didn't tell Jai's mother no when I honestly should have. I didn't want to leave in the first place. I felt disgusted with myself. When I walked back into the delivery room Jai was holding him. I slowly walked towards her. I saw a very pale looking baby.

"What the fuck?!" I thought.

I was at a loss for words. I thought to myself, "There is no fucking way was this kid mine."

I just looked at him, and then she handed him to me. The moment I touched him everything went silent. The storm in my heart was slowly dying. I never held anything so special in all my life. I was holding God's gift. As soon as he pressed his lips together, I could see the dimple forming in his left cheek. Right then I knew, "Yes, Andre you are the father." I thought.

That moment became the happiest and scariest moment of my life. The fantasy of Jai's pregnancy was now a reality. I welcomed my son Jamari Ondrej Simmons into the world. Even though I didn't have a clue on how to raise my son, I knew I would love him unconditionally; and I would never abandon him. That day was a new beginning for me as a man. I wanted to be the best father that I could possibly be. I hoped that his existence would kill my strong desire of wanting to be with a man. I wanted it to disappear forever.

29: **Flashing Lights**

November 9th, 2006

The bar and club scene were never my style. I never quite understood why people would spend outrageous amounts of money on watered down alcohol, when it was so much cheaper to just go to the liquor store. One-night Red and I had been drinking. I knew my limit because I wouldn't drink behind the wheel.

"Are you ready to go home?" I asked him as I pulled out of the Walmart parking lot in Bowie.

"No, it's only 11:30PM. I don't have to be at work until 10:00AM." He responded.

"Where should we go to next?" I asked.

"Let's go to Annapolis." He suggested.

"Alright then." I agreed.

Annapolis was only a twenty-minute drive. I took highway 50. Then I took exit 23. As I was coming off the bridge, I realized we were being followed. I never told Red because I didn't want him to get riled up. I checked my speedometer and I was going the exact speed limit. I put my left signal light on and switched over to the left lane. The cop followed. Red was just talking his little head off. I wasn't paying him any mind.

"Dre?" He said.

I didn't answer.

"Dre!" He shouted as he grabbed the wheel and jerked it.

"Red! Why did you do that?!" I shouted.

Instantly I saw the flashing lights come on.

"What the fuck?!" Red said and turned around.

Rule number 1, never ever turn around when getting pulled over by cops.

"Turn your ass around!" I snapped.

I put my right signal light on and pulled over.

"Don't worry." I said trying to remain calm; as well as trying to keep him cool. Two minutes passed, and the cops finally decided to get out their car. "Oh, fucking great they're white, Red." I said looking in my rearview mirror.

Police officer 1 walked over to my side and the other on Red's side. Police officer 2 was flashing his flashlight inside the car. He tapped on the window while shining the light in my face. I rolled down the window.

"License and registration." Police officer 1 asked.

Police officer 2 walked around the front of my car to stand beside his partner. I handed the officer my information.

"Have you been drinking?" He questioned.

"I had a little earlier, officer." I stated.

"I pulled you over because you were swerving." He explained.

I didn't say anything. Police officer 2 took my information and walked back to his car. Within two minutes he returned.

"Turn your car off and step out of the vehicle." He ordered.

I followed his instructions, turned the car off and stepped out.

"Close the door. Lift up both your arms, turn around, place both hands on the car and spread both your legs." He instructed.

Police officer 2 frisked me. After he didn't find anything, I was then given a Breathalyzer test. I didn't refuse because I knew that I wasn't over my alcohol limit.

"I want you to take a deep breath." He said.

"Ok sure." I answered.

Studies have shown that a driver who holds his breath before blowing into a Breathalyzer will increase the BAC reading by 15.7%, while a driver who hyperventilates will decrease his BAC result by 10.6%. That is a 26.3% difference. The police officer wants the driver to take a big breath and blow hard, so that they exhale as much of that alcohol-rich air in the bottom of their lungs. Do not fall for it. I blew as hard as I could anyway. I passed the test. Then police officer 1 told me to walk in a straight line, toe to toe. I passed that test as well. The next thing I knew, police

officer 2 requested to Red to step out of the car. I felt like
something wasn't right. I didn't understand why they
would ask him to do the test, when I already passed; and
furthermore, he wasn't the driver. They made Red do the
same test they asked me to do.

"To be honest with you, it's hard for me to walk in a
straight line due to my weight." He said when they asked
him to do it.

They could have careless about his reasoning. They still
made him do it. I just stood there as they laughed at him
stumble back and forth. After they were done being
amused, police officer 1 told us to get back in the car. I put
my seatbelt back on. Police officer 1 handed me my
driver's license and registration. As they were walking
away, I heard them say, "They need to just take their black
asses back to P.G. County."

"Red did you hear that?" I asked surprised.

"They need to just take their black asses back to P.G.
County." Red repeated.

We both laughed, as I drove off. I took the stripes that I
earned, lesson learned.

30: **Ghostly Holiday**

December 23rd, 2006

The upside was that Jai and I were proud new parents of 2 month and 5-day old Jamari Ondrej Simmons. Jai and I were happy as ever. Just to prove to everyone that Jai was still bad, I made sure I picked out every outfit that she was going to wear while we were down there. We were the last to drive down to North Carolina in Jai's yellow Cavalier aka Beyoncé. Jamari slept the whole ride down, which was a true blessing being that it was his first road trip. Jamari was truly the best baby in the world.

When we finally pulled up in my grandmother's yard, the weather felt more like spring, than winter. Jai was in full model mode; true fashion. I watched her as she stepped out of the car wearing her 5-inch stilettos. Strutting across the grass, she walked on the porch of my grandmother's home. Moments like that truly made me happy.

"Wait for us." I said giggling.

She looked back at Jamari and me.

"A diva never waits." She said as she flipped her permed roller wrapped hair.

I took Jamari out of his car seat. She flipped her hair again.

"Will you two hurry up!" She yelled from the porch.

"Ok, open the door." I said when I finally made it up the steps. "Hi everybody, we're here." I said walking in.

Greeting the family, I could feel that there was love and tension at the same time. Jamari was passed around like a Sunday's tithes and offering plate. The downside about that visit was that it was the first time everyone had been together since the incident with Gregory. Most of the family in North Carolina felt he shot Alfred. The family in Maryland felt it was a setup. We felt he went to jail for a crime he didn't commit. Following the shooting, Alfred later passed away. The night was full of laughter and good old times, nonetheless. Jai and I stayed at uncle Allan's house which was right next door to grandmothers.

December 24th, 2006

As much as I loved being in North Carolina, there wasn't much to do. Jai, Kendrell, his girlfriend, and I decided to go to the mall in South Carolina on Christmas Eve. We went back to my grandmother's home to speak to everyone before we headed out. Jai walked in first, and I immediately followed.

"You dress like an ole Faggot." Uncle Vonice had said in front of everyone.

No hello, no congratulations Andre on being a dad, or anything. When it came to me, I can't recall anything positive ever coming out of that man's mouth.

"Hello to you too uncle Vonice. How's Cassie?" He didn't say anything after that.

Cassie was a woman he had a previous relationship with before he married aunt Julie. It was rumored that he was still messing around with her behind aunt Julie's back. Aunt Julie was in the kitchen cooking while this conversation was going on. No fucks were given. He embarrassed the hell out of me in front of Jai and the family. I sat down on the couch and all eyes were on me.

"This is why I hate coming down here! I hate that black fat fucker! Are you guys ready to go?" I asked.

We headed out and enjoyed ourselves. Calabash seafood is a must every time we were in North Carolina. Eating food this good, made me forget about my big black bear of an uncle. We retuned back to grandmother's home later that evening. Everyone was still at grandmother's home when we got back. The children under the age of ten weren't allowed to stay at grandmother's home on Christmas Eve. That's where all the Christmas gifts were wrapped. This was also the highlight of Christmas where I would organize the Christmas tree by families and secret Santa gifts. It would literally take me hours; however, the finished product was always beautiful.

December 25th, 2006

Christmas day was beautiful. The kids came back over and opened their gifts. Seeing how happy they were, and the smiles on their faces was too precious. After the kids opened their gifts, everyone else opened theirs. Christmas music was playing, and everyone was fighting to get into the one bathroom in the home. The smell of breakfast and Christmas dinner cooking at the same time; what a warm priceless feeling. I couldn't stop thinking about aunt Janelle and what she could possibly be going through now. I glanced over at her. I smiled, and she smiled back. One thing I know for sure is that my grandmother raised some strong women. They can all hide their pain so well. That's a good and bad thing.

After all the hours of opening gifts and laughter, I had to reorganize the tree with the remaining gifts. The secret Santa gifts were opened after dinner. The evening ended perfectly.

December 26th, 2006

At some point, Kendrell and I had to go see Gregory. He was at the Complex which was only 15 minutes away. We told our mothers that we were going to pay him a visit. I took Jamari with us because I wanted Greg to meet him. I didn't know what to expect. That was my first time visiting anyone who was locked up. It was nothing like the movies. I pictured a large glass screen that divided the civilians and the criminals. There was only one chair and a 10-inch screen. We waited for a couple of minutes, and suddenly he popped up on the screen. He smiled. I smiled and turned to the side to look at Kendrell; he was smiling too.

"Hey Gregory. Merry Christmas." I said.

"This is Jamari, say hi uncle Gregory." I said holding Jamari up. He just smiled some more.

"What's going on man?" Kendrell asked him.

"Nothing." He replied and smiled.

There were so many questions that I wanted to ask him; however, it wasn't the time. It killed me inside to see our baby brother in that situation. I didn't know what he was going through. I didn't know the pain he was feeling inside.

"I love you Gregory." I told him.

He just kept smiling. He didn't say much at all, which was completely understandable. He was only eighteen and he was locked up behind bars on Christmas. On the screen I could see boys walking behind him, some of them just hanging around. I didn't want to come off too mushy or emotional because I had to remember where Gregory was. We stayed for a few more minutes, and then we left. The drive back to our grandmother's home was a silent night.

31: Got The Job!

I lost my job, as a security guard at Geico for tardiness. As a result, I was on unemployment. I was now able to babysit Jamari, collect unemployment, and clean houses because of my mother's cleaning business. I was making more money cleaning houses, than I was when I was working. On the other hand, I didn't want to get too dependent on the system and I didn't want to be up underneath my mom either. I didn't have a clear sense of direction, and I was unsure of what I wanted to do. I only wanted to become an actor, and move to L.A. Even though my dream was slowly slipping away, there wasn't a day that I didn't think about it.

Fast Forward:

Jai's brother told me about a job and its requirements on Friday, August 3rd, 2007 while I was cleaning a client's house. I was apprehensive at the beginning, and I wasn't confident about shooting a gun. It wasn't my thing. The fact that I came from a family of hunters didn't matter. Jai's brother kept pushing me to take the job, and I finally gave in.

My first interview was on Friday, August 10th, 2007 and it went very well. I took training classes for the job and the expectations of the officers. The classes also taught the proper usage and the maintenance of a gun. A 9-millimeter, as well as a shotgun was given to all the guards. When I went to the gun range to take my test, I had no idea that shooting a gun would be an issue.

The shooting targets were at 5 meters, 7 meters, 15 meters, and 25 meters. 300 was a perfect score. I had to score at least a 220 to pass. My first time shooting I scored 160. My second time I scored 175. I wound up failing. The next test that I had to take was agility test. It consisted of eighteen pushups, twenty-seven sit-ups, and I had to run a mile within eleven minutes. I was unable to complete my pushups. My arms began to burn, and I was beginning to feel weak. I got the spaghetti arms after my tenth pushup. After my nineteenth sit up, I was coughing uncontrollably in front of the Captain and Chief. It was sad because they were much older than me. They stood there shaking their heads at me.

"Mr. Simmons you said you wanted this job." The Chief stated.

"I do sir, I really do." I responded.

"Well we're going to have to let you go. You seem like a good guy, but I don't think you're cut out for this work. Try believing in yourself more Mr. Simmons." He suggested.

Maybe he was right. Maybe I wasn't cut out for that type of work. Fortunately, I was able to complete the mile.

August 20th, 2007

I was at the park with Jamari when I received a phone call. I didn't recognize the number, so I decided not to answer. I noticed the voicemail icon and realized the person left a message. It was from a woman named Stephanie. She called to inform me that they were doing mass hiring in the Washington D.C., Maryland, and Virginia area. She wanted to know if I was interested. I was hesitant, but I knew I could do it. I called her back to set up an interview. I chose the location Walter Reed Army Medical Center in Washington D.C. I knew what the requirements were, and I prepared a couple of weeks in advanced, so I wouldn't fail the agility test. When the time came, I passed the agility test and I scored a 261 on my gun range test. The training class itself was two weeks long from 8:00AM - 4:00PM Monday - Friday in Lorton, Virginia. It was a little difficult to see the targets, so the next time I planned to borrow my mother's glasses.

September 10th, 2007

On my first day at work I was like a kid in a candy store. Never in a million years did I think that I would be making that type of money. June 11th, 2007, I lost my job making $11.00 an hour and then 2 months later I was making $17.60 an hour. Everything was going great.

November 1st, 2007

There was one big elephant in the room, and it was Jai pushing the issue to get married. I just started working my new job, and it was impossible for me to take off to go to the courthouse to marry Jai. If anything, I was going to be the one to choose the date. It wouldn't be on her terms or her time. I decided to tell my mother what our plans were.

"Mom? Jai and I are going to get married on my birthday. Can you be there?" I requested.

"Andre you are a grown man. If that's something that you're sure about doing, I will stand by your decision as your mother. But I will not be there." She stated.

Did I like my mother's answer? No; however, I felt like I had no choice. I had to do what I had to do, even though I didn't want to. I wanted and needed my mother to tell me not to marry her. Deep down inside I knew if she told me not to, I would have still done it anyway. I guess I needed someone to blame for the mistake that I was about to make.

32: **Wedding Vows**

November 29th, 2007

My 24th Birthday

Jai, Jamari and I woke up early to head to Upper Marlboro courthouse. Jai couldn't stop smiling. "Damn man, I can't do this to this girl. She has been riding with me for so long." I thought to myself on the drive there. We weren't in proper attire; in other words, we didn't have the wedding look. We were dressed in casual clothes. We walked into the office, and there were two couples ahead of us; a white couple who looked like they belonged on top of a wedding cake and an older Mexican couple.

"Mr. Simmons and Ms. Richards." The lady behind the desk called us.

She led us into a smaller room where the priest was. Here goes, this was my last chance. "Dear God, please make this boy cry that I'm holding." I prayed.

As the priest began the ceremony, Jamari couldn't stop smiling just like his mother.

"We are gathered here today to unite this man Andre, and this woman Jai in the bonds of holy matrimony. To the groom, do you Andre take Jai to be your lawfully wedded wife? If so, answer I do." He presided.

I glanced at Jamari one last time, and he was still smiling.

"I do." I said.

"To the Bride, do you take Andre to be your lawfully wedded husband? If so, answer I do." He stated.

"I do!" She shouted.

"By the power vested in me, by the State-of-Maryland, I now pronounce you husband and wife." He confirmed.

We kissed and hugged each other while I was still holding Jamari in my arms. We got our wedding certificate, and on the way out the court house I put Jamari down to walk. Right then he started to cry.

"Oh, now you want to cry Jamari?" I asked.

"Why'd you say that?" Jai questioned.

"Because, if this little nigga started crying while the minster was reading, I wasn't going to go through with it." I said directly.

"Are you serious?" She asked sadly.

"Yes, I sure was. But he didn't cry. You're stuck with me forever now." I said laughing.

33: **Fool 4 U**

Flashback:

Jai suggested that we move out of my mother's home to get a place of our own. I thought she was kidding at first, but she was dead serious. I wasn't even working ninety days yet and she wanted to move. My mother was strongly against it because she felt like we weren't ready. Especially with baby number two on the way. Once again, my mother was right.

"Andre, know what you're getting yourself into son." She suggested.

"Mom we will be alright. Don't forget we're only moving next door." I explained laughing.

I was uncertain about making the move. I began to think maybe my mother knew that I truly did not want to do it. Honestly, I just wanted to prove that I was a man and that I could handle any challenge. If Superman could save the world on more than one occasion, then I could save one relationship. I told Jai that I wanted to move to Bowie, Kettering, or Largo, Maryland. We quickly became aware that Bowie was way out of our price range, and it wasn't metro accessible. We settled with Steeplechase Apartments, which was literally right across the street from where my mother lived. It was funny to me because she made a fuss about moving, and we were literally across the street. We were moving out to basically live next door.

Fast Forward:

December 3rd, 2007

I knew something was bothering Jai; however, I couldn't quite put my finger on it. It seemed like the closer the holidays approached, the more distant she became. We were moving out, so it could only be two things. Jai didn't want to have this baby, or she wasn't happy with me. We were watching TV after she came home from work that day. She didn't say anything and neither did I.

"Andre I may lose my job." She blurted out.

"What do you mean; you may lose your job?" I asked and thanking God that I wasn't the problem after all.

"I've been late a lot lately. I'm tired Andre." She explained.

"Well Jai, what do you want to do? We're moving at the beginning of the year. Remember, this is something you wanted to do. Are you having second thoughts? Say it now Jai." I pressed.

"No, I still want to move." She answered.

"Ok. I'm lost. Now tell me why you may lose your job again?" I said.

"I've just been really tired." She said.

"Then maybe you should try to get more rest." I suggested.

There was nothing left to say. Somehow, I knew there was more to this conversation. She just wasn't telling me. In due time I hoped everything would be revealed.

December 19th, 2007

Sixteen days later Jai came home telling me that she decided to quit her job.

"Andre, I put my two weeks' notice in today." She said nonchalantly.

"Why the fuck would you do that?! We're moving out soon and expecting another baby!" I shouted.

I was immensely pissed off. I wanted to talk to my mother immediately about Jai randomly quitting her job. As a result, I felt the move had to be put on hold. Despite it all, according to Jai everything would be fine. She had a plan. What plan exactly? I didn't have a clue.

"I'm going to get another job." She assured.

"You're two months pregnant!" I screamed.

"Trust me. Trust me Andre." She said trying to sway me.

"Ok." I said and headed downstairs.

I got to my room, looked at the banana boxes that I had packed, and plopped down on the bed.

"What am I going to do?" I asked myself out loud.

February 18th, 2008

I was in the booth at work watching a movie on my portable DVD player when my phone rung.

"Hello?" I answered.

"Good afternoon. Is this Mr. Simmons?" The voice of a woman asked.

"Yes, this is Mr. Simmons." I said.

"Yes. It has been brought to our attention that your wife no longer works at Chevy Chase Bank." A rep from Steeplechase.

"Ok. So, what's your point?" I questioned.

"Well Mr. Simmons, based on your income alone you won't be able to move into the two-bedroom apt. that you're requesting." She specified.

"Are you serious? Ok. Thank you. I will call my wife." I said.

As mad as I was, I tried my best to explain the situation to Jai without causing her any stress. She only said once again, that she would find something. I trusted that she would, even though deep down inside I knew she wouldn't find a job in such a short time.

March 1st, 2008

As luck would have its Jai did get a job at Aflac. This job was based on commission. The good news was that we were able to move into the apartment on the 1st of the month. Jai was 5 ½ months pregnant by then, and her baby bump was clear as day. Both of our income tax checks went towards our apartment. We bought a 52-inch flat screen TV and a dining room set. My mother blessed us with a sofa/love seat, and a bedroom set.

For the most part, things were going well. Pending the second month, I soon realized the fairytale had come to an end. I found myself asking for more hours on my job. I needed as many hours as I could possibly get. Unfortunately, the new job that Jai had wasn't much help come time to pay rent. The more hours I'd work, the more money I made only to see it go towards rent, groceries, and providing for my family.

Occasionally I would work sixteen hours a day. After a while it became pointless to leave work. I would often sleep in my car and shower at the gym on my break. To come home to a dirty apartment with no food prepared, after working didn't help either. I felt as a hardworking man, there was no reason why I should have to come home to an unclean apartment. At the time, I guess Jai was so busy with morning sickness and Jamari throughout the day that she didn't have time to cook or clean.

June 27th, 2008

I've always be very appreciative of everything that my mother's ever done for me. I was even grateful when she gave me her 1998 C280 Mercedes Benz. It overheated a lot; however, it was my only transportation to and from work. Conveniently my mother gave me every vehicle I'd ever owned. Eventually I got to the point where I wanted to find my dream car. One day while at work, after I signed a customer in, I saw it. It was a beautiful green automobile.

On the back door it read Jeep. I went back into the booth and googled it. I learned that it was a Jeep Commander.

"I will own that Jeep one day." I said out loud.

I knew it was out of my price range though it wouldn't have been if we weren't in a hurry to move. Still I wanted to do something for myself. With J'Adora on the way, we needed something bigger.

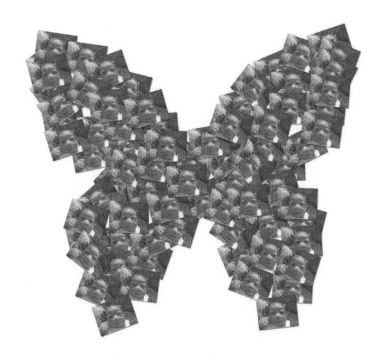

Larva: J'Adora. *July 17ᵗʰ, 2008.*

34: J'Adora Krismas Simmons

Sex: Female

Weight: 7lbs. 12oz.

Time: 17:46PM

Mother's Age: 25

Father's Age: 24

With the boy out of the way, it was exciting and such a blessing to bring new life into the world. However, nothing compares to your first born. We wanted to know immediately what the sex of the baby was.

"It's a girl!"

How awesome was that? A boy, and now a girl? Everyone, including Jai assumed that her name would start with an A. I wanted her name to begin with a J.

"Can I name her?" I asked Jai.

She smiled and agreed.

One Sunday night at work I remember scanning through the Sunday's paper. I flipped through the pages and came crossed a Macy's catalogue. I saw the perfume called J'adore, and I liked the name of it. "This could definitely work, but I need to add a twist to it to make it my own." I thought. "What if I drop the e on the end and add an a; and then capitalize the A after the J? I asked myself aloud. "The capitol J and A will stand for Jai and I. Then I will add an apostrophe between the capitalized J and A. J'Adora. I love it." I thought excitedly. That night when I arrived back home from work, I was elated to tell her.

"Jai, I think I have our daughter's name!" I said walking through the door.

"What is it?" She asked.

"J'Adora." I gleamed smiling.

"I like that." She gushed and returned a smile.

"What do you think about Krismas for her middle name?" I suggested.

"Christmas? Like the holiday? Why?" She asked with a strange look on her face.

"It's pronounced Christmas, like the holiday, but its spelled K-R-I-S-M-A-S and it's in memory of you grandmother since she passed away last Christmas." I explained.

"Andre, I love it!" She said grinning.

Everyone loved that name. J'Adora Krismas Simmons.

July 17th, 2008

"I've got this!" Nothing was going to stop me from seeing the birth of my daughter.

With Jamari's birth, we didn't find out the sex of the baby until he was born. To already have a boy, then to find out we were going to have a girl was more than exciting. I was building America's ideal family.

Seeing the feces come from her butt and her vagina stretching was no surprise to me. I knew all of this was normal for a woman giving birth. My issue was the way the doctor was handling the neck of my baby struggling to get her out. "Really sir? You're going to break her fucking neck!" I thought to myself. He was wiggling and twisting her head. He kept pulling as Jai continued to push. Then I saw her chest, arms, hands, stomach, her thighs, her legs, and finally her feet. Thank God for another healthy baby. She didn't cry right away. The doctor snipped the umbilical cord, picked her up, and stuck a tube down her throat. I finally heard her first cry. J'Adora Krismas Simmons was born.

Jamari and J'Adora. *July 21ˢᵗ, 2008.*

"To cut off the confusion and accept an answer just because it's too scary not to have an answer is a good way to get the wrong answer." - Janet Jackson

35: **Janet Jackson** *(Rock Witchu Tour)*

Flashback:

While living in Kettering, Maryland back in the early 90's, we didn't have cable. There was only one television in the house located downstairs in the living room. Most of our movies came from yard sales and we had quite the collection. I was flipping through the rows of VHS tapes and stumbled upon one that read: *Janet Jackson Music Videos "Nasty" and "What Have You Done For Me Lately."* I put the tape in the VCR and pressed play. I remember seeing the word Nasty and guys were making noises. Then a lady dressed in black Janet Jackson was leading the group of friends. She had the meanest walk that I had ever seen. Janet made her way to the front of the line and handed the guy her ticket. As he shined the light up and down her body, Janet rolled her eyes and continued inside the theater. The guys still grunting and hollering like wolves proceeded to follow the three young women. Once Janet made it to her seat, the movie was already playing with a violent shoot out scene. The guys still taunting the young women came to sit with and behind them. One of the guys rubbed his hand across Janet's thigh. She removed his hand and turned her body to her friend.

"What are you doing after the movie?" The other guy asked Janet.

Then Janet got up out of her seat.

"Stop!" She shouted.

Janet made her way to the big screen. All eyes were on her.

"Give me a beat!" She shouted as she danced, and the beat knocked.

Janet back flipped and landed in the screen where she was then the main attraction. Janet was dancing to the beat of the song with male backup dancers following her lead. The rest was history. I have been a huge fan of Janet Damita Jo Jackson ever since.

Fast Forward:

October 15th, 2008

On May 19th, 2008 Janet Jackson announced that she would be touring on The Ellen DeGeneres Show. While planning the tour, Janet started a phone line where fans could call in and request songs to be performed. I was unsure of the ticket prices, so I started saving my money bi-weekly. Jai isn't a Janet fan besides I didn't have anyone else to go with. So, I purchased her a ticket as well. When the night finally arrived, I was so nervous because Janet cancelled seven shows prior to ours. With the last cancellation being only two days ago, I didn't know what to expect. I hid the tickets under Jai's jewelry box in our bedroom and decided to play a prank on her.

"Jai have you seen the tickets?" I wondered.

"No, I haven't. You had them." She said.

"They are no longer where I left them last. Are you sure you didn't move the tickets?" I asked trying to keep a straight face.

"I don't know where the damn tickets are! Stop trying to blame me for stuff!" She snapped.

I swear I wanted to hit her. Instead, I threw the Vogue magazine Jennifer Hudson covered at her to calm her down.

"I was just fucking playing with you!" I shouted.

"I can't believe you hit me!" She shrieked.

"What?" I chuckled.

"You hit me Andre!" She continued.

"Really? I threw a magazine at you." I said rolling my eyes.

I felt bad about throwing it at her. I shook it off and we got ready for the concert. We left the house and caught the metro. We didn't bring up what happened earlier. I was too excited to see Janet to worry about a petty little argument. When we made it to the arena, we took a few pictures together and headed inside. The seats we had weren't bad at all. I was just hoping that Janet would show.

When the intro started, the crowd was on their feet. Then suddenly, "You might think I'm crazy But I'm serious…" Janet came out in a futuristic tan bodysuit and a Mohawk that had to be about a foot high. The crowd went crazy! My left leg was shaking uncontrollably; only Janet had the power to do that. It was the second greatest moment of 2008; my daughter being born was the first.

36: **Brother** (*Part Three*)

December 26th, 2008

Jai and Jamari came with me to meet my brother at Independence mall; the same mall that I went to looking for him six years previously. Five-month-old J'Adora stayed with my mother at my grandmother's home. Trying my best to go the speed limit, and sweating uncontrollably, I eventually made it. When I reached the mall, I called him.

"Hello Adron. I'm here at the mall now. Where should we meet up?" I gushed.

"Hey bro, meet me at the food court" He answered.

"Ok. Cool" I said hanging up.

As I sat there waiting for Adron, I watched as customers returned gifts and bought new things during the day after Christmas event. I had a permanent visual of Adron in my mind. There was a picture of him that I saw six years ago, and that was the image I had locked away. "Ok Adron where are you? Did you get nervous? Were you ever coming at all? What the hell is taking you so long?" My mind started to get the best of me. Then suddenly I spotted him.

"Jai there he is!" I said with a big smile on my face.

I felt like a five-year-old boy. As he got closer to me, I noticed that he wasn't alone. He was with his son and a woman. I stood up. He was taller than me, and better looking too in my opinion. "Stop it Andre, he's your brother. All that stuff is null and void."

"What's up bro?" He said reaching for a hug.

We embraced.

"This is Jai, and this is my son Jamari." I gushed pointing at my family proudly.

He hugged Jai and greeted Jamari as well. Then he introduced us to his girlfriend and son. Jai, Jamari, Adron's girlfriend and son all left Adron and I to catch up. We spoke about everything, including our father. Adron revealed to me that dad wasn't a big part of his life either. We shared our dreams with one another, shared what it's like being fathers, etc. Further into the conversation we found out that the both us were into acting. He also told me that he was an extra is the film Idlewild. I told him I starred in a promo commercial for HEW Federal Credit Union back in June 2006. The conversation was amazing. It was refreshing to finally be able to talk to someone who I had so much in common with. Even though I was smiling on the outside, I was still crying on the inside because I wanted to talk to him about my marriage. I didn't want to scare him away, so I just pushed it to the back of my mind. I didn't want it to end however, the mall was closing. Adron and I made a promise that we would always keep in touch. I thanked God that I was finally able to meet my brother.

37: Home Sweet Home

March 31st, 2009

Thirteen months prior, I left my mother's home and moved my wife and son age 3, into Steeplechase Apartments. Now I was returning to my mother's home with my wife, son, and daughter. I was unhappy about the move back, simply because it felt like I was in a time warp traveling backwards. However, the advantage of returning was a blessing financially. As expensive as the rent was, I loved my privacy. By no means do I hate my family; however, I enjoyed when they weren't around as much. Acquiring the Jeep aka Lady Gaga wasn't the smartest move after all. I had no idea that once I made the decision to buy the Jeep that things would go south.

When Jai started working in October 2008, she began paying the electric bill and decided to get the cable turned on. While living there, my mother would frequently drop by with groceries and see the babies during the week. Jai worked on weekends and I was always at home without transportation. My mother would keep the kids every weekend to give me a break.

Often Red would come over to hang out with me. I would cook for us; we'd drink, and watch movies. Jai never knew about it because I kept it from her, being that she wasn't too fond of him. Besides, when I was home alone, I kept our place spotless. When I would clean, it was really the only time I had peace. I was shattered by the thought of the direction Jai and I was headed in. I no longer saw her in my future. That dream I once had of us attending the Oscars together was gone. I didn't dream at all. I don't consider nightmares dreams. I had totally given up the idea of wanting to act. The black and white, and colored headshots that I had taken in 2006, were now in pictures frames. I felt alone, and I didn't have anyone to confide in. Time and again, I wished that God would have allowed my father to reach out to me. I needed him more now than ever. Even if it was just a shoulder to lean on, I would've been satisfied with that. I felt lost without him. My father's absence was really starting to take its toll on me. Jamari and J'Adora gravitated towards my mother; she was like milk and honey. They just couldn't get enough of their sweet grandmother. Jai always had a problem with it. Jealously was all it was because she felt like my mother was trying to take her place. I never understood why she felt that way about my mother, and I never will. In my opinion, if she felt that way about my mother then she should have stepped her motherly duties up. On numerous occasions I would hear Jamari knocking on his mother's bedroom door, and she'd ignore him every time. If I wasn't working, I would try to sleep my life away trying to escape reality. Some days I would just lie in bed until my side ached. I didn't realize it; however, I was falling into deep depression. I was existing, not living.

38: **Face Mask**

May 7th, 2009

All I wanted to do was sleep and sleep even more. I didn't have the energy to do anything else. Sadly, I was unable to sleep at home anymore. Our work schedules were hectic because we were short staffed. We were losing staff left and right. People were calling out and getting fired. There were plenty of no call, no shows, quitting, and suspensions. There was no unity on our job. Our new Chief didn't care about seniority either.

I was beyond stressed out and it would show on my skin. My skin was at its worst. I remembered being told by family members that my skin would clear up once I became sexually active, that was a lie! Having several dermatologists visits the cream prescribed was a quick fix which caused me to breakout even more due to my sensitive skin. I have probably tried every over the counter product known to mankind: Proactive, Murad Acne, Neutrogena, peroxide, alcohol, black soap; even baby piss, which I was told was an old country remedy. None of these products or remedies worked. Furthermore, the baby remedy only made my face smell like piss. You name it, I've tried it.

I became so desperate that I started searching online for pills specifically for my adult acne. In return it was the biggest mistake that I had ever made when it came to my skin. Before I made the purchase, I read up on the product. I saw many before and after photos of clients who used it. I felt if my skin could look like that afterward, the major breakouts beforehand would be worth it. I received my pills within two weeks. A week into it I developed blisters on my face. I was mortified. I became anxious to cover up the open sores. I begged Jai for her help. I asked her to buy me some makeup and she found this spice almond powder.

Even though I kept having recurring breakouts I continued taking the pills. This caused me to cake on the makeup even more.

"Did you have an allergic reaction? I know you have been known to have a break out here and there, but people are talking behind your back Simmons." Officer James said.

"There's nothing I can do. I'm just overworked that's all." I explained.

Since the age of sixteen it always bothered me when I had a breakout. People would just stare. Some of them were even bold enough to bring it to my attention. I'd feel worthless. It's not like I wasn't already aware of what my face looked like. I had to look at myself in the mirror every day. Why bring up the obvious? I knew I was bumpy, I knew my skin was irritated, and some of those pimples were very painful. White heads were the worst of them all because I hated popping them. Tyra Banks always said, "Squeeze the bump until the white puss comes out but be careful when you see the blood." I always squeezed until I saw the blood. I would also stick a straight pin inside the bump and the puss would ooze out; this led to bruising.

I felt I was being taunted at work, and I wanted to quit my job. Thankfully we were able to wear hats; and I could hide the planets on my forehead. My hair was falling out faster than ever. I didn't feel or look healthy, and I was always tired. On top of that I was extremely depressed, and I was mad at every damn body. However, while at work I continued to smile. I did my best to keep my composure. I couldn't let my co-workers know what was going on because I didn't want to be put on suicide watch, have my job threatened, or taken away from me.

39: Fireworks

July 3rd, 2009

I just needed to get out of Maryland. Trying not to look like I was running away I had decided to take Jamari with me, as a cover up, I called it a much-needed father and son road trip. I wanted to visit Delvin and Martin in Greensboro, North Carolina. I'd never been there, and Delvin always wanted me to come. Kendrell was also going to be there. I was excited to see them but all I wanted to do was get some much-needed rest.

The drive down was a vacation and Jamari weren't great company. He literally slept the whole drive. I didn't tell Delvin that I wasn't staying at her place until I was on my way down there. When I arrived that night at the Proximity Hotel, Delvin rushed over. I just wanted to talk and tell her everything, the way I used to do, when we were nine and ten years old. When I saw the way Delvin's eyes lit up while talking about Martin, I knew I couldn't talk to her then. It was obvious that they were in a good space while I was close to my wits end. We left the hotel and I followed Delvin to her to place. I stayed there for a few hours until I was ready to leave. Delvin insisted on keeping Jamari overnight and I went back to my room a few minutes before midnight.

July 4th, 2009

At 4:00AM Kendrell called me.

"What you are doing man?" He wondered.

I could tell he was drunk.

"I'm sleep." I answered.

"Wake your ass up! I'm downstairs. What room number are you in?" He asked.

"612." I murmured.

About three minutes later Kendrell was at the door. I opened the door and got back into bed. I could tell he had a lot on his mind. Kendrell is the type of person that will pour his heart out and not remember a word he said the following day. We talked about Gregory for a while and we both became very emotional. Kendrell rarely ever spoke about Gregory being incarcerated. He could only talk about his brother while he was intoxicated. He really opened to me that night and I finally realized just how much pain he was in. I knew I wasn't alone. It was obvious that Kendrell and I were and still are heartbroken because we can't grasp the idea of our baby brother being behind bars.

I wished his mother and my mother could have heard how he truly felt about Gregory. I didn't even bother telling him about my own personal problems. He finally fell asleep after 7:00AM however, I was still wide awake. Later that morning around 9:00AM we had breakfast in the hotel. That was the first time that I had ever had a Mimosa; a cocktail-like drink composed of champagne and thoroughly chilled citrus fruit juice. Usually orange juice but it was delicious. After breakfast we drove around. Greensboro was a beautiful place and the people were very friendly; especially the women. I didn't make it back to the hotel until 2:00PM. By that time, I was exhausted. As soon as I reached the door, I started peeling my clothes off as I hopped into bed.

9:47PM

POP, BANG, WHOOO, BOOM!

"What?!" I yelled as I jumped up.

I looked around the dark room. The sounds of fireworks scared the living hell out of me. I couldn't remember where I was. Then I remembered that I had fallen asleep earlier and I was in the hotel room.

"I bet Delvin is pissed!" I shouted out loud.

I got up brushed my teeth, washed my face, put my clothes back on, and headed to Delvin's cookout. When I arrived, Delvin had a house full of people. She instantly started introducing me to her guest.

"This is my cousin Andre, from Maryland." She explained.

"That's your little man?" One of Delvin's friends asked me.

"Yes." I simply said.

I wasn't feeling the atmosphere at all. I stayed for an hour and headed back to the hotel.

July 5th, 2009

When I awoke that morning, I took a long shower. As I stood there in the steaming hot water, I cried my eyes out. I couldn't take it. I was overwhelmed with the stress of it all. I cried for an hour. I didn't want to go back to Maryland, but I knew I had to. After my shower I headed over to Delvin's. When I walked in the house, I saw Kendrell passed out on the couch from drinking too much the night before. Martin was in and out of the kitchen. I didn't say much as I sat down at the kitchen table.

"What's your problem?" Delvin asked.

"I don't have a problem." I mumbled.

"Yes, you do. Your attitude is nasty." She assumed.

"Oh, it is?" I asked derisively.

"Yes!" She returned.

"Damn, really? Her too?" I wasn't even in the mood to argue. Obviously, there was something wrong but that wasn't the way to reach or address me. I got up, gathered Jamari and his things, and we left. I hopped on the road and drove back to Maryland.

"Money fucking wasted!" I yelled while driving.

When I made it back to home, I never contacted Delvin to let her know I made it back safely.

40: **Officer Snow**

Flashback:

During my orientation at Walter Reed Army Medical Center they let us know that the contract would end sometime in September of 2011. Snow began working there in the spring of 2009. Our first encounter was on April 12th, 2009 at Forest Glen Annex on Brookville. He was an exceptionally tall white guy. Snow had to be almost seven feet tall.

Since it was my first time working with officer Kwaize and Snow, I was hesitant to take out my portable DVD player. After a few minutes of small talk officer Kwaize began questioning me about my personal life. I'm nobody's fool. My personal life was off limits. So, to shift the attention I suggested that we watch a movie. I took my DVD player out and we watched Tango and Cash.

Every two hours Snow would go to the back booth. I found it to be rather strange; however, he told us he wasn't feeling well. I didn't think anything of it. Six hours passed and by that time officer Kwaize had fallen asleep. Snow still made sure he continued his rotation. If I had my DVD player, I didn't need anybody else. It was all the company that I needed.

1:23AM

There was a call-out and the supervisor called the booth needing an officer to holdover. Officer Kwaize had school later that morning and Snow still wasn't feeling well. I could use the extra money, so I volunteered to stay.

Around 3:00AM Snow started to warm up to me. He became more open and he seemed cool. I was surprised that he was even talking to me. I wasn't popular on the job and most of the officers weren't too fond of me. It was funny nobody had a problem with me, but nobody messed with me either. I was certain that he'd heard the gay rumors about me, but it didn't seem to matter. The conversation alone was invigorating. He made me feel welcomed; however, I remained reserved.

Fast Forward:

There were only a few people that I trusted on the job, but I never quite let anyone in like I did Snow. Snow wanted to get to know me and he seemed to be very intrigued by me. It was odd because he didn't seem like the type of guy to hang around someone like me. He was more than persistent, and I eventually let my guard down. I felt so comfortable with him. Snow was the first person that I revealed my sexuality to. I knew he was trustworthy because he didn't judge me, and my confirmed word never got out. I knew he was going to become a great friend and someone I could confide in.

One day Snow unexpectedly asked me what my plans were for my 26th birthday. I was taken aback at first. Clearly, he could tell I felt it was a little bizarre and he backed off. I knew that there was no way possible because he was straight, and I was married however, a part of me felt like I was being asked out on a date. In a way I wanted it to be true. Days went by and it was weighing heavily on my mind. I didn't have anything planned so I gave in. Later, in the week I asked him if he still had plans for my birthday.

We couldn't do anything the night of my birthday because we were scheduled to work. We wound up celebrating on that Tuesday.

Snow was the first man to take me to a bar at Ireland's Four Provinces Restaurant & Pub in Fall Church, Virginia. We met up on December 1st. He also took me to my first strip club at Crystal City Gentleman's Club on December 9th. Since Snow and I were officially hanging out I was no longer considered the weirdo. Other officers finally started to take some interest in me. At work people saw us as friends and that was all anyone needed to know.

December 11th, 2009.

It was another twelve-and-a-half-hour shift on a Friday night at Forest Glen Annex on Brookville gate with the best co-workers ever; Snow and officer Sanchez. Scarface was the movie of choice to start the evening. I watched as Tony Montana, played by Al Pacino leaned over to snort a pile of cocaine off his desk. He had an undisturbed look in his eyes. He was calm, relaxed, and did not have a care in the world. Officer Sanchez was in the bathroom on the first sleep break.

"I would love to try cocaine." I said giggling.

"Simmons you're not fucking serious." Snow suggested.

"Why not?" I replied.

"Let me go make a call. I'll be right back. Hold down the gate." Snow told me.

I continued watching the movie that I clearly wasn't interested in. I couldn't wait for this movie to end so I could watch The River Wild. A few minutes passed, and Snow returned to the booth. Then he told me to walk down to the Research booth and look under the temporary pass.

"Be careful when you lift it." He cautioned.

I looked at him and laugh. Snow didn't laugh. Curiosity, excitement, and fear suddenly took over me. I wanted to see what was under that pass more than anything. I couldn't get it out of my head. I walked down to the Research booth counting every step I took. I never turned around because I assumed that this was a prank. I was just waiting for Snow to shout out "Simmons!" at any second, but that never happened. I opened the door and there was the yellow pass lying face down. I looked at the pass, terrified to see what was underneath. I slowly lifted the pass and there it was; a white powdered substance. I dropped the pass immediately and backed up into the door covering my mouth. I reached for my phone and dialed Jai.

"Guess what?! We were watching Scarface and I told Snow that I wanted to try cocaine, just being silly. Why did this fool really have cocaine?" I revealed.

"What?!" She screamed.

"What should I do?" I asked.

"Where are you Andre?" She wondered.

"I'm in the research booth. It's under a temporary vehicle pass right here in front of me. That's why I'm calling you. I'm going to try it, hold on." I said.

I put the phone on speaker and placed it beside the temporary vehicle pass.

"Hello, Jai I'm about to snort it." I told her.

I leaned over breathing heavily. I pressed my index finger against the right side of my nose to snort it.

"Shit!" I shouted.

"What happened?" She asked.

"I blew it everywhere." We both started laughing. "What should I tell him? He's going to be so pissed. This shit isn't for me. I don't even know how to snort it. I'm going back up to the main booth. I'll see you in the morning. I love you, goodnight." I explained.

"What are you going to tell him?" She wondered.

"I'll make up something." I said giggling.

"Y'all are crazy. Bye boy." She said and hung up the phone.

I fanned the rest of the powder with the pass and walked back up to the main booth. When I walked in, he looked at me and I sat down. We didn't make eye contact, I just looked straight ahead. Suddenly, I started laughing uncontrollably. I just couldn't stop laughing.

"Simmons calm down man." He whispered.

"I'm good, I'm really good." I said trying to collect myself.

Snow got up to leave and told me to hold down the gate. I knew what he was about to do. Reality hit me a few seconds after. I couldn't believe what I tried. I started counting my blessings. I had an excellent job and a family. I made a vow that it would be my first and last time trying cocaine. I loved Snow. I shared so much with him in such a short period of time. I trusted him, and he trusted me. I hoped things between us wouldn't change because I wasn't trying to do cocaine again. I hoped he understood that I was never trying that again.

41: **Nose Candy**

Flashback:

Since I've known Jai, she's always liked to party. I met her when she was 19 and I was 18. To attend the clubs in Maryland, Virginia, and Washington D.C. women had to be at least 18 and the guys had to be 21. So, I couldn't go if I wanted to. Even if I could go, more than likely I wouldn't tag along. I was still traumatized by that Cabaret event in which I never brought up until years later. Jai called most of the times when she was on her way home from the club. She'd arrive between 3:00AM - 5:00AM. I trusted her. The only time I or my mother ever said anything to her was when she was pregnant with our first-born child. I on the other hand liked going to the movies. If I wasn't going with her, Lyndyann, Ava, Kendrell, and Gregory, I'd enjoy being at home watching DVDs. Jai always said she was grown and could do whatever she wanted, and that was very true. I always kept that in mind and I never forgot it.

Fast Forward:

February 2nd, 2010

I reached for my blackberry as it went off. It was a text from Snow.

"What are you doing?" He wondered.

I had literally just gotten into bed. I was about to go to sleep.

"Nothing at all." I replied.

"You want to chill?" He offered.

"How much?" I spat.

"$160.00. Hey, look Simmons you don't have to do this man." He suggested.

"I want to. I've got it." I assured.

In all reality I knew I only had $20.00 to my name, however I knew my mother was good for it. I got up out of bed and put my clothes on. My mother and Jai were in the kitchen.

"Mom can I borrow some money?" I asked.

"How much?" She wondered.

"$160.00." I declared.

"Andre, I don't have that type of money." She hissed.

I gave her the stupidest look.

"Please mom! I will pay you back! I get paid on Friday!" I snapped.

"What do you need the money for?" Jai wondered.

"I'm not asking you, so it doesn't matter!" I barked.

The only thing I was worried about was how I could come up with the money to buy cocaine for him, I mean us. Then I remembered that I could call my aunt Janelle and ask her.

"Aunt Janelle can I borrow some money? I'll pay you back on Friday?" I asked.

"How much do you need?" She asked.

"$160.00." I said.

"Yeah, I'm leaving the school in 30 minutes. Where do you want to meet me?" Aunt Janelle asked.

BINGO! I was so happy. After getting off the phone with her, I quickly called Snow to let him know that I would be on my way. I told him I'd meet him within an hour. He wasn't too happy because the guy with the goods was already tired of waiting.

I didn't reach Snow until 10:30PM. We went to his place, and when we got there his mother was in the kitchen. There was a big dog lying on the living room floor.

"Come here Roxy." He said.

"What the fuck! That's a big ass dog." I thought.

"Mom this is Simmons from work." He responded.

"Nice to meet you Simmons." She said.

"Nice to meet you as well." I replied as we shook hands.

After meeting her, she went upstairs. I felt bad being there because Snow always said she was sickly and going through chemotherapy. She was such a nice woman and it was good to see that she was doing so well.

Snow turned on the TV. A few minutes after 11:00PM Jai called me.

"What are you doing?" She asked.

"What do you mean?" I whispered.

"Where are you? Why did you go out? Who are you with?" She questioned me.

"I'm in Virginia. I went out because I wanted to. I never stopped you from going out when you wanted to. You always told me you were a grown woman, so what's the problem? Furthermore, I never called you when you were out and about. I'm with Snow." I stated firmly.

"Andre I'm not happy." She pleaded.

"Ok. Goodnight Jai." I said.

She hung up.

"Is everything ok?" Snow asked.

"Yes. Everything is fine. Snow I need you to put two numbers in your phone; Jai's and my home number. Just in case something happens to me or my phone, you will still have those contacts. I know it's early, but I would love for you and Jai to meet one day so that she can put a face to the person that I consider a dear friend on and outside of the job." I said.

"Ok sounds good to me. Simmons you want a cigarette?" He asked.

"I don't smoke, but ok." I said laughing.

We walked outside, and he gave me Roxy's leash.

"You've got to get used to her Simmons. When we go back inside make sure you keep your voice down." He demanded.

"Ok." I said.

We were outside for about five minutes and then we walked back inside. I started sweating under my arms because I didn't know what type of effect cocaine would have on me. I was nervous, and I couldn't help but think about my ride back home. He reached his hand in his left pocket and gave me 2.5 grams of cocaine.

"This is what you paid for." He explained.

"Ok." I repeated.

Snow took a small mirror that was hanging on the wall and placed it on the end of his mother's coffee table. Snow was sitting on the right and I was on the left by the window. Snow opened the bag and dumped all the cocaine onto the mirror.

"Simmons, give me a credit card or something." He requested.

I handed him my driver's license, watched as he made a mini mountain, and started chopping away at the cocaine.

"What are you doing that for?" I asked out of curiosity.

"To cut and break down the rocks into powder." He explained.

He cut two lines from the mini mountain, got up, went into the kitchen, and he returned with two cut straws. I figured it was for the cocaine. I just sat there and watched him as he leaned over and snorted the first line.

"There you go man." He said holding out the straw.

I kept sniffing trying to make sure my nose was as clear as possible. I took the straw and put it beside the line. I leaned over and snorted the cocaine up my nose. I stopped in the middle of it before I finished the line.

"Holy shit!" I hollered.

"Keep your fucking voice down Simmons." He whispered laughing.

I leaned back over to finish my line. I most definitely didn't feel that last year in the booth. I felt so good all over. I leaned back in my chair and smiled as the drug continued to take over my body.

"It's some good shit, right?" He suggested.

"Hell yeah. I guess." I gushed.

We snorted cocaine for the rest of the night until there was nothing left. When we were done, he said he was tired, so I left. I didn't make it home until almost 3:00AM. While lying down I got a call from Snow. He told me that I left my license on his mother's couch.

"Bring it to work on Friday." I told him.

After we hung up, I fell asleep without a care in the world.

My father, my mother and I. *Winter 1984.*

"We delight in the beauty of the butterfly, but rarely admit the changes it has gone through to achieve that beauty." - Maya Angelou

42: **P.S. Daddy I Love You** *(Part Four)*

April 5th, 2010

Everyone knew my mother was out the country by then, and everyone knew I wouldn't answer the home phone when it rung. That night the phone started to ring, and I wondered who could be calling that late. I looked at the caller ID and it was an unfamiliar number from North Carolina.

"Hello?" I answered.

"Is Joyce there Andre?" The man with the familiar wondered.

It was him, I couldn't believe it, after all these years, it was my father on the other end of the phone. His voice was unforgettable.

"Hey Dad, she's not here. She's overseas in Dushanbe, Tajikistan. She's been out of the country since February 27th." I informed him.

"Dushanbe?" He repeated sounding surprised.

"Yep." I responded.

"Oh, I just called to let her know my mother passed away this evening." He said mournfully.

"I'm sorry to hear that." I said without an ounce of serenity.

There was an awkward silence.

"I know I wasn't there for you as a father." He said breaking the silence.

There they were, the words I longed to hear. Time never spent together and unspoken words throughout the years. The anger and the bitterness I felt for this man suddenly vanished in that moment. I ran upstairs like a five-year-old boy.

"It's my dad. It's my dad on the phone!" I shrieked.

I told him everything. I was so excited to tell him that I was married to a woman.

"The girl I told you about the month before graduation, back in May 2002 is now my wife. We have two children together. Their names are Jamari and J'Adora. I'm also a security contractor for the military." I gushed.

"I'm proud of you son." He comforted.

My father finally heard it from the horse's mouth that his son Andre LeDale Simmons turned out better than ok without his guidance and teachings. I checked my call log once our conversation ended. We spoke for a total of 45 minutes and 27 seconds. He concluded by telling me that he would love to visit me. I told myself not to get too excited because actions speak louder than words, and I had heard it all before. In my heart I wanted to see him too. I couldn't wait to email my mother the news. Hopefully this was going to be the start of a new beginning for us. *UPDATE: As of June 1ˢᵗ, 2018, I have yet to see or hear from my father again.*

43: Mother's Day

May 2nd, 2010

Residence Inn by Marriott National Harbor

"Simmons what do you have planned for next weekend?"
Snow wondered.

I already knew what was on his mind.

"Besides working these twelve and a half hours Friday,
Saturday, and maybe 16 on Sunday, I will be sleeping." I
laughed.

"You should get someone to work for you on Saturday."
He said.

"This Saturday? As in 6 days from now? On Mother's Day
weekend? That will never happen." I replied.

"Call out then." He suggested.

"Are you calling out?" I questioned.

"I already did a switch with officer Thai. I'm going to work
his Wednesday, and he agreed to work my Saturday." He
said.

"I don't know. This is short notice. What did you have in
mind though?" I asked.

"Let's party man." He insisted.

I already knew what I was going to do. I had enough sick leave to use in case of a rainy day, and Jamari and J'Adora were the greatest excuse for not going to work.

May 7th, 2010

The following Friday while at work I purchased a bottle of Grey Goose Vodka to set the tone for the weekend. Officer OB wasn't a drinker; however, he enjoyed watching Snow and I act a fool with one another. Officer OB was very outspoken, and we never knew what was going to fly out of his mouth.

"I can only imagine how you are in bed when you're drunk Snow, with your big dick." He said unexpectedly.

Already tipsy Snow and I cracked up laughing.

"They should already know what they're getting themselves into with me." Snow declared.

My head whipped around, and I just looked at him. He looked back at me and smiled. I didn't smile at all. Simply because I felt like he was teasing me. Secretly I believe he knew that I longed for him. It was wrong for me to have those types of feelings for him because again he was straight; I was gay and married. The only thing I could think about was tomorrow night, praying that something would go down. I mean why else were we getting a hotel room together?

Later, that night Torrence, who was like a brother to me called. I hadn't seen him in a few years and he told me he was coming into town to see his mother for the weekend. I wanted to see him badly; however, I lied and told him that I had to work the whole weekend, and that we would catch up another time.

May 8th, 2010

Hours passed, and the Grey Goose was disappearing fast. Snow had totally gone over his limit. Thankfully Sgt. James was the supervisor that morning because Snow was white boy wasted. It was hilarious. I wound up giving Snow $200.00 to buy the cocaine. This had become a routine thing whenever we were together. He said he would put something on it as well. Then we parted ways for the night. As soon as I got home, I went straight to sleep. Before that I set my alarm for 12:00PM so I could call out of work.

After I called out, I called Snow to see what time he and I would meet up at the hotel. He told me to meet him after 3:00PM. I was ecstatic, and I couldn't wait to see him. I called him again before leaving my home; however, I didn't get an answer. I ran into traffic but once I arrived at the Marriott, I called once again. He didn't answer. I waited in the garage of the Marriott for an hour and a half. He called me back around 4:30PM to let me know he was on the way. He didn't arrive until after 5:33PM. I noticed he was acting differently as soon we made it up to the room. It's like he'd done a complete 180 from the night before.

"Is everything ok?" I asked.

"Simmons everything is fine man. Just have a lot of my mind." He groaned.

"Did you get it?" I asked.

"He pulled the bag out of his left pocket and dumped it on the table.

"Simmons, give me a card." He said.

Again, I handed him my driver's license. After he cut the lines, he wrapped the bag back up and headed into the bathroom without saying a word. I just shook my head. I couldn't help but think what I had gotten myself into. The moment I snorted the line all my problems ceased. Amazed at how fast they went away I sat back and fantasized; hoping something would happen between us. I felt my penis get hard and arise. I leaned back on the couch and waited for Snow to return. Thirty minutes passed, and Snow was still in the bathroom. An hour passed, and I was tired of sitting out there alone so I went to knock on the door.

"Snow is everything ok?" I asked.

"Give me a fucking minutes Simmons! I swear to God you can be so annoying sometimes!" He snapped.

I went to sit back down on the couch and continued to watch television, thinking to myself, "Why in the fuck didn't I just go to work? This damn fool asked me about this weekend, and he's acting funny and shit."

"What's your problem man?" He asked finally coming out of the bathroom.

"I don't have a problem. I just came to have a good time. That's all Snow." I pleaded.

He sat back down at the table and pulled the small bag of cocaine from his pocket. I was stunned at the amount that was left. "WOW! So that's what he was doing in the bathroom." I didn't bother bringing it to his attention because I didn't want to upset him anymore than I already had.

Within the next hour Snow mentioned that his mother wasn't feeling well and that he had to rush back home. He left, and I stayed in the hotel until the next morning. I didn't want to believe him; however, loving eyes can never see the truth. How stupid of me to think that something was going to go down in that hotel. I had to get off that shift.

May 10th, 2010

I called officer Thai and asked him if he wanted to do a permanent switch with me and he agreed. It didn't matter that officer Lucy was going to be on that shift, I knew I just had to go. That afternoon Snow called me.

"What's this I hear that you're doing a switch with officer Thai for good? What going on Simmons?" He asked.

"Everything is good. I just missed having my weekends off." I replied and lied.

"Alright. Whatever man." He said and hung up.

Five minutes later he called back.

"So, you're not going to tell me the real reason?" He continued.

"Snow, I'm honestly embarrassed, I read too much into what I thought was going to happen in that hotel. I like you more than I should." I stated.

"Simmons, I told you before I'm not gay." He declared.

"Yes, I understand you're not. I feel awkward being around you now. I have to move on from this situation." I said sadly.

"Don't read too much into this. What I'm about to tell you… I'm going to miss you." He said.

"I'm going to miss you too." I responded.

"What you got planned for tonight? I was thinking we could hit up Ireland's Four Provinces Restaurant & Pub, nothing big. Just chill and talk. No cocaine tonight." He suggested.

"I can do that. Around what time?" I asked.

"Around 7:00PM." He replied.

"Ok cool." I said hanging up.

I made my way to the bar and when I walked in, he was sitting at a table facing the door. He grabbed his head and flashed a big smile. I smiled back as I walked over and sat down. I guess that was his way of breaking the tension between us. He complimented my shirt. I felt it would be a good night. He then ordered us a couple of Amber ales to drink.

"Are you hungry?" He inquired.

"You know I love their calamari and chicken tenders." I giggled and replied.

When the bartender brought our drinks over Snow ordered us some chicken tenders. I just knew something was up with that dude that night. I kept pondering what it could be. Snow never mentioned cocaine for the entire night. I began thinking that it wasn't too late to mend our friendship. It's crazy how it was almost broken by my attraction to him. So silly of me to run from him instead of facing him like a real man. I had a change of heart and I ended up staying on the shift.

44: Run & Hide

July 11th, 2010

My mother wasn't even home from Dushanbe for 21 days yet and Jai and I hit another iceberg. I did everything in my power to avoid drowning in my own misery. My desire of being with a man only grew stronger. It affected me inside and out. Jai and I still weren't sleeping in the same bed, mainly because of our work schedules. Quite frankly I was relieved not to be sleeping with her especially when she'd try to have sex with me. If we weren't arguing about the bills she wasn't paying, it was always about the sex that she wasn't getting from me. I got to the point where I wanted to give her permission to sleep with someone else.

One day while in my mother's room I told her I needed space to think things through, and that I wanted us to still be friends. She wasn't trying to hear me, and she didn't take it well at all. By no means did I want it to be over, but I felt like a pimple that needed to be popped.

"We are not friends Andre! We are husband and wife!"

That was her response and she was more than right. It only made me feel guilty about the way I truly felt. That conversation led her to want to get a place with her sisters.

"What kind of marriage do you think this is if you move out to be with your sisters?" I suggested.

I was angry, bitter and torn. I was determined to try to make things work. However, what was I trying to make work? What was I holding on to? Was I just afraid of being alone? Was I in love with Snow? I wanted somebody, anybody to please help me. If I tell her about my past would it help our situation?

"I just want to come clean with you about something. It happened a long time ago, and I have been battling these feelings for a long time now. I can no longer pretend. It's causing me great pain. When it affects me, it also affects you too. This thing happened to me when I was a little boy during the summer of 1993 in North Carolina. I did things with boys. Kendrell and Gregory know about these things. I haven't done anything with a boy or a man since then. I do have urges though, and I fight my urges. It's sexually confusing and frustrating. I hope you're willing to work with me." I said.

"Andre are you gay?" She asked frustrated.

I didn't have the courage to tell her yes because I didn't want to be, for the sake of my family. I felt since she was the only female that I had ever had sex with, and that they were boys and not men, that there was no way possible that I was gay.

"No, I'm not." I murmured and looked away.

I nearly shut down. The thing that hurt me the most about her question was the way she said it, and the look of disappointment she had in her eyes. My mind reverted back to her telling me about her mother accusing their father of sexually molesting her and one of her younger siblings. It affected her and her sister's relationships with their father. Jai said her father never did those things, and I believed her

100%. I never threw it back in her face. Back then when Jai confessed that to me, we were teens. I remember how she broke down crying. I just knew we were going to be together forever because we had a similar history and a familiar hurt from our past.

"You like to brag about you and your mother's relationship. Your mother doesn't even know the real you Andre." She said with such hostility.

"You're right; my mother doesn't know everything about me. I've never had enough courage to tell my mother about my past. With your response I could only imagine what hers would be. I'm sharing this with you and basically, you're bringing up me and my mother's relationship. I won't be revealing anything else to you, trust me." I declared.

I left the room. I wasn't even mad; disappointed yes, however not mad.

45: Cozumel Mexico

Flashback:

October 19th, 2009

Almost four months passed, and Delvin and I still didn't have our heart to heart about what was going on in my perfect fairytale. She felt that I was angry, and the truth was that I was very angry. The fact that she didn't take the time to find out exactly why hurt me the most. Right before her birthday she mentioned to me that she felt like Martin was going to propose to her. One night she called me at work to discuss the matter. Delvin basically was giving Martin an ultimatum, *"Marry me or else."* It was a catch 22 type of situation because it took me back to my situation with Jai when we had gotten married in the court house on November 29th, 2007.

"What if he doesn't propose?" I wondered.

"Then I'm gone." She laughed.

"Damn, is this how women really think?" I asked myself while I continued listening to her map out her future. I didn't have the courage to tell her that she should let the man do it when he was ready, better yet when both were ready. I just sat in the back booth listening to her while the time passed.

November 1st, 2009

Weeks later Delvin got exactly what she wanted. Martin did indeed propose to her on her birthday, and she was on cloud 9. Delvin and Martin were both from North Carolina and initially, they wanted the wedding to be held there. That plan quickly changed and she decided that she was going to have her wedding on a Carnival cruise. She let me know that neither her father nor her brother was going to attend her wedding. It was extremely hard for me to take in because she announced that her wedding wasn't going to be until Thanksgiving of 2010. Other members in the family weren't as supportive either. They all gave her a bunch of excuses. They claimed it was too expensive to travel around the holiday season, amongst other things. I felt that it was my duty to show her my support the best way I knew how. I wanted to run the plan by Jai, so I called her while I was at work.

"We have to go to Delvin's wedding. It's on a Carnival cruise though and Thanksgiving weekend next year." I suggested.

"A cruise? I don't have money for that." She responded.

"Well I guess I have to pay for you and me then. I know I must be there for her Jai. Her father nor her brother will be there." I said.

After hanging up with Jai, I called Delvin.

"Jai and I will be there." I revealed.

"Thank you! It means a lot." She replied.

She was so excited to hear the news.

I started a payment plan for the cruise. Each month I'd pay little by little. By the third month, Jai and I were bumping heads so much that I stopped making the payments. I didn't want to tell her that Jai and I weren't going to make it. My mother was in Dushanbe, Tajikistan from *(February 27th, 2010 - June 26th, 2010)*. When I broke the news to my mother that we weren't going on the cruise, she offered to pay the balance. She said it was a wedding gift from her. A wedding gift? Are you fucking kidding me? This wasn't a marriage this was a Ménage à trois. I often wondered how long my mother was going to keep pretending like Jai and I were happy. If she loved Jai so much maybe she should fucking marry her ungrateful ass, then.

Fast Forward:

November 18th, 2010

The trip was paid for in full, but there was still one major problem. I didn't want to drive my jeep down to Tampa, Florida. Especially since I never got the fender damage fixed on my jeep. There was no other way for us to get down there because I never bought the plane tickets.

"Andre, would you want to take the Volvo?" She asked.

"Yes. I wouldn't mind Mom." I insisted.

She saved the day again. I would soon be turning 27 in eleven days and my mother was still taking care of me like I was turning 7. Sometimes I felt like I was too dependent on her however, who else was going to help me out other than my mother?

November 25th, 2010

We headed out around 5:00AM that morning. We were about 20 minutes from Kings Dominion when Snow called me.

"What's up Simmons?" I heard him say from the other end.

"Hello Snow." I responded.

"I hope you have a safe trip, and I'll see you when you come back." He said.

"Thank you, and ok." I replied.

The further down the road I drove, my issues; our issues seemed to slowly die. I was relaxed, and I enjoyed spending time with Jai. It had been four and half years since our last trip and I was still interested to see how this trip was going to pan out. We didn't stop until we were in Roanoke Rapids, North Carolina. We had breakfast at Cracker Barrel for the first time. The food was tolerable; however, it wasn't as good as I hoped it would be. I ordered a pecan log and it was tasty. Delvin called to tell us that they were leaving. Jai and I were in no rush. We stopped at Carolina Premium Outlets in Smithfield, North Carolina. I purchased a grey hoody pea coat by Guess. It wasn't in my budget, but it was my birthday weekend and I never owned a coat like that before. We got back on the road again and didn't stop until we were in Florence, South Carolina. We stopped at Popeyes before heading to the hotel. We didn't reach the hotel until 11:19PM. By that time, I was exhausted.

November 26th, 2010

The next morning, we had to get dressed for the wedding in the hotel because our room wouldn't be available until afterward. I was not too happy about that at all. It was hot, and I can't stand dressing up. It wasn't my wedding, so I had to. We were some of the first passengers to board being that we were there for a wedding. The inside of the cruise ship looked like a motel room. It wasn't appealing at all; however, the Casino area looked nice. Jai and I ordered drinks by the pool. An hour later it was time for the wedding. The highlight of it all was aunt Dollie's high-heels that Jai and I kept gawking over. It was a shame that neither Delvin's father nor her brother was there to give her away; but at least I was there. After Mr. and now Mrs. Martin exchanged their I Do's, the guests were taken to another part of the ship where hors d'oeuvers and drinks awaited us which were nice. After the reception, everyone hugged, congratulated, and told Delvin goodbye. It all made sense now to why her wedding was so early. Some of her guests were not actually going on the weekend cruise, and she signed up to have her wedding early. It was very thoughtful of her and upsetting to me at the same time because she didn't have many family members there to support her.

When we were allowed in our rooms, I was unimpressed with the décor. The focus of the room was the bed. Jai and I looked at each other. "Oh shit, there goes her *"Fuck Me Eyes."* I thought to myself.

"I'm hungry again. I didn't really care for the food there." I told her.

"Let's go back to the pool area." She suggested.

"Ok." I agreed.

We changed our clothes and headed back down to the pool. It was packed. There was a line at both food stations. On one side they had Guy's Burger Joint and the other Mongolian Wok. I chose to eat at Mongolian Wok.

"It's a stir-fry bar where you can design your own bowl." I said.

"What are you getting in yours?" Jai asked.

"Broccoli, carrots, spring onions, mushrooms, chicken, and shrimp." I said.

"And sir what kind of sauce?" The chef asked.

"Hmmmm Szechuan sauce. Oh yes. I love this. I'm happy now." I gushed.

"You're silly. Food always makes you happy." She giggled.

"Yep. I can always count on food to make me happy." I smiled.

"I can make this." I said as we sat down.

"You can?" She asked surprised.

"Yep. Fresh vegetables, meats, rice, noodles, and a stir fry pan. I'll make this when we get back home. I'm sure my mother would love it." I said assuredly.

After going back for seconds and then thirds, we made it back to the room to rest. Still docked, the boat finally started to move.

"Finally!" I said.

We were lying in bed watching TV when we decided to go meet Delvin's crew for dinner. I despised the fact that when we got there, we had assigned seats. I knew I wasn't going to be attending dinner every night if that was the case; mainly when room service was free. The food was not as enjoyable either. After dinner we made it back to the room. I was still exhausted from the drive down to Florida, so I undressed and went to bed.

November 27th, 2010

My alarm clock went off at 6:00AM. Jai and I decided we'd go for a walk. The sun wasn't quite up yet, and there was this nice cool breeze coming from the ocean. We had breakfast and enjoyed each other's company. We spent the rest of the morning out on the deck until we got ready to dock in Cozumel, Mexico.

Once we docked, I was shocked to see how clear and blue the water was. Jai and I caught a taxi to Paradise beach. It was incredible. They had these giant floats in the water, and as soon as we were situated, I ran towards the water and swam to a float. I stood on top of the float and dived into the water. It was amazing. Jai eventually got into the water with a life jacket on. She looked so funny, and the look on her face made me laugh hysterically. It was very relaxing, and the weather was perfect.

Even though they urged us not to eat the food, I ordered a couple slices of pizza and some beers. The pizza was delicious. After we ate, we headed back to the dock. Before we reached the dock, we stopped at the souvenir shops. I purchased some bracelets for my family and friends.

Later that afternoon I was told that my grandmother was in the hospital and that there had been a huge argument between my mother and aunt Julie. That night Jai and I had sex and I enjoyed it. I enjoyed it so much that we did it again and again. We skipped dinner and ordered room service.

November 28th, 2010

That following morning, we had breakfast and we spent the whole day by the pool. When we got back to the room, we had sex again and got all dressed up to walk around the ship. We enjoyed each other's company. That night we had sex again.

November 29th, 2010

I woke back up at 5:13AM because my blackberry messenger went off.

"Happy Birthday Simmons." Snow said.

He was such a liar. He always told me that he didn't remember anyone's birthdays except his son's, his mother's, and his brother's. I looked at Jai while she was still asleep, and I lied back down.

Later that morning we docked. We said our goodbyes to the family and went our separate ways. I don't know what it was, but the minute Jai and I got into the car the atmosphere was different. We didn't speak a word to each other. I don't know if it was because we were going back to what we were able to escape from while on the cruise, or if it was the fact that we came to the realization that this relationship and marriage was officially over. Instead of the 19 hours it took us to get to Tampa, it only took us 13 hours and 47 minutes to get back to Largo, Maryland.

46: **Janet Jackson** *(True You Book)*

February 15th, 2011

The book titled True You came out on a Tuesday; however, I wasn't able to purchase it until Friday. I did not know I was going to enjoy reading the book as much as I did. I couldn't put it down. It was the first book that I had read in years. I started reading it the same day and by Sunday I was done. I joined Twitter October 10th, 2010 and I didn't start tweeting until I read that book. I did not learn anything about Janet that I didn't already know, but it was still a great read. I was just happy to get something new from Janet because I, like many other fans were still waiting on a new album. Thankfully I got to see her the next month on her Number Ones, Up Close and Personal Tour.

47: The Running Man

Hampton Inn & Suite

7 grams was the usual amount of cocaine that I would purchase.

"Simmons, do you mind if I bring company back to the hotel?" He asked.

"Who Snow?" I wondered.

"This bitch. She wanted to stop by." He responded.

"I guess if that's what you want?" I said nonchalantly.

"Simmons don't worry about it man, this is just me and your night. I'm sorry that I even asked. I'm so fucking stupid." He hissed.

"Snow are you ok?" I murmured.

"Quit asking me that Simmons! Chill man!" He snapped.

"Snow if you want to bring a girl here then you're more than welcome to. One question though, where will I be?" I questioned.

"Would you mind waiting in your Jeep?" He suggested.

"I was so hurt, and I felt so stupid. Why did I continue to do that to myself? Why was I choosing to please him, instead of me? Every time we got a hotel, I always had this thought that Snow and I would have sex. I can't believe he wants to bring a girl to the hotel room that I purchased, and then fuck her in the bed that I'm going to sleep in." I thought myself.

"What time are you meeting her?" I asked.

"In about 20 minutes." He said.

"Ok, cool Snow anything for you buddy." I comforted.

I went to the bathroom to wash my face. As usual my eyes were bloodshot red. It didn't matter that a girl was coming because I knew she wasn't staying. Snow was staying the night with me, so I win.

"Hey Simmons, you're forgetting your key." He said as I was walking out.

"Oh thanks." I said turning to grab it.

"See Snow does care for me." I went to my Jeep to listen to some music while I waited. "Believing In Me" by Monica was playing. Within five minutes I saw Snow walk out of the hotel. I thought he would have walked over to me, but he never did. I watched as he got into his car, made a left, and his lights disappeared off into the night. After the second song played, I saw headlights and I thought it was him turning into the parking lot. Instead it was a red Honda. The gas station was only up the street and I wondered what could be taking him so long.

Two cars came driving up. One of these cars had to be him. A white truck passed, and car had its left signal light on. I was so sure it was him. But it wasn't. It was a silver car but not his silver Hyundai.

"Is Snow fucking her in his car?" I said laughing out loud.

Maybe he thought bringing her back to the hotel was disrespectful. Which it really was; after all it was my hotel room. 15 minutes passed.

"Something isn't right. Snow, where are you?" I said aloud.

I checked my phone. There were no missed calls from him. I decided to call him. The phone just rang and rang until it went to voice mail. I waited exactly five minutes and called him again. It rung once more until it went to voicemail. I texted him: "Is everything ok?" Snow never responded. I looked at the time and I realized I'd been sitting in my Jeep for 30 minutes. I decided to get out and head back into the room; hoping that he didn't pull up as I was walking. When I got back to the hotel room, I knocked to make sure he wasn't in the room. There was no answer, so I put the card in the room door. When I walked in everything looked the same. I walked around the room and noticed that his bag was gone. I stood there in disbelief for a few minutes and then my phone rung.

"Hey Simmons, I had to run home for a second." He said.

"Snow did you meet up with the girl?" I wondered.

There was a long pause.

"Simmons, I hate to do this to you but I'm not coming back." He explained.

I felt so empty and lost when I heard those words.

"Where's the cocaine Snow?" I questioned.

"I cut it in half, and I put yours in a bag in the vent." He said snorting.

"What vent Snow?! What fucking vent?!" I shouted.

"Look Simmons. I really feel like shit. Don't do this to me right now." He said.

I pressed the phone against my chest as I started to break down. I put the phone back up to my ear.

"What vent Snow?" I repeated trying to keep calm.

"The vent in the closet." He said.

I set my phone down and took the chair from under the desk and moved it into the closet. I got onto the chair opened the vent and moved my hand all around. I didn't feel anything. I went back to my phone and he hung up. I called him back and his phone went straight to voicemail. I texted him: *"Snow it's no cocaine here."* As I put my phone down on the bed my eyes filled with water. I blinked, and the tears just poured down my face. I got back onto the chair to look again, already knowing nothing would be there. I went back to the bed and lied back down.

"I just want to go home. God I just want to go home." I said it aloud as my voice cracked.

I was too messed up to drive. I was high on cocaine, I'd been drinking, and I couldn't stop crying. That was a recipe for disaster, and I was in the State-of-Virginia. I was hoping my phone would ring or he texted me back, but he never did. I watched the sun come up. I felt like complete shit. I had to get out of Virginia I took a shower, got dressed, and went to turn my key back in.

"I hope you enjoyed your stay with us Mr. Simmons." Said Julie the front desk clerk.

"I had a great time." I smiled and walked away.

When I returned home, no one was there. My mother was out, and the kids were out of town with Jai. I went downstairs to my room and cried myself to sleep. I didn't wake up until Sunday morning. I turned my phone over and I had three missed calls. Not one of them was from Snow.

March 14th, 2011

I was the last to arrive to work on Monday afternoon. Officer Jackson, officer Lucy, and Snow were already there. I walked in to get armed.

"Hey baby." Officer Lucy said and reached out to give me a hug.

Snow and officer Jackson turned around to look at me.

"What's up Simmons?" Officer Jackson said.

"Good evening." I responded.

"What's going on man?" Snow asked.

"Hi." I said.

It killed me to speak to him; however, we never brought our problems to work. It was a code he and I had.

"I got The Mologne House first." I said.

We signed off on our weapons, mace, and loaded our weapons at the gun barrow. We hopped in the van and headed to the Mologne House. Around 10:00PM I saw that the van pulled up. As mad as I was, I was hoping that Snow wasn't the one coming to relieve me.

"Simmons!" Officer Lucy shouted out my name.

I breathed a sigh of relief. I was praying it was her so that I could be back on the gate with Snow. I got into the van. Lt. Sr. was attempting to make small talk with me, but my mind wasn't there. When we pulled up to the gate Snow was standing outside. I didn't see any sign of officer Jackson. I figured he was either in the back booth or ran to the hospital. When I got out of the van, I didn't look Snow in the face. I sat down in the booth and faced the window. Lt. Sr. drove off and Snow stayed outside. After Snow checked them and the few cars passed, he walked into the booth.

"Simmons are you really going to act like this all night?" He asked.

"Act like what Snow?! Are you really going to act like last weekend didn't happen?!" I shouted.

"Simmons lower your fucking voice!" He snapped back.

"Why did you have to lie to me Snow? Why did you have to leave me? Why couldn't you just be honest with me? You didn't even check up on me the rest of the weekend. I was the one hurting. Now I'm at work pretending like everything is cool, when it's not. I want off this shift." I said.

"Look man I'm sorry if I hurt you Simmons, but I have a fucking problem. Can't you see that?!" He shouted.

"I know you got a fucking problem. A friend is what I have tried to be to you, but our friendship is based off cocaine. My intention is not to bring attention to our friendship at work; however, Snow I must go to another shift. It feels like I'm dying inside. I want to hate you right now; however, I don't. I love you so fucking much and it's so not fair." I cried out.

"Look Simmons, I told you before that I'm not gay." He explained.

"Yeah that's what you say, but as long as my gay ass is spending the money, you're happy right? I'm such a dumb ass." I said.

I got up and walked to the hospital to use the restroom. Snow, officer Jackson, and I spent the rest of the shift watching movies and rotating every hour to check customer's IDs. When the shift was over, I went home. Before I could even get in the bed a text came through from Snow.

"I'm sorry Simmons." He said.

"Me too." I responded.

48: **Janet Jackson** *(Up Close And Personal Tour)*

March 24th, 2011

I was doing my daily routine scanning through the blogs on the internet. ThatGrapeJuice.net reported that Janet Jackson was going back on tour. I screamed so loud in the booth. Janet announced that she was going on tour December 22nd, 2010 via YouTube. There were only three days left before Christmas and I only had one item left to purchase for Jamari. I signed up to work overtime. The last time I saw Janet Jackson was three years prior. I planned to treat myself to this concert solo, or so I thought. I still couldn't see myself going to see Janet alone and I didn't ask Jai to come with me. The tickets went on sale in January. I purchased two tickets. The seats weren't the best, but they weren't the worst either. It didn't matter because I would be closer to Janet this time around.

"Mom I'm begging you to please come with me to this concert." I said.

"Andre I'm not going." She said.

I wanted to take anyone but Jai. I was so desperate that I asked Snow if he wanted to go. I knew that would never happen. If cocaine wasn't involved, Snow wanted no parts of it. I also called family members and even asked some of my co-workers to go. Everyone had an excuse to why they couldn't attend. The day of the show I asked Jai if she wanted to go. It felt like old times again. We were having such a good time. Since we had time to spare, we walked down to Chinatown to get a bite to eat. After a couple of minutes of awkward eye contact with one another, she broke the silence.

"I noticed that you're not hanging out with Snow like you used to." She stated.

"And that's a problem?" I asked.

"I never wanted you to stop being his friend Andre." She responded.

"Damned if I do, damned if I don't. I just can't win with you. Maybe I think you're more important than him Jai. I asked him to come to the show is he here?" I said with a smile.

She returned a smile. After we were done eating, we headed back to the venue. The closer we got there the quieter the crowd became.

"Something isn't right." I stated.

We arrived at the building that I thought was the DAR Constitution Hall, it read The Walter E. Washington Convention Center.

"Oh, fuck we are at the wrong building." I said to Jai.

I asked a bystander how far we were from the DAR Constitution Hall, and they said they we were about fifteen blocks away. We ended up getting on the metro to get there. It was so much fun, just as I thought it would be.

Janet was gorgeous as ever, and her breast and body in that grey cat suit was everything. It was great to see Janet again in concert. The spark that wasn't there during her Rock Witchu Tour had returned. Janet was more personal with the audience and unlike the concert in 2008 in Washington D.C.; she gave us so much love.

After the show, as we walked back to the metro Jai kept asking me what I was smiling about. I was already plotting her birthday weekend. I just knew she was going to love the idea of us going to Las Vegas for the weekend, even if she wasn't the biggest fan of Janet Jackson. When we got home, we did the usual. I went downstairs to my room, and she went upstairs to hers. "Baby steps." I thought. "Baby steps."

49: Ocean City

May 11ᵗʰ, 2011

I was so wrapped up in work that I thought it was time I did something with Jamari and J'Adora. To make sure Jai wasn't planning anything with them I ran it by her.

"Hey, I'm going to take the kids to Ocean City on Saturday." I said.

"Ok that will be fun. What time do you want to go?" She asked and smiled.

I didn't say a word. I just stared at her bi-polar ass. Ever since Jai told me back in March that she was moving out again, she and I no longer did things together. If it wasn't related to the kids, we simply acted as if neither of us existed. That was it. I didn't question her when she went out, regardless of the time she got back home and vice versa. My mother was the only person that knew what was going on in the home.

"I signed up to work a six-hour shift on Friday. I would like to leave as early as possible Saturday morning. I'm not asking you to come, but you're more than welcome to come along. I'm telling you now, I'm spending the entire day there." I said.

"Ok. I want to go." She said.

"Ok. Cool." I responded.

The kids were excited. This would be our second time going to Ocean City together as a family. The last time we were there was July 17th, 2010 for J'Adora's birthday. We had gotten there too late to get into the water; however, we did walk on the beach.

May 13th, 2011

When I got to work Friday night, I was told that there were two callouts on the morning shift, and I was asked if I would be willing to hold over for some extra hours. Even though I could really use the money, I knew what I had planned for the next day and I couldn't let my kids down. If Jai drove that morning, then I could still work the extra hours and still go to the beach as well.

"Lt. Sr. yeah I'll take those hours." I said.

"Thank you, Simmons." He responded.

When I arrived at the gate, I stepped away to call Jai.

"I'm working a full 12 hours, and as soon as I get off, we are going to leave. But I'm going to need you drive so that I can rest all the way if you don't mind." I said.

"Yeah. I'll drive." She said.

"Ok cool. See you in the morning." I said.

May 14th, 2011

When I got home, she was packed and ready. I jumped in the shower and quickly got dressed. Jai drove, the kids were seated in the middle row, and I was in the back lying down trying to catch up on sleep. I felt awkward lying back there. This was the first time all year that we were taking a road trip together as a family.

Once we got to the beach, we still didn't say much to one another. We only communicated through Jamari and J'Adora that day. Though we did share a moment together when we were trying to get Jamari and J'Adora in the water. They were crying hysterically. It was so funny. We took them back to our area, gave them juices, and within minutes they were asleep. Jai was on one side and I was on the other. We didn't say one word to each other. Our eyes met twice during the hours that Jamari and J'Adora slept. When they woke up, I went to go dip my hot, sweaty body in the water.

Around 5:00PM when we packed our things to leave, we stopped at a local pizza place for dinner. The drive back home was the same as the rest of the day. We still weren't talking, but at least we didn't argue either. Overall it was a great day.

50: **Bang! Bang!**

Flashback:

April 16th, 2010

Hours passed, and I was still tossing and turning. Not only was I restless, but I was also mentally drained. I decided to take two Benadryl so that I could get a few hours of deep sleep. "Damn, I really hope Snow pays me back my money tonight." Even though I never felt comfortable lending anyone money, I had given him money before. He said he needed it for an emergency. The cat was out of the bag and I already knew what Snow did behind closed doors. Even though I caught him in plenty of lies before, I chose to ignore them. Snow wouldn't lie to me. He told me he wasn't using it for cocaine. This was an indication that he would use it for cocaine. My mind drifted back to work Sunday night to Monday morning.

April 11th, 2010

"Simmons do you think you can loan me some money? It's not for cocaine or anything. It's for a bill." He asked.

"Oh, so that's why he was being extra nice to me tonight. I'm so stupid." Deep in thought I didn't respond right away.

"You know what Simmons, forget about it. You're a father with a family. It was selfish of me to even ask. You have helped me out plenty times before." He said.

Then I thought, "You're absolutely fucking right. I do have a family, and yes, it's extremely selfish of you to even ask me to borrow money. We both work at the same damn job where overtime is bountiful."

"How much do you need to borrow?" I asked snapping back to reality.

"Forget it Simmons." He quickly responded.

"Snow I'm good for it, and as long as you pay me back by this upcoming Friday. I don't mind letting you borrow the money." I said looking him straight in the eyes.

"Only $160.00. And Simmons of course I will pay you back. Why the fuck wouldn't I? What do you take me for? I already told you it wasn't for cocaine. It's for bills." He said.

Once again, I never questioned what he was using it for; my only concern was if he'd pay me back. The rest of the night had its up and downs. Snow often disappeared, and I presumed he was snorting cocaine while at work. When he and I got off, I had him follow me to an ATM. I gave him $160.00 exact.

"I love you Simmons. I really appreciate it." He said.

I just smiled and drove off.

April 16th, 2010

It was almost noon and I still wasn't sleep. I needed to mail a package to my mother and I needed to get an oil change. After leaving the post office I was waiting at the stoplight.

The light turned green, and the vehicle in front of me didn't move. "What's going on?" They finally eased up, and I thought they would be going straight across the road since there was no signal. An oncoming vehicle had their left signal light on trying to make the turn. This caused the car in front of me to stop immediately, and then they quickly turned on their left signal. BANG! Just then I hit the back of their vehicle. There I was in the middle of the intersection of Arena Drive and Largo Town Center Dr. I put my emergency lights on and lay my head back on the seat.

"Are you fucking kidding me?!" I yelled hitting the steering wheel.

I got out my Jeep to make sure that the people in front of me were ok. I looked at their damage and their back window was shattered. My fender was damaged; however, nothing too major. "Please God. I hope they don't have any babies in their vehicle." I walked up to the driver side of the car. As I got closer, I realized it was a female in the driver's seat.

"Excuse me, are you ok?" I asked her.

She never looked my way. The guy in the passenger seat was screaming at her in another language.

"Are you two ok?" I repeated.

Neither one of them responded. "Fuck it then." I said as I walked back to my Jeep and hopped in. As soon as I closed my door, the police officer 1 drove up to the scene. He got out checking on the first vehicle. Then the police officer 2 drove up. It was a female; she got out of the car and came over to me.

"Are you ok sir?" She wondered.

"Yes I am. I tried asking them if they were ok, but I didn't get a response from them." I responded

I continued to explain to her what happened. We had to exchange insurance information, and the paramedics were eventually called for the other people. The female driver left on a stretcher. I was about to call my mother; however, I realized that I couldn't because she was in Dushanbe. I called my aunt Janelle and she was able to help me out a lot. I also called my job to notify them of the accident.

I told them I wouldn't be able to make it, but then I remembered when another officer called out who was in a car accident. They later found out that he was drinking and driving. He was immediately kicked off the contract. I called my job back to let them know that I would be there. I knew that was not my case; however, I didn't want to give them a reason to even come for me. I went straight home. I didn't even realize that I dozed off. When I woke up it was 4:33PM. I jumped up and I felt this extreme pain shoot down my back. I was very worried. I didn't move for ten seconds as I waited for the pain to ease up. I slowly made my way up the steps to take a shower and rushed off for work.

Due to the accident a few hours prior, I was still shaken up a bit. Regardless of the accident, pain, and nerves I knew I had to make it to work. I didn't want anyone on my case. When I drove up to the gate an officer asked me what happened.

"A warning from God." I simply said and drove off.

"Mind your own damn business." I thought. When I walked inside the PMO I didn't see Snow anywhere.

"Snow called out from work again but I'm glad you're here buddy. What's for dinner?" Officer OB turned to me and asked.

"Sleep." I answered.

Fast Forward:

For the next couple of months, I couldn't think about anything except the car accident. No matter what I tried, I kept having flashbacks of me driving behind the car. Many nights I woke up in cold sweats. I kept having the same nightmare. As a result, I became paranoid to drive, but I couldn't allow that to keep from getting behind the wheel. Besides that, was my only transportation to and from work.

Each day I was expecting to get a call, email, or even a letter concerning the accident; however, nothing came. Months passed, and I started to forget that it happened. Seeing my damaged fender every day was the only reminder.

The New Year came in and I still hadn't received anything pertaining to the car accident. I pushed the thought out of my mind, and I figured that April 16th, 2010 was behind me.

February 28th, 2011

(1st email)

Mr. Andre Simmons

Company Name: Geico Casualty Company Claim Number: 035239041-0101-017 Loss Date: Friday, April 16th, 2010 Policyholder: Andre Simmons

Dear Mr. Simmons,

Our efforts to resolve Akafayat Iashorobi's injury claim were unsuccessful. As a result, you may receive legal documents from Akafayat Iashorobi or an attorney. If you do, contact me immediately at the number below so we can take appropriate actions to protect your interest.

If you have questions, please contact me at the number below. Please refer to our claim number when writing or calling about this claim.

Sincerely,

Stephanie Hall, Examiner Code J391 1-800-841-1003x4369 Claims Department

P.O. Box 9505 Fredericksburg, VA 22403-9504

February 28th, 2011

(2nd email)

Mr. Andre Simmons

Company Name: Geico Casualty Company Claim Number: 035239041-0101-017 Loss Date: Friday, April 16th, 2010 Policyholder: Andre Simmons

Dear Mr. Simmons,

Our efforts to resolve Daehinde Ommotesho's injury claim were unsuccessful. As a result, you may receive legal documents from Daehinde Ommotesho or an attorney. If you do, contact me immediately at the number below so we can take appropriate actions to protect your interest.

If you have questions, please contact me at the number below. Please refer to our claim number when writing or calling about this claim.

Sincerely,

Stephanie Hall, Examiner Code J391 1-800-841-1003x4369 Claims Department

P.O. Box 9505 Fredericksburg, VA 22403-9504

February 28th, 2011

(3rd email)

Mr. Andre Simmons

Company Name: Geico Casualty Company Claim Number: 035239041-0101-017 Loss Date: Friday, April 16th, 2010 Policyholder: Andre Simmons

Dear Mr. Simmons,

The accident that occurred on April 16th, 2010 has resulted in at least one Bodily Injury coverage claim. Our preliminary investigation has revealed that the total claims may exceed your coverage limit of $20,000.00 per person and $40,000.00 per occurrence.

We will make every effort to settle all claims within your coverage limit. If we are unable to do so, you are hereby notified that you may be exposed personally for any amount in excess of your limits. Please be advised that you have the right to obtain your own attorney, at your own expense, to protect your interests in excess of the policy limits. If you have any other Bodily Injury coverage, please notify that carrier and us immediately.

We will notify you if we are unable to settle all claims.

Please contact us should you have any questions.

Sincerely,

Stephanie Hall, Examiner Code J391 1-800-841-1003x4369 Claims Department

P.O. Box 9505 Fredericksburg, VA 22403-9504

After reading the emails my whole body went numb. I sat there staring at the dollar signs and number of digits behind them. That's all I could see. My thoughts were all over the place. "Did I kill these people? This can't possibly be for the same car accident." As much as I didn't want to call Stephanie, I had too. It was in fact my car accident and I was devastated. I never informed my job about the matter at hand because I couldn't afford to lose my job. I wasn't a favorite any longer because I was the worker to use up his sick leave. I decided I'd keep quiet about the situation. There wasn't anything left for me to do. To relieve myself of all the anxiety and trauma, I prayed for peace and gave it to God.

June 16th, 2011

(4th and final email)

Mr. Andre Simmons

Company Name: Geico Casualty Company Claim Number: 035239041-0101-017 Loss Date: Friday, April 16th, 2010 Policyholder: Andre Simmons Plaintiff: Akafayat Iashorobi and Daehinde Ommotesho

Dear Mr. Simmons,

We are pleased to inform you that we have successfully resolved the lawsuit resulting from the claim referenced above. Thank you for your cooperation in the defense of this action.

Sincerely,

Stephanie Hall, Examiner Code J391 1-800-841-1003x4369 Claims Department

That morning when I read that email, I cried for an hour straight. I called my mother to let her know that everything was resolved. That night I was supposed to hang out with Snow to kick off his birthday weekend. However, I had no way of contacting him. It didn't bother me at all. I didn't care. I couldn't help but smile that day. I was relieved, happy, and finally able to be at ease. I slept through the night without a care or worry in the world.

51: Wish List

June 13th, 2011

"Someone has a birthday coming up. What are we doing for your 33rd birthday?" I wondered.

The minute I finished that question, I felt stupid.

"$500.00 is the limit." I said.

"Simmons you don't have to." Snow returned.

"I know I don't have to; however, I want too. Last time was way too much cocaine. This time we won't do as much. We will get fucked up, drink, probably see some strippers, and then call it a night.

"What do you think about that?" I presented.

"That sounds like a plan." He approved.

"Well a plan it is then Snow." I declared.

Snow wanted to do it big, so he ended up inviting a couple of guys from work to meet up at Ireland's Four Provinces Restaurant & Pub.

June 17th, 2011

The fact that everyone was contacting me was ridiculous. I called Snow several times and he never answered. I wasn't worried about him anyway. I already knew what he was up to. I found it amusing that he was inviting all these people to the bar, and he basically bailed out of his own get together. I was a little skeptical for the simple fact that he and I originally had plans for Saturday. I wondered if he'd cancel on me as well. Still it didn't bother me as much because I knew this time a hotel wouldn't be involved.

June 18th, 2011

5:19PM

All morning and early that afternoon there was still no word on Snow. I was on my way to get Chinese food and I finally got a call from Snow.

"What's up?" I answered.

"Sorry about that man. I had a crazy night." He said.

"I bet birthday boy." I said giggling.

"Yeah are we still on for tonight?" He asked.

"Sure, we are. I was on my way to get some Chinese food, so I'm ready. Do you want me to come right now?" I asked.

"I actually just got off the phone with dude. You think you can send $300.00 right now? And I will meet you at

Ireland's Four Provinces Restaurant & Pub with the cocaine." He said.

"Yeah that sounds like a plan. Give me 10 minutes." I replied.

I hung up and every hair follicle on my body was telling me not to go. Once I got the reference number from MoneyGram, I called Snow to let him know that the money has been sent.

"Cool, head straight to Ireland's Four Provinces Restaurant & Pub and hit me up once you get there." I said.

When I hit I-495 I was approaching the split between Virginia and Baltimore I ran into traffic. I called Snow right away to let him know I was going to be running a little late, but the phone rung once and went to his voicemail. I didn't think anything of it because I knew he was going to call me back once he purchased the cocaine. After sitting in traffic for 20 minutes I realized that Snow never called me back. I tried calling once again. I still didn't get an answer.

"Here we go again." I said getting frustrated.

6:51PM

I reached the Ireland's Four Provinces Restaurant & Pub a few minutes before 7:00PM. I still didn't hear anything from Snow. His phone would ring once and continue to go to voicemail. To calm my nerves, I decided to play some music while I waited.

7:23PM

Snow finally called me back.

"Simmons I'm still waiting on dude." He said.

"I'm here." I said in an inflamed tone.

"I'll call you when I'm on the way." He said.

"Ok." I said trying to relax.

I was just ready for him to get there.

When Snow hung up, I automatically knew he wasn't coming but I waited on him anyway.

9:34PM

Snow called again.

"Hello?" I answered.

"Hey Simmons, man tonight isn't a good night man. I'm sorry. I'll see you at work on Monday." He casually said.

"Ok." I said and hung up the phone.

By then, I was walking through the front door of my home with Chinese food that I no longer had the appetite to eat.

52: **Bon Voyage**

June 21ˢᵗ, 2011

I wanted to do something special for my mother since she was leaving on Sunday the 26ᵗʰ. She didn't want to go out to dinner; however, she told me that she would be more than happy if I had a dinner for her at home. On Tuesday I made up the menu. Then I called everyone to inform them of the dinner. As I was doing so Jai walked into the kitchen.

"Jai what dish are you going to make on Saturday?" I asked.

"Nothing. Me and my sisters are going to the D.C. Caribbean Carnival on Saturday." She said.

The funny thing was that the Carnival was there for the whole weekend. Why of all days would she choose Saturday? The party wasn't for me, it was for my mother. A woman who helped me, Jai, and our kids for years. I didn't let her arrogance and negativity stop me. I did what I had to do.

June 25ᵗʰ, 2011

I woke up early Saturday morning to get my day started. Jai was already in the shower. I was in the kitchen prepping my food. I watched her walk downstairs; grab her purse and keys and head towards the door.

"Wait a minute. You're not taking Jamari and J'Adora with you?" I suggested.

"They can stay here with you." She snapped.

"Really Jai? You know I'm having my mother's party today. Why can't you take them with you? How can I clean, cook, and watch Jamari and J'Adora?" I asked irritated.

She continued her way and walked out the door.

"Bitch!" I cried out.

Luckily my sister was in town and she assisted me with the kids. My mother ran errands throughout the day. The food was done, and the family arrived. An hour after the party started, Jai arrived back to the house with her four sisters and their appetites. I spoke to her sisters and continued with the evening. I didn't mind at all that her sisters were there. The problem I had was with Jai. I specifically asked her earlier in the week to help me with this function. Not only was she uncooperative and uninterested; however, she also brought extra mouths to feed.

Jai bought two bottles of wine and opened one up after the crowd left. I was in the living room with my sister Lyndyann and my cousin Kanika. Jamari and J'Adora had fallen asleep on the couch. Jai was still in the kitchen with her sisters.

"Andre, why you call my mother crazy?" She randomly blurted out.

"What are you talking about Jai?" I said shaking my head looking at my sister.

"Jamari said you called my mother crazy." She claimed.

"And you believe what Jamari said?" I asked in disbelief.

"Now is not the time or place for that Jai." I said firmly.

Aunt Celestine, Kanika, Djuan, Dayvon, and Ayana were the last people to leave. Jai and her sisters came into the living room. Jai sat right beside me. I could tell she was tipsy from drinking her wine. She was so loud, she made herself look ignorant. She began ranting about her mother.

"Jai you do be coming at mom disrespectful." Ava stated.

"Mom doesn't know how to talk to people Ava!" Jai snapped.

"Why couldn't they just stay in the kitchen with that conversation?" I thought to myself. I got up and started to clean the kitchen. By the time I finished Jai was passed out on the couch. I took the kids upstairs.

"Are you guys ready to go home?" I asked Jai's sisters.

They all replied no.

"I'll take you guys home when you're ready to go." I offered.

They all said ok and continued watching the movie.

June 26th, 2011

The next morning the family returned to see my mother off. They had some leftovers and spent time with my mother before her departure. My sister, Jamari, J'Adora, and I got ready to take my mother to BWI Airport. Of course, the kitchen was filthy again. Jai was still asleep. Before I left, I knocked on her door to let her know I was taking the kids with me.

When we arrived back at home Jai's car was gone. We walked into the house and the kitchen was just how I left it. Once again Jai didn't even bother to clean up. I was exhausted, and the kids and I took a nap. My sister wound up cleaning the kitchen. I woke up around 8:00PM just in time to watch the BET Awards.

My sister left that Monday on the 27th to go back to New York. Once again it was just me, Jai, Jamari, and J'Adora in my mother's home. My mother wasn't even gone 24 hours and I was already missing her dearly.

53: Sesame Place

July 12th, 2011

It was another Tuesday night on the job. Lt. Sr. asked Snow and I if we would like to pick up some extra hours on Saturday. I agreed to work the 1st shift and Snow agreed to work the 2nd shift. I didn't know what I was going to plan for J'Adora's birthday. Her birthday was the 17th and I wanted to do something with her and Jamari that Sunday.

July 13th, 2011

Wednesday night while at work, I decided to ask Snow to do a switch with me so that I could take J'Adora and Jamari to Sesame Place on Saturday. I would come in and work the 2nd shift that evening and he agreed. I called aunt Celestine and Kanika to pick their kids up as well. I asked Audrekia to come too. I was also given permission by my sister Lyndyann to taker her daughter Saniah. It was last minute, even so I was glad that I was able to throw everything together. I hoped the kids would have great time.

July 16th, 2011

8:27AM

We left out early that Saturday morning. Jamari, J'Adora, Audrekia, the twins Djuan and Dayvon, and Ayana rode with me. Saniah and Tatyana were with Jai. I was in Philadelphia passing the Lincoln Financial Field, Citizens Bank Park, and Wells Fargo Center stadiums when a text message came through. I reached for my phone and I saw

Snow's name. I just knew it wasn't good. I was hoping and praying that it wasn't bad news.

"Simmons I can't work your shift tonight." He texted.

"Why do I even bother with him?" I whispered.

"Snow I really need for you to work the shift. I'm in Philadelphia on my way to Sesame Place with two vehicles full of children for my daughter's birthday. Why couldn't you text me this fucking morning?" I replied.

I continued driving like everything was ok. My phone went off again.

"I'm sick man." He texted.

"You're not sick. You're a fucking addict!" I texted back.

I called Lt. Jr. to let him know the situation. There really wasn't anything he could do since Snow and I agreed to work the shifts. My supervisor questioned me, asking why I continued to let my so called *"Friend"* play me. I didn't have anything to say. I couldn't answer that question as to why I allowed Snow to have so much control. That should have been the last time, but it was quite the opposite. Deep down I knew I was going to forgive him like I always did. Lt. Jr. said he would do what he could to cover the shift. I thanked him for at least trying to cover the shift; however, I knew if he couldn't cover it, I was responsible to work it. I hated the fact that I had to tell Jai that we would have to cut J'Adora's day short. I decided not to even bring it up. I just prayed that Lt. Jr. found coverage for the shift.

11:34AM

After being at the amusement park for an hour, I got another phone call from Lt Jr.

"Hello?" I answered.

"Simmons, I found coverage for your shift. You don't have to come in tonight. Enjoy your daughter's birthday buddy." He said.

"Thank you. Thank you." I said.

"No problem man." He responded.

I was so happy. Now that we didn't have to rush back, I planned on staying the whole day at Sesame Place until the park closed. Depending on how I felt, I thought about getting two hotel rooms and staying for the night. It was scorching hot outside and I was the bag man. I was holding purses, towels, shoes, and all types of items while the kids enjoyed themselves.

3:22PM

My phone rang again. It was Lt. Jr. calling back.

"Hello?" I answered.

"Bad news man. Your boy just called out of his shift and the coverage that I had for you, he can't work any more than 12 hours, or he'll be in overtime. I'm waiting on two calls to see if I can get coverage for you. I'm doing my best Simmons." He explained.

"Alright. Thank you though." I said.

I was thankful because the kids were having such a great time. I had never been so tired in all my life behind the wheel. I knew I had to make it to work on time; however, I had to pull over a total of three times to wake myself up. Once we made it home, I jumped in the shower to freshen up, and got dressed for work. Rushing out of the house, I realized that I left my bulletproof vest at home. "Oh, fuck it." I said and prayed that I didn't get shot that night.

10:44PM

I pulled up to the gate just in time. Thank God I made it to work safe and sound.

54: **Party Pooper**

Flashback:

Best Western Dulles Airport Inn

Snow's lies began to catch up with him. Snow's addiction to cocaine was no secret, and Tracy wasn't having it. It was funny because the two of them were like a match made in heaven. They were both pathological liars. In the beginning Snow claimed that God had sent him an angel. She even had me fooled for a while. However, once her halo fell, she was giving him everything but peace. I thought it was hilarious until Snow's alleged health issues started taking a toll on him. It caused him to miss two weeks of work. I knew it wasn't that serious, but he blamed Tracy more than ever. He tried to drown out his pain and misery by heavily using cocaine. The supervisors and officers were constantly asking me if everything was ok with Snow. I had no choice but to answer yes. I gave them nothing. I knew he was on especially when Snow suggested we hang out soon. I stopped asking him to hang out because I always knew disaster awaited us. As usual I didn't tell him no. What was one more time? What was the worst that could happen? Just like the times before, I already knew how everything was going to turn out.

Fast Forward:

September 2nd, 2011

When I arrived at the Best Western Dulles Airport Inn, I called him to let him know I was outside. He met me on the side of the Inn and his eyes were bloodshot red. He already had my drink waiting for me and a line cut. To my surprise Snow purchased 2.5 grams. I knew it was going to be a long night because Snow did not wait for my money.

"Simmons, the fuck took you so long?" He wondered.

"Traffic Snow. I drove from Largo, Maryland to 6900 Georgia Ave NW, Washington D.C., to Accokeek, Maryland to drop off the kids. Then to Herndon, Virginia to be with you." I explained.

"You make me sick." He said.

"I know Snow that's why I'm here." I stated.

I put my bag down on the bed and took a sip of my drink. Then I snorted my first line.

"I hate that bitch Simmons. She's going to be the death of me man." He said pacing back and forth with his hands on his head.

"Snow then leave her the fuck alone. Look how she got you acting. Besides you said you wasn't going to spend this weekend talking about Tracy. You're not going to be able to enjoy this moment with her on you mind." I said.

"I know man this is our weekend." He said.

It didn't faze or surprise me when Snow snorted the rest of the cocaine that he purchased within the first hour. I was too busy going back and forth with Big.

"Who are you texting Simmons?" He asked inquisitively.

"Big." I replied.

"Oh, my fucking God! Get off his dick!" He said annoyed.

"Why, you want me on yours?" I asked sarcastically.

"Yuck!" He said with a shudder.

"We need some more Snow. Hit dude up for another 2.5 grams and let's go see some strippers to get your mind of Tracy." I suggested.

We left the hotel and stayed at the strip club for an hour. When we made it back to the hotel, I knew Snow wasn't going to spend the night.

"Simmons what are you doing tomorrow?" He asked.

"I don't have anything planned. The kids are with my aunt Janelle until Sunday." I replied.

"You want to do part II?" He gushed.

I was shocked that he asked me that. Even though I brought one change of clothes for that night, I figured what the hell. This was our last weekend. Why not go out with a bang? Plus, Snow was acting decent for once. Snow left, and I changed my clothes for bed.

September 3rd, 2011

I awoke to a knock at the door. I looked at my phone and it was two minutes after seven. "Like what the fuck?" Then Snow entered my room.

"Simmons wake up man. We need to fucking talk." He said.

"About what?" I asked sleepily.

"Tracy." He responded.

"Oh God." I said.

Snow sat on the bed across from me and rambled on and on about Tracy. The way she lied to him about having cancer; and saying she was going out of town for a business meeting when she was really having sex with another guy. I sat up and listened to him for two hours. It was pointless for me to even attempt to go back to sleep at that point. Finally, I was able to get a word in.

"Snow you want to go out and get some breakfast. Maybe eating will help. I know you haven't been to sleep?" I asked.

"Fuck no man! You see the way I look!" He shouted.

"Aright then. I'm about to go hit the shower." I said.

When I came out of the bathroom Snow was bent over snorting a line of cocaine. I guess he went to get more after he left me earlier. Something told me to just go back home because Snow was too emotional and too high to come back down anytime soon. Once again, I ignored my intuition.

"What are we about to do now?" I asked.

"Simmons I'll hit you up in about an hour." He said.

"Where am I supposed to go?" I asked.

"Simmons look man. I promise I won't stand you up or disappear. I just need an hour or two to get some rest." He insisted.

"Ok then. I need to buy some clothes anyway. And I've never been to Dulles Town Center. I'll call you in a couple of hours." I said.

I handed him the hotel key. We went to the front desk and went our separate ways.

After leaving the hotel, I stopped at the Shell gas station to get a snicker and a bottle of Fiji water. While I was there, I got the directions to Dulles Town Center. Around 2:00PM I called Snow and as usual I didn't get a response. "Ugh here we go again!" I thought. I called him again around 3:00PM and I still couldn't reach him, 4:00PM still nothing. Around 4:30PM I called him to let him know that I was about to head home. He immediately called me back.

"Hello?" I answered.

"Simmons, I can't believe this fucking bitch!" He yelled.

I didn't get a sorry or anything for ignoring your calls. I told him I was about to head back home, and once again it was about Tracy. I cut him off and asked him about our plans. He asked me to book the room. I booked a room at Homewood Suites by Hilton Dulles Int'l Airport. This had to be the best hotel that we stayed in. Perfect ending to what this whole situation was. I texted Snow the room number. I looked at my phone and it was 5:37PM there was still no Snow. What could possibly be holding him up? He lived down the street from the hotel. I called him and no answer. I laid down across the bed. I woke up to knocks on the door. I looked at my phone and it was 7:02PM. I was beyond exhausted and over it at that point. I looked through the peephole and it was him. I opened the door and he looked like shit and his eyes were bloodshot red.

"Are you ok?" I asked concerned.

"Let's go Simmons!" He said.

"What's wrong man?" I wondered.

"I'm sorry man. Let's just go." He said.

"Alright let me get my stuff. Give me five minutes." I suggested.

"Simmons, you're not fucking ready yet?!" He screamed.

"Snow, please don't, not now." I said.

"What the fuck you mean?" He asked.

"Snow I wasted my day waiting on you. This is supposed to be our last weekend together before everything changes. So please don't come at me like that. Tracy fucked you dude, just let her go Snow." I said.

"Simmons I can't. I love her. You can't help who you love man." He said.

"Snow I told how you how it feels man; loving someone so deep and they don't love you back." I explained.

We headed out and met the dealer. I purchased 7 grams. We stopped at an Exxon, parked on the side of the store and Snow cut a line for the both of us. Then we drove to the liquor store. I purchased a bottle of Belvedere. While in the parking lot he cut us another line. I was feeling good at that point. Snow was in and out of his emotions. I'd never seen him like that before. We went back to the hotel, and I fixed the drinks while he was cutting us more line. Since I had been doing this with Snow, I'd never seen him that hungry for cocaine. It was frightening. I could see his hands shaking as he was chopping up the cocaine with his credit card. I became worried and concerned.

"Snow maybe you should get some rest. We got the whole night to party." I suggested.

"You fucking disgust me! Don't tell me what the fuck to do!" He said angrily.

"Ok." I said as I sat down beside him.

"Simmons man. I told you I'm sorry. I'm just no good right now." He said.

"I understand." I responded.

My phone went off, and it was Big telling me goodnight.

"Who was that?" He asked.

"It was Big." I said.

"Oh him." He said uncaringly.

"Yes him." I responded.

Snow's phone went off. He looked at his phone. As he was reading the message, the reflection from the light danced on his face because his hands were still shaking. I didn't want to do anymore cocaine at that point. The night was finished.

"Simmons, I got to run." He said.

It was no surprise to me. This was his normal routine.

"Ok. And you can take that with you Snow." I said.

He just stared at me. I spent over $1,000.00 on this weekend and I wasn't mad because I knew this was my last time in a hotel room with him.

"I'm sorry man." He said as he was putting on his coat.

"Me too." I responded.

Once Snow left, I was finally able to sleep.

September 4th, 2011

I didn't realize that I had fallen asleep. I heard knocks at the door, and I thought it was Snow returning because maybe he had forgotten something. I looked at my phone. It was 2:23AM and I had seven missed calls from him. "Damn, what is it now?" I got up and walked to the door in my underwear. I opened the door and he walked in.

"What's up Snow?" I asked.

"I don't know man. I just wanted to apologize to you." He said.

"It's ok Snow. Really, it's ok this time. I'm not mad bro." I responded.

He just stood there looking at me.

"So, is that it?" I wondered.

"No man. I disappointed you again." He said.

"Goodnight Snow go back home or wherever you were." I suggested.

"Simmons you don't want to talk?" He asked.

"Nope." I responded and walked back to my bed.

I got in and pulled the covers over my head. Snow stayed five minutes longer and then left. The next morning after getting out of the shower, my phone rung. I knew it couldn't be anyone but Snow.

"Hello?" I answered.

"Simmons before you leave, can you please stop by my house?" He asked.

"No. I have to go pick up my kids from my aunt Janelle's and take my cousin Kendrell out to dinner for his birthday. I'll see you tomorrow at the gun range." I said.

He hung up the phone without a word. On the way to my aunt Janelle's house I felt like I was escaping a storm that I thought would never end. I could see the rainbow now that the rain was gone. I made it to my aunt's. I glanced at myself in the mirror. I knew no one would be able to tell what happened the night before because I was well rested and fresh faced. I got out of the car and walked up to the door. When I rung the doorbell, Kendrell answered the door.

"What's up man?" He said.

"Daddy's here!" Jamari screamed.

"Daddy's here!" J'Adora repeated.

Seeing their smiling faces, I realized just how beautiful my two treasures were. I knew that they loved me unconditionally and their love for me didn't cost a thing.

55: Man Up

September 5th, 2011

I took my gun range test early that Monday morning. I was proud to pass with a score of 247. That week we also had to choose our new work schedules just in case we got picked up by another security company. I knew what had to be done, and I knew I needed to choose another schedule. I knew I could no longer work with Snow. I could never tell Snow "No" when it came to cocaine. It wasn't because of the high. It was because I realized what it had done to him, as well as what it was doing to me. Cocaine was a drug that numbed my pain, but it was only a temporary repair. I felt it was time I finally stop running and face my life sober.

September 7th, 2011

When it came to choose my new work schedule, I based it on two things. I no longer wanted to be on a shift working with Snow, and I also needed a schedule that wouldn't conflict with Jamari and J'Adora's school schedule. This also meant I would have to sacrifice my weekends, and that was ok with me because I knew 2012 was going to be a year of change. The only thing about the schedules was that there was no privacy once you signed up.

"Simmons, why are you going in such a rush?" Snow wondered.

"Oh... I really got to get home. Jamari isn't feeling well." I explained.

I walked off as fast as I could to get to my Jeep. As I was walking, I started thinking to myself; "Oh shit. Snow knew I was lying because that's the same line I hit the supervisors with." I thought to myself. It wasn't even five minutes before my phone started to ring. Snow was calling, and I didn't answer. He called me right back.

"Hello?" I answered.

"Simmons I can't fucking believe you!" He shouted.

"What happened?" I asked playing dumb.

I already knew what he was referring to; even still, I pretended that I didn't.

"Why would you pick that schedule?" He asked.

"Snow I had to choose a schedule that was best for my kids. Do you honestly think I wanted to give up my weekends?" I pleaded.

"It's okay man. You did what you had to do." He said.

"What schedule did you choose?" I wondered.

"2nd shift, working Wednesday - Saturday." He responded.

"At least you have Saturday nights off to party." I said.

"Yeah Simmons. Whatever man. But look, I'll hit you up some other time." He said.

"Alright." I said and hung up the phone.

What a relief. The only day that he and I had off together was Tuesday. There was no way that he would risk doing cocaine in the beginning of his work week; and if he did, I would just give him an excuse on why I couldn't do it. Even though everything was coming to an end, it was still bittersweet. I loved him a lot; however, our friendship was too toxic. If I had the money to pay for it, Snow was never going to stop snorting it. I was the enabler, which made me feel just as guilty.

56: Off The Record

October 7th, 2011

That Friday night when I arrived at work, I walked into PMO Lt. Jr. was talking to Lt. Bryant when Lt. Jr. seen me, he paused.

"Yo Simmons where your boy at man?" He asked.

"He's in my back pocket." I mumbled.

"Tell your boy he needs to stay off that cocaine." He said directly.

I didn't respond to him; however, I knew that my face said it all.

"Simmons, what do you know man?" Lt. Jr. questioned handing me my weapons.

"I don't know nothing. I work on a different shift than he does." I said.

"But you used to work with him." He said.

"Yep, used to." I said and walked out the door.

"How in the hell did Lt. Jr. know?" I thought as I was walking to the gate. I was also wondering if they knew about me too. Once I reached the gate, I noticed that officer Lucy and officer Kilgore were already there.

"That's the luckiest damn white boy in the world. I can't believe he's still doing that shit and has a job. If it was one of us, we would've been out of here. I know its drugs." I heard officer Lucy say.

I pulled out my DVD player to set up shop. About 10 minutes later Lt. Jr. was heading out and called out my name.

"Simmons!" He shouted.

"Why you look at me like that when I said your boy was doing cocaine?" He asked.

I didn't say anything.

"Is that what it is Simmons? If Snow's on that shit you should say something. That is your boy after all. Because the way it's looking for him, Snow is going to get let go." He indicated.

"I'm not saying a word Lt. Jr." I declared.

I closed the door to the booth and sat back down. Lt. Jr. drove away. Just before midnight Snow called me.

"Simmons what's going on?" He asked.

"Snow, why didn't you come to work? They are asking me about you again." I stated.

"Man, it's a long story. Look Simmons if you're about to start bitching at me, I'm going to just hang up." He said.

"Fine then." I said and hung up the phone.

He called back, and I didn't pick up. He called again. I screened the call and let it go to my voicemail. Right after I got the voicemail notification, I put my password in and listened:

"Simmons you've been acting funny ever since we switched shifts. What has gotten into you? One minute you're my friend and the next minute you're not. I'm fucking sick of all this back and forth shit. Be a man Simmons. I have had enough shit to deal with than play your little boy games."

The question was should I, or shouldn't I? What would it take for Snow and me just to be over? Even though we no longer worked together, I still couldn't escape this hold he had on me. I texted Big until he fell asleep. 30 minutes at the top of the hour my phone rung. I looked down at it and it was Snow calling again. "Oh my god! What the fuck is it now?" I thought to myself. I stepped outside of the booth.

"Hello?" I answered.

"Simmons!" He shouted.

"Yes Snow?" I responded.

"Hi." He said.

We both laughed.

"Are you ok?" I wondered.

"Man no. I'm going down." He said.

"Shut up. Remember you're going to Florida soon." I said.

"Yep. About that… that's not going to happen anymore."
He said.

"Why not?" I asked surprised.

"Because I don't see myself making it to move down
there." He explained.

"Snow quit talking like that." I pleaded.

"I'm serious Simmons. I know I'm about to get fired
anyway. My son hates me. Tracy played me. You're
ignoring me. I don't have anyone man. I just cause
everyone pain. Maybe it's better if I kill myself." He
revealed.

"You're not serious. But Snow you got to chill man. Tracy,
she's last month news; even though I know you're still
messing with her. But as for your son, it's never too late to
fix things." I said.

I didn't know what to think when Snow talked about killing
himself. It wasn't his first time mentioning that. At that
point I was tired of hearing about it. Was he doing it for
attention or was it a cry for help? I didn't know. I knew I
wasn't a help to him because every time we were together,
we ended up doing cocaine.

Chief was someone who wanted to hang out with Snow and
I when he was just an officer before he was promoted. I
thought that if I could speak to him about the situation, he
could possibly be of service before it was too late.

October 10th, 2011

Monday morning when Lt. Jr. drove up to the gate, I checked his ID and he continued to the PMO. I decided that I was going to say something. The conversation that Lt. Jr. and I had about Snow bothered me all weekend. I went to the bathroom and once I returned, officers Tracie and Thomas were gone.

"Lt. Jr. this is off the record what I'm about to say. Snow has done drugs, and the drug that I knew of was cocaine." I said.

"Simmons this is big man. How long have you known this?" He asked.

"As long as I've been working with Snow. And the reason why I know this is because I have done it with him on numerous occasions in the past." I explained.

"This dude got you on this shit Simmons? He's no friend of yours if he got you on cocaine too." He suggested.

"I have stopped, and it never affected my ability to work." I replied.

"You got kids man!" He retorted.

"I'm very aware of this Lt. Jr. which was one of the reasons that I had to stop; in which I had no problem doing. But Snow seems to be getting worse. I worry about him, and he's told me many times that he may commit suicide Lt. Jr." I said.

"Are you serious Simmons!?" He asked stunned.

I pulled out my phone and let Lt. Jr. listened to a few voicemails that Snow left.

"Wow!" He said.

"That's it I'm going home." I said and walked away.

When I returned to work, I perceived that officer Tracie was upset at the fact that I informed Lt. Jr. about Snow. It didn't matter because what was done was done.

October 11th, 2011

I got off the next morning and as soon as I handed my weapon to Lt. Jr. and signed out, he asked me to stick around. I already knew what it was about. I knew Lt. Jr. told Chief. Officer Tracie left. I texted her immediately, letting her know that I would call her once I was finished.

"Simmons, Chief wants to have a word with you about what you told me yesterday morning." He said.

"I thought what you and I talked about was private Lt. Jr." I replied.

"Come on Simmons." He said.

I paused for a quick second. "Ok. Sure then." I said giving in.

Lt. Jr. got on the phone and told Chief that we were on our way. We left the PMO, got into the duty van, and went directly to Chief's office. Lt. Jr. knocked on the door and we entered Chief's office.

"Good morning Mr. Simmons." He said.

"Good morning Chief." I responded.

"Lt. Jr. informed me what you revealed about officer Snow. If you can write a sworn statement about the situation, this could possibly save Snow's job. Mr. Simmons everything you write in the sworn statement will be strictly confidential. You have my word." He said.

"Chief before I write this statement, I am by no means trying to get Snow in trouble. Let's be clear on that. I don't want this to fall back on me. I'm truly concerned about him, and I don't want this on my conscience if something was to happen to him by me keeping quiet. We already had 2 other officers on the contract kill themselves; officer Young due to bullying from the other officers and the other guy who I never seen or met came with issues and we don't need a number 3." I cautioned.

After being coerced of writing each letter on paper and thinking about sleep I handed the sworn statement to Chief.

"Thank you, Mr. Simmons." Chief said.

Chief began to read the statement. I got up to leave with Lt. Jr., so he could take me to my vehicle.

"Mr. Simmons you didn't write about Snow's drug use." He said.

"I know I didn't. I told Lt. Jr. that Snow and I doing cocaine was off the record." I said and walked out the door.

57: Snitch

October 12th, 2011

Around 2:30PM the calls started. Snow called me three times back to back before he left me a voicemail:

"Simmons I just left Chief's office. Give me a call." He said.

Before I could even hang up, my phone beeped. I had another incoming call from him. I still didn't answer. He sent me a text message right after:

"Simmons give me a call." It said.

I immediately called Chief.

"Snow is calling me Chief. Why is Snow calling me telling me he left your office?" I asked.

"Hey Mr. Simmons, he did just leave the office and I didn't mention your name. He did. I asked him was everything ok?" He claimed.

"Ok. What did he say?" I asked.

"First and foremost, Mr. Simmons you are not the reason why Snow isn't working today." He said.

"Chief I understand all of that, but why is he calling me?" I asked irritated.

"I never mentioned your name." Chief continued.

I wasn't shocked. I knew I was on my own at this point. My phone beeped again, and it was him.

"Chief, he's calling me right now. I'll give you a call back." I said and clicked over.

"Hello?" I said.

"Simmons, I don't know what I did to you, but I just left Chief's office and guess what? They are not letting me work today Simmons! I can't come back to work until I go see a doctor so that they can issue me a note to clear me that I'm okay to work. Do you know how much that's going to put me in a bind Simmons?! Fucking $300.00 man! That's money I don't fucking have! Simmons everyone isn't privileged to have a mother with money like you! I don't fucking believe you! How could you do this to me Simmons?!" He shouted.

"What you're saying is that you want me to give you $300.00 so that you're able to come back to work?! Is that what you're saying to me Snow?!" I asked.

"Don't you dare talk to me like that, don't you fucking dare! This is all your fucking fault Simmons! All those months I had to endure your nagging about your fucking pathetic marriage and your sexual identity! My brother wants to fucking kill you! Freddy wants to burry you! Everyone can't believe I let you of all people, a black fucking faggot like you play me!" He snapped.

"A black fucking faggot like me? The shadow of the truth eventually comes to light in the end! Snow you were never my friend! I was your black boy trick that never got the dick! You loved my money! If you were ever my friend you wouldn't have introduced me to cocaine in the first place, used your sob stories to manipulate me, your other co-workers, Captain, and every other white Chief that came through there! I would jump at your every command like a little puppy! I was so naïve, pathetic, and weak for your approval! Was Snow! I knew you were a liar the first time I went to your house back in February of last year and met your mother! I guess she wasn't sick that day, huh Snow?!" I responded.

"Fuck you, you nigger!" He shouted.

"Really?!" I laughed. "I'll give you the $300.00. That's not a problem but from this day forth lose my number. I'm done Snow. Andre LeDale Simmons is done!" I declared.

20 minutes later Snow called me again.

"I said I was coming!" I yelled answering the phone.

"Simmons can we talk?" He asked.

"Are you serious? No Snow we can't. I'm leaving here in the next 10 minutes. I'll call you when I'm on your street." I said.

"Alright." He responded calmly.

"Jai I have to go somewhere. I'll be back within an hour and half." I said.

"Andre, I work tonight." She said and rolled her eyes.

"I know that Jai. That's why I'm telling you right now. By that time, I'll be back." I said.

"You're going to meet Snow, aren't you?" She asked.

"If you must know, yes I am. And it's not for the reason you think." I responded.

"Yeah whatever." She said.

"Jai if I was going to do cocaine, trust and believe I would have called your sisters to have them watch Jamari and J'Adora for more than an hour and a half. I'll be back." I said as I headed downstairs.

I walked to the dresser, pulled open the drawer, and lifted the letters. I reached in the back-left corner feeling for the rolled up tiny plastic bag.

"Oh, shit where it is?! Oh, there it is." I said with a sigh of relief.

I closed the drawer and walked back upstairs. I walked back into the living room and kissed sleeping Jamari and J'Adora on their cheeks. Jai was in the dining room. I turned to look at her.

"I'll be right back Jai." I said and walked out the door.

I went to the ATM and checked my balance. I had $367.23 in my account. I had withdrawn $300.00 at the share branch credit union up the street from my home, so I wouldn't have to pay a fee. $67.23 is all I had left until I got paid on Friday. When I took the exit to get to his house,

I became nervous because I didn't know what was about to go down. When I drove up to Snow's home, neither his car nor his mother's car was in the driveway. I parked and sat in the car for a minute before I got out. I put the $300.00 and the small bag of cocaine in an envelope. I got out of my Jeep, looked around, and I didn't see any signs of Snow. While walking towards his mailbox, I stopped for a second looked around once more, and then continued walking. After getting back into my Jeep, I backed out and pulled up to the road to make a left turn. Right away Snow pulled into the driveway in his mother's vehicle. He looked at me and his window was down. I rolled down my window.

"I put everything in the envelope." I said once he pulled up beside me.

"Please Simmons. Can we talk?" He asked again.

"No, not this time Snow, and for the record I never mentioned that you were doing cocaine in my statement." I said and drove off.

58: **Adam & Steve** *(Part One)*

Flashback:

December 2007, right around the time Janet Jackson's new song "Feedback" was leaked. I only knew him as the faceless commentator that was on one of my favorite urban entertainment blogs called ThatGrapeJuice.net. This commentator knew more than I did about Janet Jackson. The way they were able to articulate the comments was quite intriguing, and that's all it was for four years. I never knew what the commentator looked like behind those comments. I later found out that the commentator referred to themselves as a male and he later choose a name that confirmed his allegations. Janet Jackson's tour kicked off February 4th, 2011 in Manila. The song she dedicated to the city was "Go Deep." I started connecting with more Janet Jackson fans through Twitter. Some names became more familiar to me such as @MeganAmbers aka Megan, @InAaronITrust aka Aaron, @TrellJJ aka Le'Trell, and @RockWitchuGurl aka Racquel. I would always see them on Janet Jackson's timeline. On June 2nd, 2011 I seen a familiar name that I would often see onThatGrapeJuice.net. I couldn't believe that it was him. I was debating whether to go on this page. When I clicked on the Twitter page, I noticed that it was a guy and I could see that he was a very handsome black man. In his avi *(profile picture on Twitter)* he had pictures of Janet Jackson, Whitney Houston, and Beyoncé. I followed him, and he immediately followed me back. I sent him a DM to let him know I was TheDimplePuppet from ThatGrapeJuice.net which was also my Twitter name (@TheDimplePuppet). What he and I had in common was our undying love for Janet Jackson. Everything we discussed was about Janet; Janet Jackson this and Janet Jackson that.

Fast Forward:

As time went on, we grew closer. In August 2011 our conversations went from Janet Jackson to having conversations about ourselves. At first it felt weird, but I talked to Snow about Big. I told him that I met this guy and he had 1001 questions. At times he seemed happy for me, and other times he acted like a jerk. It led me to keep the secret that Big was planning to come and visit me in October. Big knew I was legally married; however, I made it very clear to him that even though Jai and I were living together we weren't intimate or even sleeping in the same bed for that matter. Big knew Jai was moving on with her life, and I was obviously moving on with mine. The first and last time I was intimate with Jai was February 6th, 2011.

October 14th, 2011

It was almost 7:00PM and I was so excited and nervous at the same time. That's when my mind started to get the best of me. "I can drive away now. It's not too late. However, Big is here, I can't leave him stranded at the Greyhound until tomorrow." Big came all the way from New York to see me. I told Jai I was working a double that night, so I didn't have anywhere else to go. "I trust this, it feels right. I just can't believe Big is here though. My body needs this." I looked down at my phone and it was Big calling.

"Hi." I said.

"Hi, I'm walking out now." He responded.

"Ok. I see you. I'm in the white Jeep Commander across the street." I responded nervously.

He walked across the street with a book bag on his back. "He's here." I thought to myself. "It's too late to turn back now."

"Hi Big." I said as he opened the car door and got in.

"Hey babe." He said looking right into my eyes and smiling.

We lean in for a kiss. It was quick and sweet. I drove to the area of the hotel. We kept our conversation to a minimum. Once we were close, a guy flagged us down from the street to let us know that he had available parking spaces. I rolled down the window, "How much?"

"$20.00 for overnight." He said.

We got out and headed towards our destination. As we started walking, I felt that every person I passed was looking right through me. I felt like they were judging me. "Oh, look at him! Yeah, they're both gay. Definitely!" After shutting the voices off in my head, we finally made it to the Hyatt Regency Washington on Capitol Hill. I hoped that he was impressed with what he'd seen so far.

"Do you like it?" I wondered.

"This is really nice babe." He said.

He walked into a convenient store that was inside the hotel. There were two older black women that were inside the store. One was behind the counter and the other was standing on the side talking to her. I just stopped at the entrance and observed. One woman said something to Big and I could hear him giggling. I bet she was flirting with him. Then she looked at me and I backed out of the store until he returned. When we got to the elevator, I stood there looking at my reflection. The door to the elevator opened and we entered. He came closer to me, and I held my head down as I began to blush. He smelled so good. The elevator door opened, and we walked side by side until we got to the room. I opened the room door and walked in first. As he was looking around, he stopped and looked at me. "Oh shit." I thought to myself. I walked to the window to show him the view. I could hear his footsteps coming nearer. I turned around and he was right on me.

"I don't know how to kiss." I said bashfully.

"Babe it's ok." We kissed again. "Awwww." He gushed.

I started to get a little excited down below. I needed to calm my nerves.

"Would you like a drink?" I wondered.

"Sure babe." He responded as he was taking off his shoes.

"I'm going to run a bubble bath for us." I said smiling after handing him his drink.

I took my clothes off until I exposed my new fitted briefs. I was very comfortable around him. He preferred his guys thick, so I felt beautiful and confident around him. I watched Big as he started to take his clothes off. His body was dark, smooth, and clean. I walked into the bathroom so that I wouldn't reveal that I was getting a hard on. I was bent over running my hands under the water to make sure the temperature was perfect. I heard him behind me. I turned around and I could see his dick peaking from the left side of his boxers down his leg. He took off his boxers and I stood up with my back facing him. I bent over in front of him, pulled my briefs down to my ankles, and stepped out of them. I got into the tub full of bubbles and he jumped in right after. He put my legs over his thighs to make more room. I felt his dick rub my balls. We started kissing. I was more than ready to have sex. We talked for a little while, laughed, and just enjoyed each other's company. We were looking into each other's eyes and smiling. He kept grabbing my thighs. I could feel the Ciroc Peach kicking in. I was buzzed and ready for whatever Big had for me.

"I'm ready now. Are you?" I asked anxiously awaiting.

"I'm ready when you are babe." He gushed.

"Ok, let's take this somewhere else then." I said.

I got out of the tub dripping wet and grabbed a towel. I dried off and got into the bed. He came out of the bathroom rock hard. I was lying on my back when he crawled onto the bed and got onto his knees. He tried to flip me over and I resisted.

"Big, what are you doing?" I asked nervously.

"Babe just relax, I got you." He said softly.

I knew what Big was trying to do, and I wanted him to. He wanted to taste it. I never had that done before. I was extremely uncomfortable. He attempted to flip me over again. This time I didn't resist. He spread me open and stuck his tongue inside of me. The feeling was nothing like I'd ever felt before. My body was trembling. I turned around and sat up. I wanted to taste myself too. We kissed passionately.

"I want to suck you Big. Let me taste your dick." I said pulling away from the kiss.

I got on my knees and bent over. His dick was already standing at attention. I put it in my mouth, wrapped my lips around it, and began sucking him. He started to moan. I held back. I didn't want to give him my all too soon. Especially since he swore up and down that this wasn't my first time with a man. I came up for air, and we kissed once more.

"I'm ready for you. I want you inside me now." I demanded.

"Ok babe." He said.

He got up to get a condom. I watched him rip it open and slowly put it on; the magnum covering each inch of his dick. I turned over to lie on my stomach. He slowly crawled back into bed and kissed me on my neck, my back, and down to my ass cheeks. He opened me up and fondled my insides. He got on top of me and started grinding me slowly to relax me. He paused for a second, took his fingers to spread my butt cheeks once more and I felt pressure on my rectum. I tensed up. He started kissing me on my head, neck, and back.

"Relax baby. Relax." He whispered.

"Ok." I said.

Big started off gently sliding in and out me. Each time he went deeper and deeper. The deeper he went, the tighter I gripped the sheets and started to bite down on the pillow to relieve some of the pleasurable pain. My hole gripped his dick. He was going too fast.

"Slow Big, slow baby." I requested.

"Ok baby, your pussy is so good." He moaned.

The stroking continued.

"Baby I'm about to cum." He said.

He released his load inside of the condom while he was still inside of me. He slowly pulled out. I turned over to look at him as he was looking at me. I reached down and gently took his condom off with my left hand. I pulled him closer kissing him with deep passion. We then laid down; our naked moist bodies touching skin to skin. He pulled me closer to him and wrapped his arms around me. His dick rubbed against my ass, his stomach pressed against the small of my back. I arched my back, my ass into his groin area. Breathing heavily on the back of my neck. I was ready to go once more. It was getting late and because I wasn't familiar with the area, I thought it would be best for us to go out and get a bite to eat.

"Babe we should get up before it gets too late. Besides, the longer I stay in this position with you we're going to get started up again." I said feeling like I was in heaven.

His dick jumped.

"I'm ready to go right now." He replied.

"Come on boy. Let's get up." I said.

I turned to kiss him. I got up and walked into the bathroom to grab a towel to dry off my sweaty body and the lube around my hole. As we were getting dressed my phone started to ring. I looked, and it was Snow. I put my phone down as it continued to ring.

"What do you feel like eating?" I asked.

"What do they have around here to eat?" He asked.

"We are near Chinatown and they have plenty of restaurants to eat at or we can get a bite to eat here at the hotel." I said.

"We should definitely get something to eat outside the hotel because I'm pretty sure the prices are high." He replied.

I felt like I walked into the hotel as a boy and walked back out into the same streets as a man. I didn't care if people were staring at me or not. I was grown, and nobody could tell me any different. I felt like I blended in with the people of Washington D.C. We didn't walk too far, and I suggested that we eat at Five Guys. I sat down while he ordered our food. He glanced over at me while he was in line and I started to smile. I couldn't wait to get back to the room. We ate our food hastily and as soon as we got back to the room, the clothes came off. We made it to the bed and we started kissing.

"I want you to fuck me raw this time and I want you to cum inside of me." I said.

I shoved him back onto the bed as I took his penis in my mouth, only pausing when I felt him reach the back of my throat. I teasingly licked and kissed the tip. He was hard and wet with my saliva as well as his juices; and I was ready. I laid on my back as he slowly slid inside of me. It felt different, but I loved the feeling. I was more relaxed. Clearly, he opened me up since the first round. He continued to slowly dig inside of me, giving me another inch with every stroke. I arched up as I attempted to throw it back. As painful as it was, I could tell he liked the fact that I was more aggressive the second time around. Somehow, I wound up on my hands in the form of a push up. Big never missed a beat, he was still going strong. I started giggling at the fact that this dude wasn't stopping. I quickly stopped laughing because with each laugh I tensed up, which put more pressure on my hole. I got on all fours, and he grabbed me by the waist as he plunged deeper.

"Baby, slow down now! Never mind don't slow down." I said in between moans.

Big kept going, as he forced me back into my original position. "What the hell?" I thought to myself. This man was totally taking over my body. He made me feel things I'd never felt before.

"Baby I'm about to cum!" He bellowed.

"Yes, cum inside of me. I want you to fill me up with your love." I whispered.

He started to shake, letting go. I could feel his juices flowing as he released his load. I didn't like it, I loved it. He laid on top of me for a few minutes trying to regain his strength. I turned over on my side to face him, as I wrapped my arms and legs tightly around his body. We laid there staring and smiling at each other. We eventually fell asleep. I woke up about an hour later.

"Babe, come back to bed." He said.

"I will as soon as I finish cleaning and organizing our clothes." I responded.

I got back into bed and I fell asleep with his arms wrapped around me.

October 15th, 2011

I woke up to look at the time and it was after 8:00AM. Big was still asleep. I kissed him on his forehead.

"Come on babe. Let's get some breakfast." I suggested.

He pulled me closer to him.

"Oh babe. Come on let's go." I said smiling.

"Babe, I'll be quick." He said smiling.

"Big, you and quick don't belong in the same sentence. Babe I'm sore." I returned.

"Awe babe I'll be quick." He said begging.

"Big, the meat has been beat, pounded, and tenderized." I said.

But of course, I gave in to temptation. I wanted it too. As soon as he stuck the head in, I tensed up. I was so tender.

"Baby this hurts, and I mean really bad." I said.

"I'll be quick." He said.

"Oooohhhh!" I cried out.

"Shhhh…" He said.

I seriously hated him at that moment. I buried my face into the pillow. I had no choice but to take it. It was so damn painful. Big wasn't quick at all. When he finished I went into the bathroom. I lifted my leg and spread my cheeks to check myself. It felt so funny. I sat down on the toilet to wipe and there was a little blood. I wiped myself again to make sure it wasn't a steady flow of blood and it turned out that I was ok. I took a nice hot shower. I came out of the bathroom in my underwear and laid on the bed. He moved over and laid his head on the small of my back as I was checking my messages. Five minutes later he had fallen asleep. That was such a special moment and I didn't even want to move.

"Big?" I called out his name.

He didn't respond. I just laid my head back down on the pillow to let him rest. 10 minutes had passed.

"Babe?" I said.

"Hmmmm?" He responded.

"It's time." I said.

"Ok." He responded.

"Is there something you need me to iron for you?" I asked.

"No babe I'm good." He said.

Reality started to set in that I only had a few more hours with him.

"I don't want you to leave today but I work a 12 hour shift tonight, and you have to return back to New York." I said.

"I wish I could stay too." He said.

The good news was that I was going to see him again late November early December for a getaway to the Poconos. He got up and went into the bathroom to take a shower. As we were leaving the room, I turned around as I reminisced about last night and that morning. I smiled and closed the door. When I checked out, he waited on the side.

"Did you enjoy your stay?" Asked Maria the front desk clerk.

"Yes, I did. It was fun." I said.

She handed me my info.

"Thank you, Mr. Simmons. Come again." She said.

"Thank you." I responded.

Big and I walked back to my Jeep.

"Thank God it's still here." I said as we both laughed.

After we put our bags in the Jeep, we walked a couple of blocks to grab some refreshments. Then we headed back to the Greyhound station.

"Are you coming in?" He asked.

"Yeah I have some time." I said.

"Ok" He responded.

Truth is I didn't want to go inside because I hated to say goodbye. Besides I didn't want him to see me cry. He had about 30 minutes left before he boarded. We walked inside and sat at a table. We talked about the future and the possibilities of this turning into something more; however, in due time. Around 1:40PM he started to board. There was a white heterosexual couple kissing and hugging one another. We both looked at them and looked back at each other and started to smile.

"Alright Big." I said and smiled.

He looked at me.

"Alright I'll hit you up in a little bit." He said and smiled back.

I extended my arm to shake his hand and he shook mine. We both smiled at each other because that's not what we wanted it. It's all about discretion when it comes to men and their public display of affection. I watched him get on the bus and I walked back to my Jeep and waited until his bus drove away. Still waiting in the parking lot, thinking about what I had just done. What we shared was very special. It was exactly what I needed. It was what I wanted, and he was a perfect gentleman. Big texted me, and I looked at the time. It was 2:00PM. Those were the best 19 hours ever.

59: **Goodbye**

October 22nd, 2011

It was after midnight and I was working on the gate. My phone rang, and I saw the number I dreaded seeing for the umpteenth time. I memorized the number due to the excessive calling.

"Simmons I'm not calling you to argue, but when am I coming back to work Simmons?" He wondered.

"I don't have anything to do with that." I explained.

"You do fucking have something to do with that! You have everything to do with that, you good for nothing fucking faggot!" He shouted.

I knew Snow was high as a kite.

"Are you finished?" I asked.

"Fuck you Simmons!" He yelled.

I hung up the phone and called Jai.

"When I get home in the morning, I need my number changed." I requested.

"Why?" She asked.

"Snow just called me again asking when he's returning back to work." I said.

"Why won't he just leave you alone? But ok I will." She said.

I could never understand why I let Snow have so much power over me. I did trust him; however, I was the fool because I never told him no. Not one time did I ever blame him for our uses of cocaine. I chose to spend my hard-earned money on moments of pleasure. Towards the end of our friendship I came to my senses. I became the bad guy out the situation because I knew he had a problem. I had to stop enabling him. It was the only way he'd get better. Whenever we were together, I'd always hope that he would get so coked up out of his mind that we would finally sex. I didn't know my worth. I felt that I wasn't even worthy of anyone's love or for someone to make love to me.

60: **Adam & Steve** *(Part Two)*

After meeting and linking up with Big, I already had my future mapped out. I just knew he was going to be my last stop. It was so amazing how we shared the same dreams. I was certain that God sent and made him just for me.

October 23rd, 2011

Following Jamari's 5th birthday party, Big texted me the next morning letting me know that he had received the pictures I'd sent him.

"Good morning babe." He said.

"Good morning to you." I responded.

"Everyone looked like they had a good time." He said.

"We did. It was a lot of fun. I can't believe Red didn't show up though." I said.

"Babe, I'm sorry but I can't do this anymore." Big said.

"Ok." I responded.

"Thank you for understanding." He said.

I literally couldn't move. That was completely random, unexpected, and out of the norm. How did we get here? Was he fucking kidding me? What the fuck did I just text him? What did I do or say wrong? I re-read our messages and there was nothing unusual about the conversation. I didn't understand and there was nothing left for me to do, so I deleted his number.

November 1st, 2011

Jamari, J'Adora, and I put up the Christmas tree and it felt like I was being given a fresh start. Here I was starting from the beginning all over again. 9 days passed, and I hadn't heard from or had any communication with Big. I was really bothered by it and I needed some answers. I wanted closure. I did not want to believe that this nigga was only good for giving me a sore wet rectum. I didn't want to be that guy that would blame the next person for the last person's repugnant behavior. I refused to be that guy. I no longer had his number; however, I still had his email address. When I finally got up the courage to email him, we went back and forth for a couple of days. I was tired, and I realized that we weren't getting anywhere. He kept giving me a bunch of excuses. He claimed he ended things because he thought I said I couldn't believe that Snow didn't come to the party, when I obviously said Red. Big read what he wanted to read. I had never mentioned Snow, which was why I didn't understand what exactly was going on. In the beginning of our relationship it seemed like everything went from 0 to 60 overnight. He later revealed to me that he didn't have an issue with the pace of our relationship. That's what concerned me the most. As fast as we were going, I knew it would end in disaster. That's exactly what happened.

After he sent that text on Sunday, I became a wreck. I blacked out. I just couldn't understand what I did that was so wrong. I repeatedly replayed the scenario in my mind. I couldn't sleep, and I was constantly eating to numb my pain. I let him know that he came along in the middle of ending the friendship between Snow and myself. Big wasn't budging. He didn't want to work things out with me. What was I supposed to do? I eventually got the picture and thanked him for everything that he had done for me. He said he loved me, and I told him I loved him as well. I concluded that I wasn't in love with Big; however, more in love with the idea of being in love. I was trying to prove myself to him. I later found out that he had trust issues. They stemmed from his past, and it had nothing to do with me. Big dealt with a man who had children and it didn't end well. He often compared me to his past relationship. He didn't recognize the hurt that it caused. In turn it made me more determined to prove that our union wasn't going to be a déjà vu, but something everlasting. In the beginning I made the choice to walk into that situation being truthful and completely honest. I can say I did just that.

61: Broken Candle

November 28th, 2011

The day before my birthday while working the booth, I got a phone call from Lt. Jr. notifying me that I needed to meet up with the Chief before leaving. After I got off, I drove over to the Chief's office and knocked on the door.

"Come in. Good morning Mr. Simmons." He said once he saw me.

"Good morning Chief." I said.

"It was random, but you have been selected for a drug test." He informed me.

"Ok." I responded.

After he issued the drug test and I was finished, I made my way to the door.

"Chief my birthday isn't until tomorrow, but I won't be surprise if I get randomly selected again next week too." I said before leaving.

"Oh Simmons, I thought it was last week." He said.

"Nope, you're one day early." I said and closed the door.

I drove to Jai's mother's house to pick up the Jamari and J'Adora. By the time we made it home they were wide awake. I fixed them a bowl of cereal and put them to bed. To get a few more hours of sleep, I went into my mom's room to keep an eye on them. Before I dozed off Jai called me.

"Hello?" I answered.

"I'm holding over at work. They want us to start standing outside with the kids from now on." She said.

"Why is that? They have never missed a day of school before. Why the sudden change?" I asked.

"I don't know." She said.

"Are you sure Jai?" I asked.

Yes, I'm sure!" She snapped.

"Aright then." I said. Then she hung up.

I got the kids ready for school and stood outside with them until the bus came. After seeing the kids off, I went back to bed.

Later that afternoon I woke up to get situated because I knew the kids would be coming home within the next hour. I greeted them once they got off the bus. I then made them something quick to eat.

"Daddy can we watch Inuyasha?" Jamari asked.

"We sure can." I said.

I put the HP Desktop on the floor and turned on Inuyasha. Jamari and J'Adora raced upstairs and came back down in their underwear and blankets.

"You ready daddy?" Jamari asked.

"Yeah." I responded as I was making popcorn.

"J'Adora no!" Jamari shouted.

"What's going on?" I asked.

"J'Adora keeps trying to press play to Inuyasha." He said.

"Well Jamari show her what to press then." I said.

I returned to the living room and we watched Inuyasha until late that evening. Jai came home and went straight upstairs. I eventually took Jamari and J'Adora upstairs, so they could sleep in their beds. I went back downstairs and got on the phone until I dozed off. As I was dozing off, a text message came in. It was my sister wishing me a happy birthday.

November 29th, 2011

I knew when I woke up, I wasn't going to have the red carpet rolled out. However, to wake up to absolutely nothing; I didn't expect that. I decided to call Red, so I could vent.

"You won't even believe this shit!" I said as soon as he answered.

"What happened Dre?" He questioned.

"That girl didn't get me shit for my birthday. Well my kids. I got her something from the kids Red." I said.

I heard footsteps on the kitchen floor. Then I heard the front door open and close. I didn't care if she heard me. What's right is right and wrong is wrong. Thirty minutes later the kids came running in.

"Happy Birthday Daddy!" Shouted Jamari.

"Happy Birthday Daddy!" Shouted J'Adora.

"You see, she didn't forget." Red said laughing.

"She heard me talking shit. I'll call you back." I laughed.

I hung up with Red and went upstairs. When I walked into the kitchen there was a chocolate cake on the table.

"Thank you, Jai, Jamari, and J'Adora." I said smiling.

"The kids and I would like to take you out to dinner for your birthday. Any restaurant of your choice." Jai said.

"Ok that will be nice." I responded.

My co-worker Sgt. James texted me. I thought he was sending me birthday wishes. But I thought wrong.

"Simmons I will never forgive you for what you have done but I wish you and your family the best." Sgt. James texted.

I was a little confused and taken aback by that message. Then he sent me another text message.

"Simmons that was from Snow he texted me that this morning and he wanted me to forward it to you. I don't

know what he's up to, but don't trust him Simmons. Please don't trust him." Sgt. James texted.

"Oh well today is my birthday James. I guess he wanted me to feel some type of way on my day. The last time I heard Snow's voice was October 22nd, 2011. Don't worry that door is closed. His number is still blocked, hence the reason for him texting you. Snow knows that we are both your friend. Thank you, James." I texted.

"No problem man. Happy Birthday." Sgt. James texted.

"Thank you, James." I replied.

Dinner never happened. However, the idea was cute.

November 30th, 2011

The next morning while I was on the computer Jai walked into the kitchen.

"I will be moving out around New Year's." She informed me.

"Ok cool." I said and continued surfing the blogs.

I got up and walked into the kitchen behind her. I had to know something. I just had to ask.

"Jai, do you still love me? I just want to know." I asked looking into her eyes.

"Yes Andre. I do love you." She said.

"Just to let you know, for what it's worth; I never stopped loving you Jai. I wish you well." I said.

"She's leaving. It's her choice, and I'm not stopping her from making that decision." I thought to myself. I went back to my desktop. Big texted me a day late sending me birthday wishes. Even though he was late, I was glad that he remembered; especially since he and I were no longer.

"We go to the past to lay the blame - since the past can't argue. We go to our past selves to account for our present miseries." - Glen Duncan

62: Female Imposter

December 9th, 2011

December was the most peaceful month that Jai and I had all year. With my mother returning home from Egypt the next week, there was absolutely nothing left to fight about. When the New Year rolled around my life as well as hers would be officially reset. My alarm went off and it was 5:00PM. I had exactly 4 hours and 45 minutes before I had to be at work. I decided to go to T.J. Max. When I walked upstairs Jai was watching TV in the living room. I continued upstairs. I checked in on the kids and they were asleep. I took a shower and started getting dressed. While getting dressed I heard knock on the bathroom door.

"Yes?" I asked.

"Daddy where are you going?" Jamari wondered.

"I'm going out." I responded.

"Daddy can I go with you?" He asked.

"Yeah Jamari." I told him.

I quickly got him ready and went back downstairs.

"I'm taking Jamari with me to T. J. Max keep an eye on J'Adora." I said.

She didn't respond. She just continued laughing at a rerun of Martin that she had probably watched 100 times already. Jamari and I left. 25 minutes down the road my phone rung, and it was Jai.

"J'Adora's wet. Why didn't you change her?" She asked.

"Both of them were asleep when I checked on them, and I didn't want to wake Jamari or J'Adora. Jamari woke up by himself. Besides what can I do if I'm out? Change her Jai." I told her.

My mood went south. "Thank you God I work tonight." I thought to myself. As much as I loathed working on that job, it was still a place I'd much rather be than at home with her. When we arrived at the store a remote-control helicopter caught Jamari's attention.

"Daddy can you buy me that?" He asked.

"Jamari this is for 14 years and older, and you're only 5 years old. What are you going to do with this?" I asked laughing and walked away.

I headed over to the men's department to check out some clothes. I started thinking, "Maybe I should purchase the helicopters one for me and one for him." I headed back over there. I picked up a blue one and a red one. I put them on layaway, so Jamari wouldn't think I was going to purchase them right then. On the way back home, I stopped at Krispy Kreme and ordered a dozen glaze donuts. I knew the kids would love that. As soon as we got back home, I had to rush to get ready for work. J'Adora was eating cereal and of course Jamari wanted a bowl as well. I fixed him a bowl. Jai walked into the kitchen to see what I had purchased.

"I put two helicopters on layaway for Jamari and me. I know he's too young for it, but I think he will enjoy flying them together with me. You can have some donuts if you want." I said.

"I really don't care for my mom." She explained.

"What did she say or do this time?" I wondered.

"She called me asking about the kids. I told her J'Adora was here with me and Jamari was out with you. Then she asked why I would let Jamari go with you by yourself." She explained.

"Got damn! Got damn! Got damn!" I thought to myself.

"Jai I don't have anything to do with your mother. I keep my distance from that woman. Now that she's saying shit like that, I have a problem with her." I informed her.

"I told her, Andre spends time with his kids. Just because you and dad didn't spend time with us as kids doesn't mean Andre can't spend time with Jamari and J'Adora." She said.

"You told your mother that?" I questioned.

"Yes. I'm not having anything to do with her when I move." She said.

"Well Jai, as much as I don't care for her you will still need your mother." I said.

I could have easily phoned Jai's mother and got her straight; however, I didn't because the many pages of Andre and Jai were coming to an end. It was only in a matter of days. Once there is nothing left for either party to fight for, it's over. I continued to get ready, kissed my kids' goodnight, and went to work.

December 10th, 2011

The following morning around 6:45AM I arrived back home. I immediately hopped on the computer. Jai's phone started to ring. When her phone stopped, my phone started to ring. I thought it was my supervisor. I turned my phone over to see who was calling, and surprisingly it was Jai's mother. "Why in the hell is she calling my phone?" I wasn't going to pick up, but then I remembered what she said to Jai the night before. I answered.

"Hello?" I asked.

"Good morning Andre. I'm trying to reach Jai." She said.

"Jai is asleep, and don't be calling my phone!" I snapped.

"Excuse me?" She gasped and responded.

"Yes! I said don't be calling my phone! Jai told me what you said about me when I was out with my son last night! Know your place and keep my name out of your mouth!" I ordered.

I hung up the phone. That woman had been dipping her sticky fingers in our business since I met Jai. I never confronted her out of the respect I had for Jai. If there was a family function at Jai's mother's house I wouldn't go. I never stopped Jai from taking the kids to see her family as bad as I wanted to. I just refused to take any part of it. What made matters even worse was that the psychopath had the nerve to say Jamari was her favorite, and J'Adora wasn't because she thought J'Adora cried too much! I wasn't worried because I knew that one day when Jamari and J'Adora were old enough, they would see Jai's mother for who she really is. Jai woke up and walked downstairs and into the dining room.

"Jai just to let you know, your mother called my phone and I let her know about herself. I'm not trying to come in between you and your family, but I needed to remind her who I was." I stated.

"It doesn't matter. Mom is always saying things like that." She said.

"That's very true. But when it comes to things like that, I take that as a serious matter." I said.

Jai went back upstairs and closed her room door. Within 30 minutes the doorbell rang. I got up and went to the door. It was Jai's father.

"Hey Andre." He said.

"Good morning. Jai your dad is here!" I yelled.

Jai came back downstairs and gave her father her car keys. She closed the door and went back upstairs. I shut down the computer and went downstairs to the basement to get some sleep. I had to go back to work at 1:45PM that afternoon to work 16 hours.

63: **Band Aid Love** *(Part One)*

Flashback:

Besides Janet Jackson, I also loved Destiny's Child and Kelly Rowland was my favorite from the group. Kelly Rowland was killing the music R&B charts with her number 1 hit "Motivation" which was released April 8th, 2011. I began connecting with a lot of Kelly Rowland fans on Twitter. I wasn't looking for anyone or anybody at the time; however, I reached out to Tarantino in a DM. He stood out to me because of his hair in his avi, and our friendship went from there.

Fast Forward:

December 17th, 2011

I didn't know what made me so nervous to meet Tarantino. I couldn't sleep that morning when I got off work. I felt like a cocktail mixed with several ingredients between butterflies, excitement, and being enormously nervous. I was secretly hoping that he was going to stand me up. The last couple of months was full of disappointments, but he didn't. Even though I knew Bowie, Maryland like the back of my hand, I got lost trying to locate this man. I gave him a call and he stayed on the phone with me until he saw me pull up. He opened the door and came outside to meet me.

"What's up?" Tarantino said.

"Hello." I responded.

Damn, he had a beautiful smile. He was wearing a grey pea coat with a maroon Mohawk like I never seen before. I thought that he was brave and comfortable in his skin. We walked around Tysons Corner Center and tried on coats in Macys. The funniest moment was when he and I were walking, and he heard Kelly's Rowland song "Commander" playing in the clothing store Express. We only walked in to hear the song and walked out. It was hilarious because that's exactly what I would've done if I heard a Janet Jackson song playing. We went to the Disney Store where I purchased J'Adora Tiana paraphernalia. Tarantino wanted to go to the movies, but I was extremely tired. We decided to eat at The Cheesecake Factory where I ordered shrimp scampi and he ordered shrimp & chicken gumbo. After dinner I dropped him off in Silver Springs. There was no kiss goodnight; however, I couldn't wait until the next time we'd be together. I just knew from the first time Tarantino sat on the passenger side of my Jeep that he was someone very special. The energy I felt from him was more than what I expected it to be. Looking back, I'm happy that he didn't stand me up because I believe that I could've missed out on a memory. His presence is still vivid in my mind like it was yesterday.

"Andre?"

"What is it?"

"Do you remember what you told me when you were 12 years old?"

"Referring to what?"

"About you having kids?"

"No Delvin what did I say?"

"You said, "Delvin one day, and if it doesn't work out with me and my wife, my kids will live with me."

"I said that? Are you sure Delvin?"

"Yeah you did. The conversation started when you felt some type of way about your father being involved in your brother's life and not yours."

"I remember everything, but I don't remember that for some odd reason. Thank you for reminding me. I needed to hear that."

"You're welcome."

64: Reset

December 30th, 2011

New Year's Day was on a Sunday. I knew Jai had gotten her keys earlier in the week. The secret was out. The cat was out of bag. Everyone knew she was moving out. It was a Friday night and I was on my way to work, so I decided to call her.

"Hello Jai. Congratulations once again for getting your new place. I'm happy for you that you're moving on with your life. One question though; how are we going to work this thing out with the kids? You're moving things out little by little and you have yet to communicate with me on where you reside. I'm not trying to get in your business, but I need to know these things, so I will be able to pick up my children." I explained.

"Well Jamie is staying with me, and she will be helping me with the kids." She explained.

"Ok we will talk more about that. I just wanted to be clear on the actual day that you were moving out. It's hard to tell because you keep popping up at my mom's home." I said.

"Well, I have been doing a lot of cleaning of my new place." She explained.

"Basically, tonight is your official night to move in?" I asked.

"Yes." She responded.

"Ok. What I'm going to do is go half on a TV with you so that Jamari and J'Adora can have some entertainment over there. I will also give you the extra Wii since I was shipped two. I want to keep things as normal as possible for Jamari and J'Adora. You can keep the HP desktop too. What about beds?" I said.

"Thank you. You can keep the HP desktop. No, they don't have beds yet. I'm working on that." She stated.

"So where are they going to sleep then?" I asked.

"I'm getting a bed really soon. Also, my dad is going to bring the couches from their garage that your mother gave us when we had our place." She said.

"Ok cool. Well I'm at work now soooo… have a good night." I said.

"Alright." She responded.

"Thank you, Andre." She said.

I could tell she was smiling. I got out of my Jeep and headed inside to work.

January 1st, 2012

"Andre?!" Paula yelled downstairs.

"Yes Paula?" I answered.

"Can I have a minute of your time please?" She asked.

"Damn that was some good sleep." I said as I got up to go to the door.

"Andre do you need any help with the kids?" She asked.

I paused, looked down at the floor, and then looked her in her eyes.

"Yeah sure Paula. Since Jai moved out and my mother's leaving on Friday, I wouldn't mind you sticking around for about a week; just until the kids get use to not having their mother and grandmother around." I said.

"Ok. Your mother was about to take me back to Baltimore, and God laid it on my heart to ask you that." She said.

"Thank you, Paula." I said.

She went back upstairs, and I closed the door.

"Damn you mom. But thank you. Maybe I'm not the bad guy in this situation after all." I said aloud.

So much was just lifted off my shoulders. I didn't know who the fuck I was fooling. I had no idea how Jai and I were going to pull this separation thing off. Even though Jai moved out on December 30th, 2011 it occurred on me that half of her shit was still in my room. I went back to sleep because I had to rest before work later that night.

January 2nd, 2012

When I got home that Monday morning her shit was still there. I fell asleep and later awoke that evening. I got out of bed, went to my Jeep and laid my second and third row seats down. I took the rest of Jai's clothes from the hangers; her heels, boots, papers, and other items and put them in a pile. After making several trips to my Jeep, it was fully packed with her belongings. On my way to work I stopped by Jai's apartment unannounced.

"Hello? Jai it's me, and I'm outside." I called to let her know.

Her sister Jamie came to the door and opened it.

"Hi Andre." She said.

"Hi Jamie." I responded.

Jai came from the back.

"Yes?" She asked.

"You left some of your belongings at my home and I thought maybe you could use them." I said and walked back to the Jeep.

Jamie followed me. I popped the window to my Jeep up.

"That's all Jai stuff?' Jamie wondered and started laughing.

"Yep." I said.

Jamie and I started taking arm loads of the stuff out of the Jeep. Jai just stood at the door with her arms folded. Jai didn't lift a thing. Within 10 minutes we were done. Jamie walked me back outside and I handed her Jai's mail that was on the front seat.

"Here you go Jamie and good luck to you." I cautioned.

January 6th, 2012

I took my mother to BWI Airport that Friday afternoon. I knew it was harder for my mother to leave this time because of everything that was going on between Jai and myself. I tried my best to make everything look like it was going to be ok. But on the inside, I was crying, and I was still in disbelief that my life had made a 180. I wasn't afraid of the change, it was just scary not knowing how things would pan out anymore. My aunt Janelle came to pick Paula up for the weekend, which was a relief. I also wondered how long I was going to be able to keep up this "I'm ok" act in front of Tarantino. I had already pushed him away once, and I should have never tried to pursue him again. He wasn't doing anything wrong. I just knew that things were going to get much worse for me before getting better. I just figured I'd enjoy this ride with him if I could. I knew he would crack under pressure. He was young, and he didn't need me polluting his life. I tried not to dwell too much on the negatives because I knew it would be great seeing him on that Saturday.

January 8th, 2012

The doorbell rung, and I knew it was Jai dropping off the kids. I opened the door.

"Hi daddy." Said Jamari and J'Adora.

"Hello." I responded.

The three of them walked passed me. I was shocked that she walked into my home. I closed the door behind them. Jamari and J'Adora followed me into the kitchen. Jai got on the computer. I was thinking to myself that this girl had gone mad. I wasn't going to say anything at first, but then I remembered how happy she was to move out around the holidays. She was telling everybody she was moving out.

"Jai what are you doing?" I wondered.

"I'm doing my homework." She stated.

She didn't even turn to look at me when she said it. Oh no! I wasn't having it.

"Oh, so that's why you didn't want the desktop when I offered it to you? You think you're going to come here whenever you feel like it? You have another thing coming. Baby girl you gave my mother back her house key. You have nothing here. You must leave. You have to go." I demanded.

"I can't use the computer?" She asked.

"No, you can't! What kind of game do you think this is?! You moved out! Your only reason for coming over here is to pick up and drop off the kids! You don't need to enter to do so!" I clarified.

"I don't even believe this. Where's Paula?" She asked sounding disappointed.

"Girl stop it. Paula isn't your concern." I told her trying to rush her to leave.

"Why are you paying her to watch Jamari and J'Adora?" She asked.

"Paula's dependable. Paula cooks, cleans, she helps the kids with their homework, she reads to them at night, she prays with them, she treats them like they are her own. The best thing that I have seen so far is that she loves them equally. She doesn't show favoritism like your mother did and does. Besides, when I work overtime, I will always know that someone is home taking care of Jamari and J'Adora. I no longer worry about which one of us is going to have to watch them. The problem is now solved." I enlightened her.

Jai got her things together and left. About 30 minutes later Paula arrived back home.

January 9th, 2012

Paula and I were now a team. We had Jamari and J'Adora Monday - Friday and Jai had them on the weekends. Things were starting to come together. I finally had some sort of relief with Paula being there.

65: **Band Aid Love** *(Part Two)*

January 13th, 2012

Tarantino was my angel of the night and I was so anxious. I couldn't wait to make love to him. He went to church that evening, which gave me a few hours to get everything set up. Once Paula left for the weekend to go to aunt Janelle's, I immediately started. I wanted his first time to be gentle, romantic and special, so that's exactly what I set out to do.

January 14th, 2012

He called me a little after midnight to pick him up at Largo Town Center *(WMATA station)*. When he got into my Jeep, we lean in for a kiss. Before long we arrived back at my home. I got out of my Jeep and he followed not too far behind to enter the house. Once inside I told him to have a seat on the couch.

"I'll call you in a few." I said and headed upstairs towards the bathroom.

I ran a nice bubble bath for us and lit candles all through the bathroom while soft music played.

"Tarantino." I called.

He came upstairs and when he entered the bathroom he smiled. I slowly took my clothes off and got into the warm water. His body was a work of art. Nice chest, flat stomach, thick tight thighs, and a nice ass. His penis wasn't circumcised, which made him even more special to me. He got into the water, reached for my phone, and turned my music off. *"Depressing Music"* as he called it and started to change the mood. Tarantino was the best kisser. It was evident what he wanted when our lips met. His lips were so soft. He moved closer to me; his body in between my legs. We continued kissing as our erect dicks played sword fight with one another. As we kissed some more, Tarantino reached down and began playing with my asshole. I grabbed his ass and pulled him closer. The kissing only became more intense. Tarantino pushed me against the wall of the tub and wrapped his soft lips around my dick; gently sucking me up and down. It felt so good that I was so close to exploding.

"No not here." I said stopping him.

"Where?" He asked.

"My mother's bedroom." I suggested.

He obliged, we kissed again and got out of the tub. With our wet bodies ready, I lead him to the bed.

"Lay right here on your back." I whispered.

I got on top of him and we continued kissing. I reached for a condom, put it on, and lubed it up. I pushed his legs back towards his shoulders, his ass in my face; and I tasted him. I slightly brought his legs back down and stuck my finger in his ass to loosen him up.

"Are you ok?" I cautioned.

"Yeah." He replied.

"Am I being too rough?" I wondered.

"No." He assured.

Given the green light, I slid the head of my dick inside of him. He was tight, and it felt different. The moment I was inside of him I was reminded of Jai's pussy after giving birth to J'Adora. I started off slow. The excitement had me ready to cum. I went in and out slowly, and his moaning turned me on even more. When I was ready to cum, I exploded inside the condom while still inside of him. I pulled out and he took the condom off and instantly started sucking my dick again.

"Stop, stop, stop. It's sensitive right now." I said laughing.

We cuddled under the sheets of my mother's bed until we fell asleep. When I awoke the next morning, the sun was up. I turned over, looked to my left and he was still lying next to me. I leaned over and kissed his lips.

"Good morning." I said smiling.

"Good morning." He replied.

Tarantino and I decided to take a shower. As we were washing our bodies, our dicks became erect. We started kissing as the warm water ran down our soapy bodies. Tarantino bent down and begin sucking my dick. He started off slowly and I leaned my body against the wall of the shower. I always warned him right before I came to take his mouth off my dick, common courtesy; however, he never listened. I came in his mouth, and he sucked me dry until there was nothing left.

After our quick little sexual activity, we got ourselves together and went out to get breakfast at IHop. He was the only person in the world that I didn't mind picking off my plate. That's a lie, I hated when he did that shit as well. Yet I tried to remain cool about it. Afterward we went to Tysons Corner and watched The Iron Lady starring Meryl Streep. When the movie was over, we headed back to my home; where we made love again on the living room floor and fell asleep.

January 15th, 2012

When Sunday morning came, I was upset at the fact that he had to leave for church. I had to work that night; however, that was the best weekend that I had had in years. The best part about it was that I knew I was going to see him again. I just hoped that what I was feeling for him was mutual.

66: Clarity

March 5th, 2012

I was downstairs washing dishes after Paula cooked dinner. She was upstairs giving the kids a bath.

"Andre?!" She yelled.

"Yes Paula?" I asked.

"What is it now?!" I thought. Paula was just extra annoying that day.

"Can I have a word with you please?" She asked.

I stopped doing the dishes and walked upstairs. She was standing outside of my mother's bedroom.

"As I was giving the kids a bath, I caught J'Adora doing something inappropriately to Jamari." She said.

"What was she doing to him?" I questioned.

"Jamari had his butt in the direction of J'Adora's face and J'Adora was looking between his cheeks. I said Stop! Where did you learn that from? And they both replied mommy." She said.

"Ok. I don't want to believe what I think Jai may or may not have been checking for, but from this day forth I would like for them to take baths separately. I will call Jai and ask her about this." I confirmed.

I went back downstairs, grabbed my phone, and texted Jai to call me. The situation took me back to what her mother would do to her daughters when they were children. I just hoped Jai wasn't doing anything on that affect. When Jai eventually called me, I asked her about the situation.

"Hello. Paula was giving Jamari and J'Adora a bath and she said J'Adora was looking in between Jamari's butt cheeks. When she questioned them, they both said they got it from you. I'm not jumping to conclusions, but could you tell me what you may or may not be doing?" I asked.

"I was only giving them a bath, but Jamari and J'Adora are always playing with each other." She said.

"In what way Jai?" I asked.

"Just some of the things kids shouldn't be doing." She responded.

"Do you watch them while they take baths together? It just doesn't seem like you do." I said.

"Yes, I do Andre." She replied.

"Ok this is what we are going to do in my home, and yours. Since Jamari and J'Adora are getting older, and it's only natural for kids to get curious about their bodies; they will no longer be taking baths together." I said.

"I only have them take baths together, so my water bill isn't too high. I do always watch them though." She clarified.

"Well this situation calls for a change Jai. I hope you understand where I'm coming from. I'm not trying to tell you what to do, but as a parent I hope you do the right thing." I said.

"I will." She assured me.

"Ok." I said.

"Sooo is that it?" She asked.

"Yes, that's all." I said.

"Alright." She answered and hung up the phone.

67: Access Denied

Flashback:

I eventually lost count with the amount of times I was called dumb, a fool, stupid, or weak for keeping Jai on my health insurance policy. I would often hear these insults because she no longer lived in my household, and the fact that I was struggling finically. I got sick of it.

Fast Forward:

June 18ᵗʰ, 2012

I decided to write a letter of concern to the Humanomics Insurance Services Inc.to see what I could do about removing her from my insurance plan:

"Good Morning Mr. McCray. My name is Andre LeDale Simmons, I'm an employee with the WSI guards, here in Silver Spring, Maryland at the Fort Detrick Annex. I'm going on my 5ᵗʰ year serving on this contract. I'm married in the middle of a divorce my wife and I have been separated since December 30ᵗʰ, 2011. We have two kids together and I have them Mon - Fri and she has them on the weekends. I need advice with taking her off my health insurance plan. I have more finical responsibilities for the kids, and I can really use the extra money without my wife being on my health insurance plan. Please contact me at 301-XXX-XXXX or give me the steps that I need to resolve this issue. Thank you for your time." - S/O Simmons

He emailed be back:

"Andre,

You cannot drop your wife from the coverage until open enrollment, or if you have a qualifying life event. Divorce would be a qualifying life event, but you cannot drop here until the divorce is final, and you can show proof. Your open enrollment period will be sometime in October if you would like to drop her then. This would take effect on November 1st, 2012. If the divorce goes through before then, please give us a call at 877-XXX-XXXX, and we can send you the forms to drop her from your coverage."

Thanks,

Ken Miller

Account Executive

Humanomics Insurance Services Inc.

That was the response I got. There was nothing I could do about it.

68: **Team Player** *(Part Two)*

June 23rd, 2012

Player 6 had a kid, and his life hadn't turned out so good. It had been years since I last saw player 6, but I wound up running into him at my cousin Audrekia's graduation party. When I spotted him, the flashbacks of torment came back to me at once. I tried my best not to be seen.

"Andre!" Delvin shouted.

"Aw shit!" I turned around and there he was staring at me, standing there with his hands on his hips. "But I'm the faggot?" He looked like shit. The Prince-of-Supply well at least that's what he was in my eyes had fallen and fell. I reached out to shake his hand hoping he wouldn't cause a scene in front of the family.

"Check you out. You filled out nicely." Player 6 said.

"Shut up." I reacted.

"Nice firm handshake." He said.

There I was 28 years old and Player 6 was still intimidating. Then something started happening. The more Player 6 and I spoke, I noticed he was missing teeth. How could I not see his huge belly appearing in front of me? He looked sick. The things that I had heard he'd gone through over the years made me not only pity him; but in that moment, I forgave him. At the end of over conversation, he made a smart remark. I just smiled and walked away because I no longer allowed his words to have power over me.

The summer of 1993 was my first and last summer being sexually active with the boys of North Carolina. What made me do it? A lot of the boys were doing it. I was the boy with the high-pitched voice, I was fat, and I switched when I walked. So of course, I was the target for ridicule.

I want to be clear; it wasn't rape. I knew exactly what I was doing. The summer of 1994 Player 4 begged me like a dog for some ass. I threatened to tell, and he eventually backed off. Of course, I continued to hear things here and there, but I left that back in the summer of 1993. I started being a kid again, and I was careful not to venture off too far from my grandmother's property. I became super protective over Kendrell and Gregory from that summer on.

69: **Brother** *(Part Four)*

June 23rd, 2012

All my grandmother's children, her grandchildren, and great-grandchildren all gathered together in the state of North Carolina for Audrekia's 2nd graduation celebration. Due to my grandmother's illness, she couldn't travel such long distances. Aunt Janelle brought the 2nd function back home where it all began. Even though the party was right in the front yard, my grandmother was still unable to come outside because of the blistering heat. It was a family reunion nonetheless. I was also very excited to see Adron again. This time he was driving all the way from Wilmington, North Carolina to visit me. I was also looking forward to my mother meeting him. My phone rung, and it was him.

"Yeah man." I answered.

"Alright bro, I'm pulling up now." He said.

"Ok." I said with a big smile on my face.

I saw a couple of cars driving up. One passed us, and a gray BMW drove up after. "Is that Adron's car?" I said to myself. It parked, and a door opened. Mr. Morris Chestnut in the flesh stepped out of the car. I couldn't help but think of the movie The Best Man.

"Damn who the hell is that?" Someone said in the background.

I laughed as I walked towards him.

"That's Andre's brother." Someone else said.

"Hey bro." He said.

"Hey Mister, fresh ass." I said giving him a hug.

We stood by his car and talked for a while. Eventually we made it back to the party. I made sure I introduced him to all my aunts; Patricia, Dollie, Iris, Celestine, and Janelle. Then I introduced him to Paula. He smiled and shook everyone's hand.

"I saved the best for last." I told him as I walked over to my mother.

"Now this is the famous Joyce Simmons, my mom." I gushed.

My mother got up as he extended out his arms to hug her. Not only did my brother stick around to watch the fireworks, but he stayed until the wee hours of the morning. We stayed up all night, just he and I talking and catching up. I still had so many things that I wanted to share with him. I wanted to tell him about the special person in my life and let him know that I was gay. I figured that I would break all the news to him the following month, since he informed me that he was coming to Maryland for a vacation. I knew I wasn't going to be up for the 7-hour drive on Sunday, so I called out of work and hung around the family for one more day.

"The more you try to crush your true nature, the more it will control you. Be what you are. No one who really loves you will stop." - Cassandra Clare

70: True Colors

July 4th, 2012

I was lying in bed just listening to the birds outside my window. "Andre are you going to get up today?" I heard my mother yell to me downstairs.

I flipped my phone over to look at the time. "It's only 11:30AM woman!" I shouted back.

"We still need a grill! You are the one who wanted to have this cookout so get your ass up!" She retorted.

"Ugh." I said as I got up, got dressed, and went upstairs. I walked into the kitchen where she was. "I guess Ken isn't coming, let me season these ribs. Mark can grill them. I'm just going to run back to Lowes and buy that blue grill I saw last night. It will do. I'll be back." I said.

The cookout was not the main thing on my mind. I couldn't sleep the night before. I knew today was the day. I couldn't help but think about how yesterday my life was headed in one direction, and today it would forever change. "I hope this change is for the better." I thought to myself on the drive home.

Once I arrived back home with the grill, I went in the house to find my mother to show her; hoping she'd approve.

"You like it mom?" I asked.

"Yeah that's more than fine." She said.

I was just looking at her with the biggest smile on my face.

"What? What are you smiling at?" She asked.

"Nothing mom." I quickly responded.

"Now isn't the time Andre, but it has to be today." I told myself as I took the grill out to the backyard. I went through the back door of the basement to change clothes, so I could cut the grass. I got the lawn mower from the wash room, pushed it through the open basement door, and around to the front of our home. Then I tried to crank it.

"Damn! Really?" I said out loud.

The lawn mower wasn't working. I had it for over 6 years. "Oh well, I guess that's the end of that." I said.

3:34PM

The food was prepped and ready to be cooked. Mark had the grill hot and the family was in the backyard in lawn chairs just gossiping. Mark was grilling, and I was sitting in a lawn chair beside him iMessaging Tarantino and drinking a beer. I didn't realize that I was smiling to myself while looking down at my phone. Before I knew it, Paula walked over literally scaring the shit out of me.

"Andre the person you're texting right now is the one for you." She stated.

"What the fuck? You are straight killing me right now." I thought to myself. "Paula this isn't Jai." I said rolling my eyes.

"I never said it was Jai." She answered back and went back to her seat with the rest of the females in the family.

"Mark she is so nosey." I said disgustedly.

Mark just shook his head, took a sip of his beer, and flipped over the hot dogs and hamburgers.

9:27PM

When my mother walked into the living room, I thought to myself, now or never Andre. I took a deep breath and walked over to my mom.

"Hey, mom can you come downstairs?" I asked.

"Yeah." She said heading towards the basement.

"Ok." I said.

I walked downstairs to the basement, then walked to the last room, pulled out a bar stool and sat down on it. She was standing up looking at me and I was just looking at her.

"Yes? You have something you want to tell me?" She wondered.

I was trying to read my mother; however, she wasn't inviting at all. I got the feeling that she knew whatever I was about to say, she wasn't up to hearing it. I was so scared to tell her. I didn't know if she was going to scream, shout at me, or even try to fight me. I was still unable to say a word, but I kept smiling. My mother began to pace the floor back and forth.

"Hmm-mm." I paused and immediately broke down crying.

"Andre what is it?" She asked.

I just cried even more. My mother started pacing back and forth again.

"This is really hard for me to say mom." I said in between tears.

I inhaled and then exhaled as I began to speak again.

"I have always tried to be the best son in the world. I have always wanted to be the son that other mothers wanted, and other boys envied. I'm just tired of you not knowing who your son truly is." I said.

"What are you telling me?" She inquired.

"It's just so hard for me to tell you in the right words." I said as I continued to cry.

"What... Are you gay?" She blurted.

"Yes, mom I'm gay. I'm gay." I revealed.

There it was. It was over. I finally said it.

"What do you want me to do? I figured it was something like this from the way you said it in the email you sent me before I came. You explained to me that you had something to tell me. Andre I honestly don't know what to say." She expounded.

"Well I am. I won't say this is the reason why my marriage came to an end. I honestly did try up until the very end, but I told myself if Jai and I didn't make it I was going to come out and start living for me." I returned.

"If Adron was in your life would it have helped?" She asked.

"Even if Adron was in my life, it really wouldn't have made a difference. It's not like he had a magic wand to turn me straight. I would hope as a father that his purpose would have been to love me unconditionally. Honestly the only thing my father could have done was teach me what it's like to be a black man living in white America. On the other hand, that's something Jamari and I will have to experience together; not that coming out makes it any easier, but I'm up for the challenge. This is just something that's inside of me mom, and it has been as far as I can remember. It's part of me." I expressed.

"Have you ever been with a man?" She questioned.

"Yes, I have before." I proclaimed.

"You know it's a sin. I don't know how to take my only son being gay." She explained.

"Not only am I your son, but I'm the only child birthed by Joyce Simmons. So, you can imagine the pressure of trying to do the right thing. I've always tried to make you proud. Your happiness was all that mattered to me. Yes, it is a sin and that's the one sin that society tends to focus on. I am a believer of God, I always was, and I always will be. I must answer to him on judgment day. I gave you two grandchildren. That's what most grandparents want. I'm healthy, I'm not sick, and I'm safe. I have never brought my lifestyle around my children. Besides, I want and need Jamari and J'Adora to know who their father truly is when the time comes. I never told you this; however, I was ousted at work by Snow last fall. My co-workers believed that Jai left me because I'm gay. What people failed to realize is that Jai was planning on moving out long before Snow said anything. On top of that, Snow took it upon himself to call her." I added.

"How did he get her number?" She asked.

"I gave Snow Jai's number along with our home number. Snow was the main person that I was always hanging with, and I wanted him to be able to contact my family."
I instantly paused. "Mom let me ask you something, did you always know about me or were you going to let me carry this thing by myself?" I asked her with furrowed brows.

"Andre I would have taken it to my grave." She said with sincerity.

I wasn't shocked by her response. It hurt like hell, but the cat was out of the bag. The one person that I needed and wanted to know was my mother; and now she knew pretty much everything about her son.

"Well I'm glad I finally had enough courage to tell you." I said breaking the silence.

"Is that all you have to say or is there something else that you would like to tell me?" She asked with concern.

"No, that was it." I replied.

"Well I'm glad you were able to tell me." She said.

"So am I." I replied.

My mother went back upstairs, and I went straight to my room. I couldn't wait to iMessage Tarantino and tell him what I had done.

Flashback:

On June 5th, 2012 after leaving work that Tuesday morning I drove to Tarantino's house to pick him up. Then I drove him to Largo Town Center *(WMATA)*, so he could go to work. This was another way of getting the chance to not only see him but spend time with him as well. I asked him if there was anything that he felt I should or needed to work on. He informed me that he wanted me to work on my attitude. He also mentioned that he didn't like the sneaking around. I completely understood. I also felt like if he and I were going to be together he shouldn't have to come to my home while Jamari and J'Adora were sleeping at night and must leave before they awoke for school the following morning. I knew I was going to tell my mother about myself when she came back from Egypt because I felt Tarantino was worth it. He'd been by my side even when he should have left because of the things I was putting him through emotionally. He didn't really give me the response that I wanted which made me feel uneasy.

Fast Forward:

Coming out to my mother was the hardest thing that I'd ever done in my life; and the man that I was falling in love with wasn't the cheerleader that I thought he was going to be. "What the fuck did I just tell my mother? Why wasn't he supportive or enthused as I thought he should be once I told him that I came out to my mother?" I thought. I kept trying to convince myself that I came out for my sanity and not for Tarantino. Either way what was done was finally done and I was free; however, why did I feel so empty?

71: **Happy & Nappy** *(Part Two)*

July 5th, 2012

I was in the bathroom shaving my head when Jamari and J'Adora walked in.

"Daddy I want haircut like yours." Jamari said as he and J'Adora were leaning against the door observing me.

"Like mines Jamari? Are you sure that's what you want?" I asked laughing.

"Yeah daddy, just like yours." He said.

"Ok." I responded.

Once I was finished shaving my head, I gave Jamari a low fade. When Jamari walked downstairs, my mother cheered with excitement.

"Look grandma. No more black hair!" He shouted with excitement.

"Thank you, Jesus! Awwww Mari you look so handsome." She said as she threw her hands up.

July 10th, 2012

I decided to take Jamari to get his hair professionally cut. I sent everyone a picture, including his mother.

"I love it." Jai texted.

Then she called.

"Hello Andre." She said.

"Hello Jai." I responded.

"Guess who called me?" She asked.

"I don't know. Who?" I wondered.

"Snow called my phone. He wants you to call him." She insisted.

"Jai I have nothing to do with him. Why do you still have his number in the first place? I'm surprised you don't have his number blocked. Block his number Jai! Did you forget? That man threatened me. Remember your kids stay here, and he knows where we stay at." I declared.

"I know. There is also something I would like to talk to you about." She said changing the subject.

"Like what?" I asked.

"Can I take you out to dinner on Thursday?" She asked.

"You mean the kids?" I questioned.

"The kids can come too." She said.

"I don't know. I guess. We shall see." I said.

I wondered what she had to say. What could she possibly say that she couldn't just tell me over the phone? I figured maybe she would present me with the divorce papers at dinner.

"Beyond the door there's peace I'm sure and I know there'll be no more tears in heaven." -
Eric Clapton Lyrics Tears in Heaven

72: **Grandma's Hands** *(1933 - 2012)*

July 11th, 2012

"Andre!" Yelled Audrekia.

"Yeah?" I responded.

"Grandma died!" She said.

"Alright." I responded.

I didn't move. I didn't want to deal with it at the moment. I heard what Audrekia said but I didn't receive it. I didn't allow it to sink in. I didn't want to believe the woman that started it all was now dancing with granddad in heaven. My grandmother had always been in and out the hospital over the last 15 years after having several strokes. Due to that, she lost her ability to speak and walk. Nevertheless, her mind was healthy, and she was still the most respected woman of Supply, North Carolina. Our family admired the fact that she always pulled through and I looked at it as another visit at the hospital. I guess we don't live forever after all. I sent an iMessage to Tarantino to notify him that my grandmother had passed away, soon after he called me.

"I'm sorry to hear that." He said.

"Are we still going to the movies?" I asked.

"Yeah if you're up for it." He responded.

"Yeah I don't want to be home." I said.

"Ok." He responded.

I got up and put on my clothes to go jogging. It was quiet when I went upstairs. I walked outside. It was so hot; however, it was sunny, and the skies were clear. I jogged across the street where they were building a church. I took my hat off and looked up at the sun, put my hat back on and continued to run. When I returned, I got my clothes together and took a shower. I just wanted to get out of the house as soon as possible. As I was walking to the door, I heard Jamari talking to my aunt.

"Aunt Janelle why are you crying?" Jamari asked.

"Jamari go sit down and watch TV." I said.

Aunt Janelle's daughter, Audrekia was outside with her mother along with Kanika. I walked passed aunt Janelle and turned back around to face her. I reached out and gave her a hug. I got into my Jeep and my eyes filled with water.

"Dear God, let me reach Tarantino in time. He always makes me feel so much better." I prayed.

July 16th, 2012

Getting ready that morning was bittersweet. This was the first time Jamari and I ever dressed alike. It was heartbreaking and unfortunate that it had to be for my grandmother's funeral. To make matters worse, I hadn't received an iMessage from Tarantino at all. I decided to shake that off. I was particularly nervous about my funeral reading. "God, please let me get these words out today." Reality set in when I saw the two white limousines pull up outside. My grandmother's 8 children and the first grandchild, Tamara were all set to ride in the limo. Pastor Rowe gathered the family outside for a heartfelt prayer. Everyone was present except Gregory. Even though he wasn't, I could still feel his presence. The sun was hot, and the sky was beautiful. I felt sick and I wanted to cry. Jamari was holding my left hand and J'Adora was holding my right. Damn my heart was just so heavy. So many things were on my mind. After the prayer, I went back into my grandma's home. Aunt Janelle already had tears in her eyes. That did me no good. To see aunt Janelle, one of the strongest women I know hurting like that just broke me down inside. I was the last one to leave my grandmother's home. The floral deliverer dropped more lilies off for my grandmother.

When we got to the church there were so many people. There were even two state troopers outside. They had the family line up first to enter the church, and everyone followed suit. Entering the church was like walking to an edge of a cliff to our own demise. When I saw my grandmother's casket tears just streamed down my face. On the inside I wasn't only crying for my grandmother. I was crying for Tarantino as well. I know I shouldn't have been thinking about him at that specific time, but I felt like he and I were over. I tried to keep my composure because I knew what I had to do. After a few minutes everyone was seated. The preacher started to speak, then there was a song selection. The preacher gave the floor to the family. Bryan helped his sister Tamara up to sing.

"Thank you, lord

Thank you, lord

Thank you, lord

I just want to thank you lord."

Tamara sung.

It was beautiful. I knew my grandmother would be proud. Keisha got up to read a poem that she had written. It was very nice. At first, I didn't want to, but I stood up anyway. I took the microphone, looked at the people, and my vision became cloudy. I kept sighing. The words wouldn't come out. I was so frustrated and disappointed in myself.

"Fuck! Shit!" I thought to myself.

I couldn't get my words or my thoughts together. I took a deep breath.

"Today…" I started. Suddenly I fell to the ground and cried my eyes out.

"What's wrong with daddy?" I heard J'Adora cry out.

I just wanted to get out of there. After lying on the ground crying for what seem like a lifetime, I was escorted back to my seat. Upon leaving, Kanika lost it. Every time someone would cry, it would trigger everyone else's emotions; and there would be more crying. We finally made it to the burial site to pay our final respects to that amazing woman. No one stayed to watch her coffin get lowered. The family met back up at the church for the repast where dinner awaited us. I couldn't help but think of the movie Soul Food, and how food brings a family closer together.

Following the repast, I went to Walmart to pick up J'Adora's birthday cake. We had a little party for her, and we all sung her happy birthday. Later that evening we picked Secret Santa names. Even though my grandmother was gone, she would never be forgotten. That night the family asked me what I had written for my grandmother. I tried to play it off because I really didn't care to share. I gave in and read it anyway:

"Good afternoon everyone and thank you for being here. (Aunt Patricia, mom, aunt Dollie, aunt Iris, aunt Celestine, uncle Allan, uncle Vonice, and aunt Janelle). Today we are here celebrating the life of my legendary grandmother Katie Ruth Simmons. The last time I saw my grandmother was 24 days ago June 23rd, 2012 for my cousin's Audrekia's graduation celebration. That moment would have never been possible if it weren't for the baby of the bunch, aunt Janelle wanting to share that moment with her mother. I thank you aunt Janelle for bringing us together for our last family reunion with Katie Ruth Simmons (grandmother). Thank you for getting me out of Maryland for a much needed, much needed vacation. When I heard the news that the Lord called my grandmother home last Wednesday, I was in bed doing what I do best. I was

sleeping. I tried jogging that afternoon, and it was hot. I wanted to cry, I wanted to scream, I wanted to rob a bank, but I didn't. I couldn't, my grandmother wouldn't let me. Tamara grandmother's in heaven. We all must stay strong more than ever and we all need to come together and get this family in order more than ever. Whatever issues we have with one another, leave it outside of this church. It's a new day. This is a new beginning and it starts now. We are 8 children: we are 18 grandchildren, and we are 13 great grandchildren. We're celebrating you, we're honoring you, and we will always love you."

The family really enjoyed what I wrote. I was just a little saddened that I was unable to read it at the funeral. When I was finally alone, I decided to pour myself a glass of wine...then another, and then another. The saying goes "A drunken heart speaks a sober mind." I decided to iMessage Tarantino everything that I wanted to tell him over the past couple of weeks. To get his attention, I made up my mind that I would end things with him. When he didn't respond, I couldn't believe what I just did. "Oh my God, he didn't iMessage me back." I was starting to regret it all. Maybe he just needed time to think. By no means did I want to end things. I just wanted him to know how disappointed I was in him for the past couple of weeks for not being there for me. "Lord, please let him respond back to me." I thought to myself.

July 17th, 2012

The following morning, I was no damn good. I didn't sleep at all, and just when I started to doze off it was time for us to get ready to go back to Maryland.

"I know you miss your grandmother Andre. You will be ok." Paula said.

I just nodded my head. I was too tired to drive back to Maryland, so my mother offered to drive first so that I could rest. I was so upset with myself, but I simply didn't have the strength to drive. I kept dozing in and out of sleep. Every time I looked down at my phone, I was hoping that I had an iMessage or a missed call from Tarantino.

"Boy what kind of phone call are you expecting?" Laughed my mother.

I looked at her and rolled my eyes. She laughed even more.

When we returned to Maryland my emotions were all over the place. Not only was my grandmother gone; however, I didn't have Tarantino to return to. I just wanted to mute the noise of the world, disappear, and not deal with anything. That same day Lt. Shore asked me if I could come in to work. I didn't want to; however, I agreed. When I got there, she told me that I needed to shave my beard. She then asked me to return home to shave.

"Lt. Shore, if I go back home tonight, I'm staying." I told her.

"Well Simmons, what do you want me to do?" She asked.

"If you want me to work, you need to go to the CVS off Georgia Avenue. I'll give you the money to purchase a Gillette shaving razor for me." I said.

"Oh, Simmons you're such a diva." She said and laughed.

"Oh ok Lt. Shore. Goodnight." I said and proceeded to the door.

"No, Simmons wait! I'll go. Jeez give me the money." She said.

73: He Said. She Said.

August 1st, 2012

Red and I hadn't seen each other in a couple of months, but he stopped by to see how the kids and I were doing after the funeral. You could always tell when Red had something to say, and I wondered what it was.

"I knew you were ok." Red said.

"How did you know?" I asked.

"Because Jai's mother still talks about you." He said and laughed.

"What?! Where?! Most importantly why?!" I shouted.

"She still works at Target." He said.

"Which Target? Not the one in Largo, she moved to Waldorf last year remember?" I asked.

"Yes, the one in Largo." He confirmed.

"Oh Wow! I've never seen her up there and thank God I haven't." I said laughing.

"What exactly is she saying though?" I asked.

"How you left Jai, and how you moved another woman into your home." He said directly.

"Ok." I said. We both looked at each other and laughed. "But how do you even know that?" I quickly asked him.

"Because, I'm talking to a girl that works out there part-time. Jai's mother is known as the *"Crazy Lady."* She works in the back, and she's always putting her family on blast. Especially her husband. I never knew it was her until the girl I talk to pointed her out. That's when I was like nooo! That's Dre's monster-in-law! Then I put two and two together." He explained.

"Got damn! Got damn! Got damn! I will be making a call!" I screamed.

Red stayed for 30 more minutes and then left. I decided to call Jai up.

"Jai why does your mother continue to run her mouth about me?" I asked.

"What are you talking about?" She asked sounding baffled by my claims.

"I was informed that your mother is telling people on her job that I left you. It's been over 7 months. Why is she even talking about me? Please don't say it isn't true, because she did it back when we were pregnant with Jamari." I said.

"Who told you, Red?" She asked.

"It doesn't matter who told me. Just tell her to stop, and that it's a small world." I said harshly.

"You can call her and tell her yourself." She said unconcerned.

"Ok. I did it before and I don't have a problem doing it again." I stated.

Jai gave me her number, and we hung up. I immediately dialed her mother.

"Hello, this is Andre." I said.

"How can I help you Mr. Simmons?" She asked cooperatively.

"First things first, I didn't leave your daughter, she moved out, as in moved on with her life. That was almost 7 months ago. I think it's time you do the same…" I explained before she interrupted me.

"Let me tell you something! You are a disrespectful…" She screamed into the phone.

I refused to be disrespected by her; and I wasn't going to allow her to yell at me. Without hesitation I pressed the end button on my iPhone. She called me right back. I looked at my phone as my ringtone, Janet Jackson's "Doesn't Really Matter" played. About two minutes later my voicemail notification went off. Oooo she left a voicemail:

Clears throat… "You know I thought it was very immature and rude of you to hang up on me like that. Umm… but I just want to let you know Andre, again like I was saying before I was so rudely interrupted; You have a lot of disrespect for my daughter, as well as myself. And I'm not going to put up with your insaneness anymore. It's best that, and I want to say this with as much respect and

*Christian love that I most possibly can; it's best that we
just keep our distance and not converse. Your accusations
of me spreading rumors of you and my daughter on my job,
or something or whatever, or anything like that is
ridiculous. I shouldn't even be giving this whole thing the
attention and time that I am. I know the devil is truly busy
and I guess if he wanted to upset me well, (laughs) he truly
did. I'm going to try to look beyond that and pray for you. I
hope that God gives you a heart of flesh, and that you will
stop this harassment of me and my daughter. And the best
thing that I can say is that I'm praying for you. And I hope
that whatever you're going through, any stress or trouble,
that you are relieved from it. And I do apologize for
screaming at you earlier. I am human. Again, Andre take
care and God bless. Alright goodbye."* She said.

I was very unaware that I was harassing Jai and her mother.
Most of Jai's and I conversations and text messages as of
2012 were Jamari and J'Adora related. The last time I even
had any verbal contact with Jai's mother before that day
was December 10th, 2011. The last time I saw her was on
September 6th, 2011. She didn't have a car, and I was nice
enough to let her borrow my Jeep. That same night the P.G.
County's police pulled her over because my taillight was
out. The only reason I decided to talk to her since then is
because I found out she was talking shit about me. I'm sure
God doesn't like that. I did appreciate the fact that she said
she was going to pray for me because I did need it. That
being the case, what she could do for me was mind her own
marriage and children. I went back in my home and
informed Paula about the situation that occurred and my
short phone conversation with Jai's Christian mother.

"Guess what? Red just told me that Jai's mother is running her mouth about me on her job. That woman still works at the Target in Largo, Maryland. I never knew that. I thought she transferred to one closer to Waldorf, Maryland." I said.

"The devil is always busy, but Andre let me ask you a question. Were you mean to Jai?" She asked.

"What do you mean by mean to her?" I asked.

"That's what people are saying." She informed me.

"Who Paula?" I asked getting serious.

She didn't say a word. My motto is, if you come at me; please come correct with facts and receipts. I have no fucking problem stepping to anyone. Not any fucking more.

"The people Paula? Where did you hear it from?" I proceeded.

"From North Carolina." She finally answered.

"Really? That's funny. How would anyone in North Carolina know what was going on in my home? I was just down there. How come no one stepped to me then? People are always quick to run their fucking mouths, when they don't know shit about the situation! It's cool though fuck them down there!" I said.

I left the house to go to the credit union. My phone rung, and it was Jai.

"Hello?" I answered.

"Where are you?" She wondered.

"On my way to the credit union." I replied.

"What time are you going to be home?" She asked.

"When I finish. The kids aren't with me, they're at home."
I specified.

"Do you think we should see a counselor?" She asked.

"For what? For whom?" I asked.

"For us." She responded.

"Hmmmm no. I'm good." I said uninterested.

"Ok, I will be over there soon." She said.

"Ok." I said and hung up.

About 7:00PM that afternoon Jai stopped by. I went outside
to meet her. She didn't have any papers in her hands, I
wondered what it could be because I was over this fucked
up day.

"Yes?" I said.

"I don't want to walk away from this." Jai said.

I just looked at her and smiled. I didn't know what to think.
Really? Is she on drugs?

"Quit smiling. I'm serious." She said.

"But you did Jai." I responded.

"Are you seeing anyone?" She asked.

Tarantino instantly flashed in my head. Damn!

"Not that it's any of your business, but I'm not." I explained.

"Who did you take down?" She questioned.

"What the fuck was up with these questions?" I thought.

"What are you talking about? Take down what?" I asked getting irritated.

"Jamie said you tweeted that you took some girl down." She responded.

I started laughing at the fact that Jamie would even tell her that I took some girl down. That was so far from the truth. I didn't realize I had an audience. My intentions were not to entertain her family members, so they could report back to her.

"That's not true at all. Let me ask you this; who would you be getting back together for, the kids or us?" I wondered.

I was awfully nervous to hear what she was going to say. If she said me, I wouldn't know exactly how to handle it. It felt like November 29th, 2007 all over again.

"The kids." She stated.

"Ok. I'm such a better father and man overall without you being in my life. The best part of it all is that Jamari and J'Adora no longer have to see mommy and daddy argue. You may or may not believe me, but I'm happier than I have ever been in a long time. You married into the Simmons family, I didn't marry into your family. Jai you moved out and you felt that was the best decision for you at the time. I know things were far from perfect between us, but you chose to leave. You knew how things turned out with Snow and I during the month of October. I was honest and upfront with you about the whole situation from the beginning. Even though I didn't owe you an explanation, I kept you informed, especially when he threatened to sue me. Paula came along during the final stages of your transition. I didn't know what your motives were, or what you wanted to happen by your decision to leave. When you did, I never folded. Now two weeks ago you told me Snow contacted you and wanted my number. I was shocked more than anything. I wondered why he was calling you, and then the light bulb went off inside my head. It basically confirmed that Snow was indeed the one who called you back in January of this year. When you and I were having an argument through text messaging, you accused me of cheating on you last year. I asked you to tell me who told you because at the time only two people knew the name of the person who I identified as *"My friend"* my sister and Snow. You said, "Your boo told me." I didn't know who you were talking about. I just thought you were trying to call my bluff. I was going to keep it 100% with you since you asked the question. I was going to tell you the whole truth and give you details since you wanted to know. I told you if you tell me the person's name that I did something with, I would tell you; however, you never could, and neither could Snow. He didn't know with whom because I stopped trusting him long before I ever did anything sexually with anyone else. To be honest I stopped trusting you a long time ago. I don't trust what you're trying to do today. I would like to proceed with this divorce. Jamari and J'Adora are here now, and they understand mommy have a home and daddy has a home. We will both love them, just not physically under one roof together." I said.

She just looked at me, and I looked at her. "I've said my peace. There's nothing more to say." I explained.

I called Jamari and J'Adora outside to come see their mother before she left. I wanted to say much more; however, I stopped. Even though I fucked up things with Tarantino, I knew who had my heart; and it wasn't Jai. It was now or never. I truly needed to get myself together emotionally and mentally. I made up my mind, no more alcohol for me.

74: **Band Aid Love** *(Part Three)*

Flashback:

The audition had come to an end back in April 2012. I had a job interview to go to, and I didn't have any money to purchase a shirt. Even when Tarantino offered to help, I either rejected or acted like I had it, trying to impress and make up for my emotional baggage.

"Let me help you." He said.

"No. I've got it. I'll manage." I said trying to convince him.

The truth was that I didn't have it. I had to put my last $20.00 in my Jeep. Even though I didn't want to, we stopped at K-Mart on the way to his house to look for some cheap shirts. I already had in mind what I was going to do. I knew it was wrong, but I snatched the tag off this black sweater I liked and wrapped it around my waist. I walked right out of the store. Once I got back to my Jeep, he called me.

"Where are you?" He wondered.

"I'm back in my Jeep." I said.

"I thought I was going to buy you something to wear." He said sounding confused.

"I took care of it. Just come back when you get ready Tarantino." I told him and hung up.

Fast Forward:

I had never fallen so hard for anyone in all of my life. I was truly in love. I felt like God sent me someone I needed; and not who I wanted. Tarantino was like a complete 180. I never had anything or anyone in my life like him before. All he tried to do was love me for me, while I was still learning to love again. Tarantino didn't use profanity, didn't drink, he was focused, and dedicated to the church. I was so intrigued by him that I even started attending services and bible study sessions. However, I wasn't going to hear the word of God, I was only going to see and spend time with him.

Every time things were going well between us, I would push him away. The closer we became, the more I would pull back because I was terrified of getting hurt again. The final straw for him was shortly after my grandmother had passed away. Right after I started to really miss him. For the next couple of months, I tried hard to get him back. I sent him house warming gifts for his new home. One morning leaving work I had decided to go to the grocery store because, I wanted to drop him off something at his home. I didn't know what, so I left a flower with a card on his doorstep, so he would see it before he went to work. I would send essays of iMessages confessing my love for him, emails, and sometimes calls. I did everything in my power, even still he wasn't having it. As hard as it was, I figured I needed to move on. If it was meant to be, then it would be. If I had my way, I would have chosen to spend the rest of my life with him. If only he wasn't the one that got away… but I will always love him.

75: **Timeout**

October 1st, 2012

I for one was more than excited for the contract to end October 1st, 2012. I had a plan and I knew I had 1 year to make my wildest dreams come true. I was going to become a star before October 1st, 2013. I had all the tools to make that happen. I told myself that I would have my headshots done in November before my 29th birthday. I knew that I was the only one to prevent that from happening. I wasn't seeing anyone at the time and I was 100% focus. Originally my mother was supposed to go to Egypt for a year in 2012. I wasn't going to leave my kids in Maryland with Jai; I refused to. At one point I wanted them to come with me to L.A., but deep down I knew that wouldn't work either. Jai moved out December 30th, 2011. My mother went back to Egypt on the 6th of January in 2012. Before my mother left, I told her I wouldn't leave for L.A. until she came back from Egypt and was home for good. My mother was pleased to hear that, and she extended her contract until the summer of 2013.

2012 turned out to be a time for me to grow up for the sake of Jamari, J'Adora, and most importantly myself. With three months and a day away from the New Year, I hoped and prayed that the storm was almost over. For the last 12 months and 16 days *(September 15th, 2011 - October 1st, 2012)* that I had left on the contract; my regular hours were a flat 34 a week. That placed me at 68 hours every two weeks without overtime. Making $25.28 an hour, my paycheck was around $1,200.00 weekly after taxes and a grand total of $2,400.00 monthly. Out of $2,400.00 a month I had to pay my car note/insurance, electricity bill, gas bill, groceries, pay Paula $400.00 *(monthly)*. The water bill only had to be paid every three months which came out to be $250.00. Just putting gas in my Jeep alone averaged out to be about $400.00 a month. By October 1st, 2012 I already knew what I would be receiving from unemployment. Every week I would be collecting $430.00. That would give me $1,700.00 a month. I would no longer have to buy groceries because I would be getting food stamps. I was still uncertain of exactly how much it would be. Instead of paying Paula $400.00 a month, I would now be paying her $200.00. I would no longer have to spend $400.00 on gas to travel back and forth to work. I would be saving money while being out of work.

My plan for the next 3 months was to investigate different auditions in the area. By the time the January 1st, 2013 came around, I would only have until June 22nd, 2013 before my mother would officially return. I didn't know where I would be by then; however, I was excited for the future. I wasn't worried. I was confident, and I was sure things would be so different for me. As far as jobs were concerned, I had all the certifications I needed to get another good paying security job. I would always have that to fall back on. I was more than ready for a change in scenery. I was going to give the acting thing a shot, and if it didn't work out, I wouldn't have any regrets. It sounded like a great plan, but only God knew what was ahead and what was in store for my future.

76: **Breaking Point**

October 2nd, 2012

From the beginning, I never wanted the schools involved in any situations between me and Jai when it came to the kids. When my job contract ended October 1st, 2012, I filed for unemployment. Being that I was still legally married to her at the time, while filling out the application I noticed that they asked me for my spouse's social security number. With Jai being the last person that I wanted to talk to, I decided to put my pride aside and make the call.

"Hello, Jai I need your social security number." I requested.

"For what, so you can put more stuff on my credit report?" She responded.

That response did it for me. At that moment I felt the need to tell her about herself.

"Excuse me, how am I able to do that? Jai let me tell you something, if I wanted to put something on your credit report, I would have transferred over the shit you neglected to pay. Like the $1,500.00 electricity bill or how about the $1,000.00 cable bill that you agreed to pay while we were living together in Steeplechase Apartments. You remember Steeplechase Apartments, right?" I asked.

"Yes." She said.

"The same place you wanted to move to when I started working in security. The same place when you and I got approved to move; you quit your job knowing you were pregnant with our daughter. Now give me your social security number." I requested.

She gave it to me. "Thank you." I said.

Then I hung up the phone. Within 5 minutes she was calling me back.

"Hello?" I answered.

"Akin told me yall contract ended." She stated.

"Yeah it did. What's your point?" I asked annoyed.

"I thought we were going to be open with one another." She said.

"Jai I'm 100% open with you when it comes to Jamari Ondrej Simmons and J'Adora Krismas Simmons. The contract ending has nothing to do with you. You have a great evening Mrs. Simmons." I returned.

"Yeah, at least I won't be sitting at home on my ass! I have a job! You have a great evening Mr. Simmons!" She snapped back.

"Jai, I'm still making more money than you just sitting at home. So, what's your point? Please don't test me because I have been called dumb and stupid by plenty of people for letting you off so easy." I replied.

"What do you mean?" She asked surprised.

"How stupid I am for having our kids five plus days a week. How stupid I am for letting you carry J'Adora, when I should be the one claiming the both of them on my tax returns. It's also been said that it's stupid of me for not going after you for child support." I said sternly.

"I will be picking my kids up and keeping them seven days on and seven days off." She said.

"When you get a schedule that will allow you to do that, then you're more than welcome to. It's pretty damn funny how I mention child support and income taxes; and suddenly you want the kids." I said coldly.

"You're threatening me, so I will be picking up my kids and keeping them for seven days and you will have them the following seven." She responded.

"How am I threatening you Jai?" I wondered.

"Because you said you're going to go after me for child support." She said.

"Once again you're not listening. I never threaten you, I was just telling you what people have told me I should do. My mom doesn't think I should, and I truly think that's only because she truly still cares about you. Truth is Jai, you know you don't help me with the kids like you should. Things you say you'll do, you don't. Take J'Adora's birthday for instance; you said you were going to take her to have her pictures made and you never got around to doing that. It's now October 3rd, 2012 at 12:35AM and your daughter's birthday was July 17th, 2012." I said.

"I was sick and stressed Andre. Did you ever stop to think about the reason I was sick in the first place?" She asked.

"Why were you sick Jai?" I asked.

"You, because of you!" She shouted.

"You're a liar! I wasn't the reason you were sick! As a matter a fact on Thursday, July 12th, 2012 when my mom let you and your sister Jamie into her home so that you could tell Jamari and J'Adora bye; you for some strange reason shouted down stairs for me to have a good trip! My mom, Jamari, J'Adora, my sister, Paula, and I left later that evening to go to North Carolina! My whole family was in North Carolina for my grandmother's funeral! My grandmother's funeral was Monday, July 16th, 2012 and J'Adora's birthday was Tuesday, July 17th, 2012! We didn't get back to Maryland until Wednesday, July 18th, 2012! I paused and then I continued, "So how was I the cause of you getting sick?!" I shot back.

"When Snow called my phone wanting to get in contact with you." She responded.

"Jai that's not fair at all. I haven't spoken to that man since October 22nd, 2011. I haven't heard his voice since that early morning while I was on the gate; the same day as Jamari's 5th birthday party. As soon as I got off work, I came straight home to let you know that he was still calling me, cursing me out, and asking me when they were going to let him come back on the contract. Since you were only paying my phone bill at the time, I had you call Verizon to have his number blocked. The number was blocked for two months from October 22nd, 2011 - December 22nd, 2011. You moved out December 30th, 2011. I changed my number January 1st, 2012. I never gave it to him. I even asked my co-workers who had the new number not to give it to him either. So just because you never changed your number like I asked you to, his reasoning for calling you isn't my fault. So, come up with another excuse... and guess what Jai your number is still the same. Hello, are you there?" I asked.

"Yes." She said.

"Get back to work Jai; and you may have your kids when you present me with a schedule that will not conflict with Jamari and J'Adora's school schedule. Like I said before you left, you walked away. Now you need to make a way to see your children, or things with stay the same. Have a good night." I stated.

I got off the phone and that was that.

October 5th, 2012

Jai and I didn't have any contact with one another until she sent me an email on Friday evening. The email read:

"This is a friendly reminder that I will be picking up my kids tonight, and I will be dropping them back off next Friday."

As I was reading the email I paused to think. All I could do was shake my head. If this woman thought I was going to let her get my kids in the middle of the week just like that, then she had another damn thing coming. I responded back with:

"That's not happening, but ok."

I left my home and went to Staples to get some ink for my printer. When I got back, I decided to type up a Letter of Agreement. Jai arrived around 12:45AM Saturday morning to pick up Jamari and J'Adora, and I opened the door. "I need you to sign this Letter of Agreement if you want the kids seven days on and seven days off." I said.

"What letter? I'm not signing anything without a lawyer present." She said assertively.

What the fuck? I just looked at her and took a deep breath before I continued.

"The Letter of Agreement is a 50/50 contract. I think you should read it first." I said.

When I allowed Jai to enter there were five printed copies laid out on the table in front of her. Five total copies. One for Jamari's school, J'Adora's school, Andre's copy, Jai's copy, and Paula's copy. She took her copy and began to read it. She giggled the whole time while reading the letter. I found nothing funny about the situation for the simple fact that Jamari and J'Adora had fallen asleep on the couch waiting for their mother to pick them up for the weekend. I also felt like if she went through with this, everything would once again change for the kids and not in a good way.

The purpose of writing the letter was to protect myself. Meaning when Jai fucked up like I knew she would; the schools would know who would have the kids on that week. Jamari and J'Adora had been on a steady schedule for 9 months and now their mother was about to alter their schedules for reasons of her own. After Jai read the letter, she signed each one. Before she left, she started requesting things she bought that she felt were never given back to her; such as a pair of black tights and a pair of grey tights that belonged to J'Adora. Paula usually handled things like the kid's clothes. I called her to come downstairs to ask her to go search for the items. Jai was just sitting down smiling. I noticed how impatient she was becoming.

"I can go upstairs and find them myself." She said implying that Paula was taking too long.

"Oh no, not today you will not. I'm here now and I'm not Paula. I will not allow you to walk throughout my home scoping and being nosey." I said.

It turned out that Paula couldn't find the grey tights. It was after 1:00AM and I wanted the kids to be in their own beds sleeping, instead of sleeping on the couch. This was getting ridiculous.

"Jai you can go up there and search for the items, but I'm coming with you." I insisted.

We walked up stairs to find Paula still up there searching. Jai pulled the closet door open and started looking for the grey tights that she could clearly see weren't there. I just looked at her as she was going through the clothes on the hangers. Something came over me, and suddenly, the words began to flow out of my mouth...

"I tried to give you the fucking world! My family said I spoiled you, and that I'm the blame for the way you turned out. As you know my family is full of women, and I disagreed with what they said because my job was to love you like you'd never been loved before. I know your story better than anyone. I loved you on purpose, shame on you for taking advantage of a great thing. I sacrificed so much of myself for you. I supported you when you wanted to move out. When you quit your job, you told me to trust you; and even though I knew you weren't going to find another job, especially being pregnant, like a fool I ignored my intuition because I loved you that much. My mother advised us not to move out. I went against my mother's pleas because you were and still are my wife. I was and still am your husband. I was working 12, and sometimes 16 hour shifts to make it and provide for our family. There were plenty of days I would come home to uncooked meals, a filthy apartment, and sometimes both while you were home all day long. I had fewer taxes taken out my check so that I could see most of the money each pay period. Due to that, it affected my income tax and now I owe the IRS thousands of dollars. I'm in fucking debt because I was irresponsible! I never told you this, but I felt horrible about moving back into my mother's home. The main reason I told you that I would pay for the utility bills in my mother's home wasn't because I was better than you, as you claim; it was because I was the man and I hoped that you were going to pick up the slack with the cleaning and saving money for us. Moving out the first time was strike 1 for me when it came to you. Yes, you put up $2,000.00 of your income tax money to help furnish the apartment that you insisted we move into back in 2008, but guess what so did I. Yes, you helped pay for the paint job for my mother's home back in June of 2010 but guess what, you were living here too. So, let's be clear on that. You never gave me $2,000.00 as you like to tell people. You put money into the place where you were residing. You mentioned that you were moving out back in July of 2010. That was strike 2 with me; and not one time did you mention taking Jamari and J'Adora with you. You were only thinking of yourself. You just wanted to get a place with your sisters. On January 1st, 2011, you and I sat down to talk about us; which became very awkward because you kept talking about the different guys that liked you on your job. I remember that married male supervisor that you strongly disliked when you started working with Allied Barton, who ended up becoming your friend, the same friend who later gave you advice on what was best for our relationship and wound up promoting you. I remember you also mentioning to me that your co-workers were gossiping about how you two were more than friends. Hell, I was happy when you got the promotion; more money for you. I guess you wanted to make me jealous or make me feel inferior, but it didn't work. I thought it was cute. On March 25th, 2011 the day after seeing Janet Jackson we had an intense argument about you helping me clean the home. You usually didn't, but that day I felt you should have especially after spending all that money on us to see Janet. I thought it was like any other argument. I ended up calling you at work on Tuesday, March 29th, 2011 and I was telling you that I wanted all of us to go to Walmart to purchase Jamari a bike, and you responded with we need to talk. When you arrived home, I was on the desktop, and you walked in with a smirk. Directly I knew something was on your mind. Jamari and J'Adora were upstairs sleeping. You said hello; however, I wanted you to get straight to the point. You proceeded to say that you felt it was time to get your own place. I asked, well what about Jamari and J'Adora, you said we would talk more about that as you got closer to getting a place. At that moment I knew it was strike 3, and I was officially done with us. You kept telling me you were leaving, it was threatening me; and I was done. *(June 29th, 2002 - March 29th, 2011)* we no longer mattered to me. On April 25th, 2011 it was your 28th birthday and I had no intentions of buying you shit! On Sunday, April 24th, 2011 the family had Easter dinner at aunt Janelle's home. I called to ask you if you wanted a plate, you said yes so, I fixed it. On my way home, the fact that I didn't get you anything for your birthday bothered me. Reason being is because I had hoped to be spending it in Las Vegas with you. With everything being closed, I ended up stopping at Walmart, and since you've never made it to a Beyoncé's concert, I bought you the I Am Sasha Fierce Live Concert DVD from Jamari with a birthday card and Bruno Mar's cd Doo-Wops & Hooligans from J'Adora with a birthday card as well. We were all waiting for you to get home. J'Adora had already fallen asleep on the floor…while Jamari and I were still up watching Inuyasha. Once you got in after midnight, I had

Jamari run to the door and greet you with your gift and birthday card. You told him thank you and then you walked in the living-room and I gave you your gifts from J'Adora. You never thanked me, but you took your stuff upstairs and went into your room. I will never forget July 19th, 2011 when I was short on cash and didn't have enough gas in my Jeep to make it to work. I asked you for $20.00 and you in turn asked me what I was using the money for. That was the first time I asked you for any money that entire year. I had to end up calling out of work and using my sick leave. From that point on I never asked you for any money ever again. Even though you and I were done and because my mother was in Egypt, I specifically asked you not to switch your work schedule due to the contract allegedly ending. What did you do? You switched your schedule anyway to accommodate your school schedule. I had to pay your sisters and your mother to watch Jamari and J'Adora. You didn't pay shit back then! I was on the brink of losing my job because I was always running late because of our schedules clashing, but you didn't care; which eventually caused us to have the biggest argument ever on September 6th, 2011. I called you all types of bitches and you called me all types of faggots. I wanted to kill you. The worst part of it all was to hear J'Adora crying! When I finally made it to work that night I cried like a fucking baby! I couldn't believe that I acted like that in front of my daughter! I was so disappointed in myself! With all of that finally being said, I want you to know that Paula helps me with our children more than you do. I pay her, and you have not given her one red cent! Every Saturday morning when you pick up my kids, my daughter's hair is done nicely and neatly. I can't even count on my right hand how many times J'Adora returns with her hair done. I always make sure Jamari has a haircut. You don't take him and neither does any other member of your family. You're always complaining about the way Paula styles it; the rubber bands she uses, and the hair bows she uses. If you don't want Paula doing her hair, you need to do it! If you're not going to, why complain? Unless you do it purposely to piss me off. I find this whole situation sad. I hope and pray that you are doing this for the right reasons; however, your timing is questionable, and the Letter of Agreement is to protect me." I pleaded.

Jai's smile disappeared. The things that I wanted to tell her face to face were finally said. I felt so much better. It was lifted from me. She never found the grey tights. She turned, went back downstairs, and walked out the door. I rushed down to wake up the kids.

Jamari and J'Adora, your mother's here. Wake up." I said shaking them.

I walked them to the door. They walked to her car and I closed the door.

Letter of Agreement:

I Andre LeDale Simmons with the assistance of Paula John have my kids Jamari Ondrej Simmons and J'Adora Krismas Simmons 5 days out the week since the beginning of January 9th, 2012. Their mother Jai has them on the weekends due to her work schedule. Jamari Ondrej Simmons and J'Adora Krismas Simmons schools are registered at my home address. As of October 5ᵗʰ, 2012 (both parents) have decided that Jai will have Jamari Ondrej Simmons and J'Adora Krismas Simmons for one week and I Andre LeDale Simmons will have them the following weeks during the rest of 2012. Jai's responsible for dropping Jamari Ondrej Simmons off at school before 7:45AM and picking him up by 1:55PM. Jai's responsible for waiting with J'Adora Krismas Simmons until her bus arrives in the morning between 8:55AM - 9:20AM. Jai's responsible to be present when her bus drops her off from school between 3:55PM - 4:05PM. Jai's responsible for putting money on Jamari Ondrej Simmons and J'Adora Krismas Simmons's lunch accounts or providing them with a lunch to carry to school on the week she has them. Jai is responsible for purchasing Jamari Ondrej Simmons's school uniforms and J'Adora Krismas Simmons's every day wear. If Jai can't follow these rules, then this Letter of Agreement will be void and the kids will be back on their regular and more stable schedule.

Jai October 7ᵗʰ, 2012 - October 14ᵗʰ, 2012

Andre LeDale Simmons's October 14ᵗʰ, 2012 - October 21ˢᵗ, 2012

Jai October 21ˢᵗ, 2012 - October 28ᵗʰ, 2012

Andre LeDale Simmons's October 28ᵗʰ, 2012 - November 4ᵗʰ, 2012

Jai November 4ᵗʰ, 2012 - November 11ᵗʰ, 2012

Andre LeDale Simmons November 11th, 2012 - November 18th, 2012

Jai November 18th, 2012 - November 25th, 2012

Andre LeDale Simmons November 25th, 2012 - December 2nd, 2012

Jai December 2nd, 2012 - December 9th, 2012

Andre LeDale Simmons December 9th, 2012 - December 16th, 2012

Jai December 16th, 2012 - December 23rd, 2012

Andre LeDale Simmons December 23rd, 2012 - December 30th, 2012

_____

_____

October 8th, 2012

I woke up around 8:50AM to make sure Jai was outside parked waiting on the bus to pick up J'Adora. She wasn't out there. I thought maybe she was running a little late. 9:05AM the bus came and there was still no sign of Jai. The bus beeped its horn, waited for a couple of minutes, and then drove away. I got up and went upstairs.

"Paula, J'Adora missed her school bus." I said.

"Jai could have brought those kids back last night if she knew she couldn't bring J'Adora in time." She said through her room door.

"I don't know." I said.

As I headed back downstairs, I glanced at the 4 letters on the dining room table that hadn't moved since early Saturday morning. I was drained. I was at the end of my rope with it all. I emailed my mother: *"J'Adora missed her bus mom."* Sent the email, put my phone on silent, laid down, and drifted off. I didn't care anymore. I opened my eyes to see my iPhone flashing. I turned my phone over and it was my mother.

"Hello." I answered.

"Did you go to the schools to make sure they were there?" My mother asked.

"No mom I didn't." I replied.

"Are you going to go?" She wondered.

"I don't know mom. I'm tired." I said.

"Ok. I'll talk to you later." She said.

My mother hung up the phone. I just laid there. It was unusual for my mother not to push me on something as important as such. I looked at the time and it was 1:30PM. I got up and took a shower. I grabbed the two letters that was issued to Jamari and J'Adora's schools. I got into my Jeep and drove across the street. I took a deep breath, said a little prayer to myself, and I walked in the school through main entrance. When I walked into the office I was instantly greeted by the secretaries.

"Can I help you sir?" Secretary 1 asked.

"Yes, is principal De-Souza in?" I questioned.

"She's in a meeting right now. Is there something I can help you with?" Said secretary 1.

"I'm Andre Simmons, the father of Jamari Simmons. His mother and I are separated and over the weekend we came to an agreement that she would keep them one week on and I would have him and my daughter the following week. What I'm trying to say is I had my kids for 5 days a week and she had them on the weekends. She's challenging me, and I typed a Letter of Agreement to protect myself, so when things fall apart on her week it won't fall back on me." I stated.

"Mr. Simmons is that a legal document?" Secretary 1 asked.

"No, it's not but it's a Letter of Agreement that I typed, and both of our signatures are on it." I said.

"I can't accept this letter if it's not issued by the courts." Said secretary 1.

"With all due respect, this is why I requested to speak with the principal. Well can someone at least tell me if my son was present in school today?" I explained.

"What's his name sir?" Asked secretary 2.

"Jamari Ondrej Simmons. He's in kindergarten and Ms. Poole is his teacher." I replied.

"Oh, sir you can't be on your phone." Said the random black woman standing behind the desk cosigning the entire time.

I never knew the trick's name; however, I would see her in the mornings when I would drop Jamari off at school.

"I'm not on my phone, I just checked the time." I responded.

She rolled her eyes and no fucks were given by me.

"Yes, he was at school today." Said secretary 2.

"Thank you." I said and walked out the office.

I felt some type of way about what had just taken place in that office. I knew for a fact; things would have turned out differently if I were a woman. As extremely emotional as I was, I was glad I was able to keep my cool and not flip the script. "Thank you, God, that my son was in school. Now I have to make sure J'Adora was in school." When I arrived at J'Adora's school I took another deep breath and said a prayer before I entered the building. I walked into the main office.

"Can I help you?" I went through the whole routine again. The secretary walked in the back and within a couple of minutes the principal walked out.

"Mr. Simmons, we don't get involved with situations like this." The principal stated.

"I'm not going to address this in front of everyone. Now what you can do is take me to your office and we can talk about this in private if you have the time." I said boldly.

"Let him back, I know dad." She responded.

I followed her into her office.

"Look, I just left my son's school and they wouldn't even take the Letter of Agreement. No, it's not issued by the court, but it's an agreement that their mother agreed to sign. It's protecting me. One, I must protect myself now, because financially I just can't afford to do anything else. All I need is for the school to keep an eye on my daughter on the weeks their mother has her." I pleaded.

"Ok Mr. Simmons. I will accept the letter. She responded. "But you have to understand schools are not allowed to get involved in situations like this." She continued.

"I understand, I do; and trust and believe me I never wanted the schools involved." I said. As I was getting up to leave, I remembered that I didn't ask her whether J'Adora was in school or not. "And one more thing… I also need to know if my daughter was in school today." I continued.

"Who's her teacher?" She asked.

"Ms. Tyson and Ms. Deez are her morning teachers." I revealed.

"Ok J'Adora should now be with her afternoon teacher Ms. Bangura." She said.

"I've never met her before. I've only met her morning teachers." I said.

"I will walk you to her class." She responded.

We got up and I followed her down the hall. A young woman was walking towards us. My phone started to ring I flipped my phone over and it was my mother. I guess she was testing me after all to see if I did in fact get up and handled the situation. I answered the phone.

"Hold on." I said to my mother.

"Ms. Fenty this is Mr. Simmons, J'Adora's father." The principal said.

"Hi. It's nice to meet you. You and J'Adora look alike." She said.

"Hi. It's nice to meet you too." I said.

"Why wasn't J'Adora in school today?" She wondered.

"J'Adora wasn't in school today?" I asked surprised.

We stared at each other for a minute. Then I turned to look at the principal.

"No." She whispered.

I just wanted to break down and cry. I was so heartbroken for the simple fact that I didn't know what the future now held for my kids. Another lady came out of the classroom.

"Ms. Bangura, this is Mr. Simmons, J'Adora's father and he needs to run some things by you concerning J'Adora." The principal said.

"I have to go and set up for school departure." She replied.

"Hello and it's nice to meet you. J'Adora's mother and I are separated and have been since December 30th, 2011. I have J'Adora 5 days a week and her mother has her and her brother on the weekends. J'Adora has been going to school from my home since the beginning. I have an elder son who attends Phyllis E. Williams. I also have help with my children. J'Adora may or may not have mentioned her to you, but her name is Paula. She is my live-in nanny. Due to a situation, her mother felt the need to have the kids 7 days on and 7 off. If it didn't affect our children's schedule, that's something I didn't have a problem with. I have written a Letter of Agreement that I and her mother both signed. Both our signatures are on the letter. It's to cover myself if something goes wrong. It will show each week which parent has the children. I have also stated in the Letter of Agreement that if her mother breaks the contract, then everything will be void and the children will resume their regular schedule. Hopefully by this week, since her mother failed to make sure her daughter was in school." I explained.

"Whoa that's a lot." Ms. Bangura said. "We will definitely monitor the situation." She continued.

"Thank you. I appreciate that." I replied.

"Is there anything else?" She asked.

"No that's it. And I will keep the schools updated if there are any changes. Have a good evening." I said.

"You too, and I hope everything will work out. J'Adora, you have a very smart daughter and she's in good hands." She said.

I smiled.

"I know she is." I said.

When I walked away, I put my phone to my ear.

"Mom?" I answered.

"Yeah I'm here." She said.

"Hold on." I said.

I couldn't get to the door fast enough. As soon as I touched the door I busted into tears. I didn't care who saw me. I was just so hurt and disappointed. I was so careful not to make too much noise.

"Andre?" My mother said.

I could hear my mother calling my name. I didn't say a word. I didn't want her to hear me crying.

"Andre are you crying?" She asked.

I put the phone back up to my ear.

"Yes." I cried.

"Let it out, you're always holding so much inside. Let it out so you can think clear." She said.

I got into my Jeep. The tears just poured down my face. After a couple of minutes of letting it all out, I got back on the phone.

"Mom what am I going to do? All Jai had to do was take J'Adora to school. Why would she take Jamari and not J'Adora? She wanted this arrangement and she failed. It's stated in the Letter of Agreement that if she can't abide by the rules then it will be void and the kids will return back to their regular schedule." I cried.

"Andre, you need to talk to her." She said.

"I am too damn angry to talk to her! We don't talk to one another, we argue!" I explained.

"Well Andre you want your kids back, right?" She asked.

"Yes, I do very much." I responded.

"Well then you have to reason with her. Jai knows she isn't capable of having them that long by herself." She explained.

"I know this. She knows this. Everyone knows this. Hell, Jamari and J'Adora even knows this." I said.

She laughed, and I giggled too.

"I'll keep you updated mom. Thank you for everything. I love you." I said.

"And I love you." She replied.

I drove back home.

Later that evening I met up with Red for a couple of drinks just to clear my head. The temporary fix lasted for a couple of hours before I closed my eyes and went to sleep. I knew the next day was going to be hell on earth.

October 9th, 2012

Around 3:20PM I received a phone call from J'Adora's school. Her morning teacher informed me that Jai's father was there to pick up my daughter. That wasn't in our agreement. I didn't like it; and I didn't like the fact that Jai never informed me of the last-minute change.

Because her phone was off, I was unable to contact her. I didn't allow that to happen. I informed J'Adora's teacher to put my daughter on the bus, and if Jai's father wanted to pick her up, it would be at my home. J'Adora's teacher agreed with what I wanted. Within 5 minutes I received another call from J'Adora's school. When I answered the phone, it was J'Adora's principal.

"Hello dad?" She said.

"Yes." I answered.

"You have to work with us here." She said.

"Trust me; I am working with you guys. Jai's father picking up J'Adora wasn't in the Letter of Agreement, the same Letter of Agreement that you have a copy of." I stated.

"I understand that dad, but you know him." She said.

"That's correct. I do know him. He's my daughter's grandfather. This is the situation; if I bend my words for Jai now, before you know it the Letter of Agreement won't be respected by her. I'm protecting myself and my children." I said directly.

"I'm going to send a release form home to you in J'Adora's book bag, so her mom can put who she wants to pick up J'Adora. What do you think about that dad?" She offered.

"Well, she won't be putting any and everybody on that form, but I understand where you're coming from." I responded.

"Ok thank you." She said.

"No problem." I responded.

We hung up.

I went outside to wait on J'Adora to arrive home. As I was walking to the bus stop, I noticed that J'Adora's grandfather was parked on the side of my home. He got out of his van. J'Adora ran up to me smiling.

"Daddy!" She shouted.

"Hey J'Adora! You have to go with your grandfather, ok?" I comforted.

Her whole demeanor changed. I took J'Adora by her hand and walked her to her grandfather. I unzipped J'Adora's book bag, looked into her folder and handed her grandfather the release form.

"Hello." I said.

"Andre, I don't have no-nothin' to do with yo-you and Jai." He said stuttering.

"I understand that, and I respect you for not getting involved. But this is a release form that Jai needs to add you on, so it won't be an issue with you picking J'Adora up in the future." I explained.

"Oh ok. You ready J'Adora?" He asked.

He took her by the hand. As I stood there watching my daughter walk away, J'Adora turned around and looked at me. I smiled to let her know everything was going to be alright. Then they got into the van and drove away.

October 10th, 2012

3:37PM

As I was heading out my phone rung, and I noticed that it was J'Adora's school calling.

"Hello?" I answered.

"Yes dad, Jai's brother is supposed to pick J'Adora up from school today and he's not here." The principal said.

"Ok, what would you like me to do?" I asked.

"I know this is mom's week, but we are unable to reach her." She said.

"Why is that?" I asked.

I already knew what she was about to tell me, but I let her continue.

"Mom's phone is off." She responded.

"So yesterday it was Jai's dad, and today it's her brother? What do you want me to do?" I asked.

"If mom's brother doesn't show, is it possible that you can pick J'Adora up from school since the bus has already left?" She asked.

"Of course, I will. She's my daughter." I stated.

"Ok dad. Please stand by." She responded.

I sat down on the steps and shook my head. During emailing my mother, J'Adora's school called again.

"Hello?" I answered.

"Jai's brother is here. He was a little late, but everything is ok. Thank you for your cooperation." She said.

"No problem." I responded.

That evening I realized that Jamari and J'Adora weren't with me or their mother at nights because she had to work. The last place I wanted them to be was with Jai's mother, of all people, not her. Before I went to sleep, I prayed to God.

October 11th, 2012

The next morning, I awoke to my phone ringing and it was Jai calling from her sister's cell phone. I didn't know what she wanted; however, I couldn't help but think about my mother and me praying to God that Jai comes to her senses.

"Hello?" I answered.

"Hello Andre." She responded.

"Let me ask you a question. Where do Jamari and J'Adora stay at night?" I asked.

"At my mom's." She responded.

"You mean to tell me that I'm at home and Paula is here, but our kids are at your mothers? What was the point of you wanting to get them again?" I asked.

"You threatened me Andre." She said.

"I think you were scared because I was telling you the truth. I was telling you what people were suggesting for me to do when it came to you and this situation. I never acted on it and even though I wanted to, I didn't. Just like I told you when you left on December 30th, 2011, if I work and since you and I are still married you will be on my health insurance. I kept my word until my contract ended this month October 1st, 2012. Did I not?" I explained.

"You did." She confirmed.

"Can you tell me why Jamari was in school on Monday and why J'Adora wasn't?" I asked.

"What do you mean?" She wondered.

"Monday morning, J'Adora missed her school bus. I went to Jamari's school to find out if he was there, and they said he was." I explained.

"Jamari wasn't in school on Monday either. Wait they had school on Monday?" She asked.

"Yes, they were both supposed to be in school on Monday. It was Columbus Day yes, but P.G. County schools were open. That lying ass woman told me Jamari was in school. I'm going to fix her." I said.

"I didn't know." She said.

"You messed up on your first day. You are the parent, and it's your responsibility to know these types of things. Didn't you pick up a school calendar at the beginning of the school year? Another thing, I don't like the idea of your father and brother picking up J'Adora from school, and I don't think you do either. It wasn't in the agreement. Are you going to abide by our Letter of Agreement since you failed?" I asked.

"Or what?" She asked.

"Or am I going to take this thing to the next step?" I asked.

She didn't say a word.

"You lost Jai. You couldn't follow through with the Letter of Agreement. Now the schools know what's going on. Besides I'm home and why wouldn't you want the kids with me?" I asked.

"Let's go back to the way it was for now." She said.

"Alright, I will pick Jamari up from school today, and J'Adora will be riding the bus home from school. I will update them once I get off the phone with you. This is what I need for you to do. You will drop Jamari off at school every morning and if you can't, you will call in enough time to let Paula or myself know that you will not be coming. You will call Jamari and J'Adora every day to speak with them. You can either call my phone, Paula's phone, or the home phone to speak with them. We must pick up the phone when you call, and I will let Paula know. One more thing, I know in the past you wanted Paula to come over there so that you would be able to see the children more often. This is the thing, if you are willing to pay Paula what I pay her then she will do it. If not, Paula will not be doing it for free. You don't have to decide now but think about it." I said.

"Ok." She said.

"So, is that it? Do you have anything else to ask or say?" I asked.

"No." She responded.

"Alright then." I said and hung up the phone.

I never fought so hard for Jamari and J'Adora in all my life. It suddenly hit me just how much I loved my children. I was proud that I didn't give up the fight, and I will never stop fighting for them if there is air in my lungs. I was relieved that Jai and I came to an understanding for once. When I picked Jamari up from school at 2:00PM, my poor boy's uniform wasn't ironed, and he was wearing church shoes that were one size too small for his feet. He looked pitiful, and my eyes started to water but when he spotted me, he smiled, and I smiled back.

"Daddy can I go to McDonald's?" He wondered.

"Sure, when J'Adora gets home I'll take you both to McDonald's." I gushed.

77: **HIV**

Flashback:

Dreads was someone whom I have known for over a year.
We met on Twitter, just casual talk every now and then;
nothing serious. I always thought he was attractive, and I
loved his style. One of the other things I loved about him
was that he could sing well.

Fast Forward:

Dreads and I reconnected a couple of days before his
birthday on October 9th. I wasn't seeing anyone, I was
lonely, and I needed someone to take my mind off
Tarantino. Dreads told me that he was having a birthday
party to celebrate his big day; however, he ended up losing
his job before his big weekend. I felt extremely bad for
him. I decided to go to Hallmark and I spent about 20
minutes in the store trying to find the perfect card with
words of encouragement. I didn't have money to give him,
besides he and I only reconnected recently. So, I put an old
dime I had in the card. I hoped he would appreciate the
good deed; and he later said that he did.

Often, he would post different pieces of clothing that he
sewed on Instagram, even though I didn't have an
Instagram account Dreads would link his photos from
Instagram to Twitter. The man had skills. I always wanted
some drop crotch pants. I sent him money to make me and
my friend Aaron a pair. I was so excited to see him try on
my pair and he uploaded the picture for all to see. A lot of
people liked the picture and requested orders. Weeks
passed, and I still didn't receive my pants. I would often

bring up the fact that he didn't send me my pants. I thought maybe he was waiting for my birthday or something.

October 26ᵗʰ, 2012

When Dreads and I decided to Skype for the first time, he mentioned that he had something to tell me. I didn't know what it was, and quite frankly I was nervous.

"Babe I'm falling for you, and there's something I need for you to know about me." He said.

"What is it?" I asked.

He took a deep sigh.

"I'm about to cry… I'm positive. I know if you don't want to continue this with me, I will completely understand." He said looking directly into the camera.

Chills went up and down my spine. I didn't want to react because we were looking right at each other. I couldn't help but think, "How? This man doesn't look like he has anything." Nice smooth skin, his dick was gorgeous, and he was nicely groomed from the pictures and videos that he sent me. I came to the realization that HIV doesn't have a look. It isn't prejudice, and it doesn't have respect for a person. Anyone could become infected by the careless killer. I understood how important it is to protect yourself. I just listened as he went into detail about how he contracted the disease. He was infected by someone he loved and trusted a great deal. It took me back to October 14ᵗʰ, 2011 and how much I cared for Big. I trusted him to the point where he and I had unprotected sex. I felt for Dreads. Even though he told me he was HIV-positive, my feelings towards him were no different. I was curious, so I decided to ask him some questions as well.

"Thank you so much for telling me. I know that was a lot for you to get off your chest. I want to ask you some questions though. Obviously, you're still sexually active, right?" I asked.

"Yes, bae I am." He responded.

"I mean obviously you still use a condom, right?" I wondered.

"Yes bae, I always protect myself." He stated.

"Ok, that's good. Do you tell everyone before you sleep with them?" I asked.

"Yes, but there haven't been that many guys. To be honest with you, sometimes when I tell guys that I am positive they run. I'm really getting to the point where I'm tired of telling them. It doesn't seem like I'm going to ever find anyone. I take my pills daily. I'm also undetectable. I don't mind topping if I was in a relationship with a guy that is versatile, but I prefer to bottom. If I was in a long-term relationship with a guy that I trusted, and if the guy was comfortable, I wouldn't mind going raw." He said.

"What do you mean?" I asked in shock.

"Meaning, he could fuck me and cum inside me; but I couldn't fuck and cum inside of him since I'm the carrier." He said.

"Oh." I said and shook a little.

"Bae, why you make that face?" He questioned.

"Because I'm trying to take in all of what you just said. That doesn't even sound right. I hope my questions aren't coming off disrespectful, but I really must know what I'm getting myself into. That's all." I said and smiled.

For him to even consider or think that I would even have unprotected sex with him, he had to be crazy. He had me up until that very moment. We continued Skyping for the rest of the evening until he got tired. I didn't know where to go from there or what to do from that point. So, I called a couple of my friends to ask them what they would've done in that situation. The feedback was all the same, and it wasn't good.

"Run nigga run!"

"I know you're lonely, but you're not desperate Andre."

"You two don't even live in the same state. Just leave it where it is."

"Boy stop! Two names, Jamari and J'Adora need their daddy to be around. This is what I fear about that lifestyle the most. Please Andre, no baby."

With everyone telling me what I needed to do, I didn't know what to do. Well I did, but I was scared to. I didn't want to let him down, and I hoped that he would just end it first, before I did.

"Why do I still feel like I'm in prison? I thought my chains were finally broken." - Andre L. Simmons

78: **Handcuffed**

November 2nd, 2012

The past seven days were absolute hell. I was still entertaining Dreads as if he and I had a real chance. Red could tell something was wrong with me. He was asking me questions and I was being very brief with him. I didn't know where I wanted to go that day; however, I knew vodka would be in my system for sure. I didn't know what possessed me to go to Potomac Mills in Woodbridge, Virginia however, I did anyway. I remembered the last time I was there, and I was with Tarantino.

"Red this store is such a bore." I said giggling.

"You were the one who wanted to come way out here Dre." He suggested.

The costume jewelry caught my eye but there was no way I was going to pay those prices. Red and I continued throughout the department store and walked around the mall for about 30 minutes. Neither one of us purchased anything. We proceeded to head back through the Department store to leave and go back home. Once again, I stopped at the costume jewelry section.

"I like this long chain. Bingo!" I said out loud.

I grabbed the chain.

"Alright Red, I'm ready. Let's go." I said.

I started walking through the clothes as I ripped the price tag off the chain. Then I balled the chain up in my right hand. I was so close to the door. "This boring ass store wasn't a total waste of my time after all." I thought and smiled to myself.

"Dre, I think we're being followed." Red stated.

I looked back on my left. I didn't see anyone. As soon as I walked out of the store I was stopped.

"Excuse me sir. Do you mind coming with me? We can do this the easy way or the hard way. I don't think you want the cops involved." The undercover officer said to me.

My body went numb. I could feel the coldness taking over. Everyone was looking at me. I was humiliated and very embarrassed. I couldn't believe I was caught. Red looked at me and kept walking.

"I will obey you." I said surrendering to the officer.

"Thank you for your cooperation. Put both of your hands together in front of you." He said as he put me in handcuffs. "Walk back into the store; walk straight, keep walking, make this first left, make the next left, and stop right their sir." He ordered.

He unlocked the door, and I walked into the room where there were video cameras.

"I need your wallet." He said.

He grabbed my bill folder and went through my wallet. He grabbed my driver's license and placed it on the table in front of him. He also removed my hat, grabbed a camera and took a picture of me. He called someone to do a price check on the item that I had stolen; however, he never let the employee into the room.

"What brings you out here?" He wondered.

"I don't know. I actually dislike this mall." I responded.

"Were you in here earlier?" He asked.

"No sir this was my first time in this store tonight." I said.

"Are you sure? Weren't you looking at the same necklace 30 minutes prior?" He questioned.

"Oh yeah I was actually. I thought you were talking about earlier in the day." I replied.

"What made you do it?" He asked. "You seem like a guy who has a lot going for himself." He continued.

"The thrill, I guess I wanted to see if I could get away with it. I had the money to pay for it." I said.

Truth is, it wasn't my first time stealing. I had been doing it for years. Walmart didn't owe me shit between the DVDs, Wii, and Wii U games I stolen there. It had always been the thrill of getting away with it.

"Have you ever stolen anything before?" He wondered.

"Not from this store. This is my first and last time getting caught I will tell you that much. My lesson has been learned." I declared.

"What type of work do you do?" He asked.

"I was an armed contractor for Walter Reed Army Medical Center. Our contract ended October 1st, 2012." I told him.

He let me know that I was banned from the store for the next two years; and that I was not allowed to order items online from the store.

"I wish you all the best. Take care of yourself Mr. Simmons." He said as he gave me my hat and shook my hand.

I walked out of the store with my head down. I called Red to see where he was. He was at the diner across the street. I walked to my truck and got in. When he got in, I couldn't even look Red in his face. I couldn't help but think about Jamari and J'Adora, and the stupid mistake that I had just made. Having handcuffs wrapped around my wrist wasn't a funny matter.

"WOW! What were you thinking?!" Red yelled.

"I don't know what's wrong with me Red. I'm just tired. I'm so tired of it all. I'm tired of being lonely. I'm tired of not knowing if I'm going left or right. I'm just tired of giving a fuck every second of every fucking day!" I said with tears in my eyes.

"Dre, I told you the guy was right there walking behind us." He said.

"I know you did Red. I didn't see him. I just didn't see him." I said.

"What's going to happen?" He asked.

"I have to pay a fine which will be mailed to me and I'm banned from the store for the next two years. I'm not even aloud to purchase anything online." I said.

"Damn. I hope this doesn't fuck up your security credentials." He said with concern.

"I hope not either. Let's go home." I said.

"Straight the fuck home!" He said. Then he paused for second. "I know you're lonely, but you have to wait on love man. Quit looking for it. You're a handsome guy, great father, and you're my true best friend. I don't know where I would be without you. I love you Dre." Red said comforting me.

"Thank you, Red. I love you more." I responded and drove off.

79: 29

Flashback:

On August 29th, 2012 I was on the phone with my sister driving home from the cleaners. I was sitting at the traffic light waiting for it to turn green so that I could make my U-turn to go home.

"I'm about get a tattoo." I said.

"Yeah right Andre." She said.

"I am. I really am." I replied.

"Ok boy, whatever." She said brushing me off.

I drove up to Red Octopus and on the door, it read that they did not take credit cards; cash only. I went to the ATM right next door. "$40.00 should do it." I walked inside with a big smile on my face. There was only one lady sitting down, and she was covered in tattoos; or as we say in slang *"Tatted Up."* I walked up to the counter.

"Hi, can I help you?" The woman behind the counter asked.

"Yeah, I'm here to get my first tattoo." I said smiling.

"Do you have any idea what you would like?" She asked.

"I want the number 2 tatted on my left wrist, and the number 9 tatted on my right." I told her.

She handed me a book of different numbers and fonts. When I found what I wanted, I had to sit and wait on the tattoo artist. I was finally called to the back, and the tattoo artist asked me where I wanted to be tatted.

"I want the number 2 on my left wrist, and the number 9 on the right." I told him.

He took the alcohol pad and wiped my left wrist. He placed the paper on my wrist, and when he took it off, I looked at what he had done. "Why is the number 2 crooked?" I thought to myself. I looked at him, and he looked back at me.

"What's the matter?" He finally asked.

"Is it straight?" I asked.

"Yeah." He said and laughed.

He then explained the way they place it. So far everything was going well, until the needle touched my skin. It felt like someone was taking a knife and slicing my skin open. I was too intrigued to look away; however, it only lasted for a couple of minutes. When he started with the number 9, it was a different story. I thought that if I looked away, the pain wouldn't be as bad. I was very wrong. I wanted to kill that tattoo artist! I was bleeding even more while the number 9 was being done. After he finished, I was very happy with the results.

The number 29 represents my past, present, and future. My mother gave birth to me at the age of 29 on November 29th, 1983. Jai and I officially became boyfriend and girlfriend on June 29th, 2002, when Joshua's Temple hosted a cruise on the Spirit of Washington. Lyndyann moved from Trinidad to Maryland on June 29th, 2002. Jai and I had sex for the very first time on my 21st birthday in 2004. I originally wanted to get married on Jamari's first birthday, October 18th, 2007. Since I had just started a new job on September 10th, 2007. Jai and I decided to go to the courthouse on the 29th of November instead. On March 29th, 2011, Jai told me she was moving on with her life. Jai and I were supposed to have an official wedding on April 25th, 2012, on her 29th birthday however, that never happened.

Fast Forward:

On Thursday, November 29th, 2012, I turned 29 years old and it was the best birthday of my life. My children's nanny, Paula cooked me a birthday dinner. I enjoyed it by watching episodes of Inuyasha with Jamari and J'Adora on the living-room floor. On Friday, November 30th, 2012 while I was out celebrating my birthday dinner, with my best friends Aaron and Red, that's when God whispered in my ear "Andre it's time for you to tell your story." I obeyed and my writing journey began.

80: Word On The St.

March 31ˢᵗ, 2013

Delvin hosted Easter dinner at her home in Greensboro, North Carolina. Most of the family that lived in Maryland traveled down, along with Paula. My mother was still in Egypt. Plus, aunt Janelle's daughter Audrekia was going to college down there so it all made more sense. It was bought to my attention by Delvin that my name was brought up in conversation and the topic at hand was my sexuality. Nothing was bad said but my truth which I never confirmed to any of my family members except for my mother on July 4ᵗʰ, 2012 and to my cousins Delvin and Kendrell during Audrekia's graduation weekend back in June of 2012. My aunt Celestine said that my sexuality didn't matter, and I seem to be much happier since me and Jai's separation. Not only that they were curious about what I was quote on quote writing about. I often wondered did Paula talk or say something because only she seen Tarantino come to my home. None of their opinions mattered though however, aunt Celestine's love not changing because of me living my truth made my heart smile.

81: **Lonely Tony** *(Part One)*

Sunday, April 28th, 2013

His first words during our monologue exchange were "Hey, how are you?" He immediately brought up *'Butterflies Hitting Home Runs'* he had questions to ask me. Like what made me start to write, was it my first book, and who was I published with etc. At that time, I could only answer him the first two questions since I was still in the beginning stages of writing. However, I was flattered that he was interested in something that mattered so much to me. "I'm Tony." He later introduced himself. He was an interesting character for sure. We exchanged phone numbers. Tony revealed to me his love for music, his favorite song by Whitney Houston, and that he could sing as well. The conversation was refreshing I was excited that he lived near me. Everything was going well until he said, "Andre I'm HIV-positive." Fuck not again I had thought to myself. Once again, same as Dreads he contracted the disease from his partner that he loved and trusted. Nothing changed about me wanting to still meet Tony though. I had to tell Aaron all about him.

82: **Rihanna** *(Diamonds World Tour)*

April 29th, 2013

Aaron had purchased tickets for us to see Rihanna in concert. He met me at my home, and we caught the train from Largo Town Center *(WMATA station)* that took us straight to the Verizon Center. She was about 30 minutes late however, Rihanna did put on a good show, she was entertaining. Production was nice. I loved when she said, "Heeeyyy D.C., I love D.C." However, the highlight for me was always just spending time with Aaron. I love and appreciated this man more than he will ever know.

83: **Lonely Tony** *(Part Two)*

Monday, May 6th, 2013

I was awakened to what sound like a car alarm. I immediately jumped out of bed and walked swiftly to the window. What my eyes then witnessed could have made me cry. It was a tow truck with my Jeep lifted in the air on the back. I ran outside.

"Aye!" I yelled. "Why are you towing my vehicle?" I then continued.

Come to find out I was behind on my Jeep payments. All I could think about was Valentine's Day and the money I spent that night on Tarantino.

Flashback:

Tarantino and I had connected again in December. Tarantino, Red, and I also went to the movies to see The Desolation of Smaug. He had never missed the chance to wish me a happy birthday since knowing him. In my mind we were back on again.

Everything was going well or so I thought. Valentine's Day was approaching. I was doing my best trying to pick his brain about what he wanted. He needed a full-length mirror for his bedroom which I had found one at Kirklands at the Waldorf, Maryland location. It seemed like the closer we got near it, something was just off, Tarantino was distant. I still had made hotel reservations at the Grand Hyatt Washington in Washington D.C. The same place when Big had traveled down to visit. I had also made dinner reservations at Ruth's Chris in Crystal City, Virginia. I had bought a bottle of Ciroc Peach and a special order of chocolate covered strawberries. I was hype about the night.

Valentine's Day

I wore an all-black turtleneck, black slacks, and some white shoes which his pastor would often ask where the guy with the tic-tac shoes was. I made sure that my head was freshly shaven. Dinner at Ruth's Chris was good. I expected more due to the hype that I've always heard about the hot spot. Later that night I was so intoxicated, and it was on purpose. You see I had wanted to suck his dick until he cummed. The plan was for me to attempt to do it while we were in the tub together to distract from the taste of it all. Well that didn't work either. It still made me gag so I was forced to stop. We ended up fucking though. The following morning, we had breakfast at a local D.C. diner.

March 2nd, 2013

Tarantino and I had gone to the movies to see Jack The Giant Slayer at Columbia Mall which came out on March 1st. Later that night he had came over and I wanted to talk about us and where we were headed. I felt like I had put it off long enough. I got down on my knees pleading with him. I wanted to know what I could do to make things better. I couldn't believe that I was going through this with him again. We could have just remained friends. I would have been good with that. After a couple of days had passed, I had drowned myself in my writing. The more I wrote the better I was beginning to feel. I knew my worth and I was worth it to someone out there. I owed myself the type of love that I was always trying to give other people. The love for him that I had would never die even though a romantic relationship would never be, not anymore.

Fast Forward:

Now back to that early morning. My Jeep was towed, and I ended up getting the information to where it was being towed to. I had emailed my mother letting her know what had happened. She called me that morning.

"Andre, we need to get your truck back. You are too close to it being paid off." She comforted.

I was too ashamed to reveal to my mother that my Jeep payments was spent on a man back on Valentine's Day and it was the same guy who I came out to her about on July 4th, 2012. My mother paid the full balance to where I was all caught up on my payments. I had revealed to Tony what had happened. He offered to pay the balance for me to pick up my Jeep from the towing location. I was taken aback. I still have yet to meet him in person, and he offered to pay for my Jeep, which was $250.00 due to it being over 40 miles from my home. I was very skeptical about that.

"Tony why are you doing this? You barely know me." I stated.

"Well Andre you have a son and a daughter for one. Two I can afford it." He explained.

No one has ever done anything like this for me other than my mother of course.

"Are you sure this isn't going to cost me later? What do you want Tony?" I wondered.

"A kiss." He gushed.

"You want a kiss from me?" I asked confused.

My mind was all over the place. Why did this nigga want a kiss?

"Andre?" He whispered.

"Yes Tony?" I answered.

"You won't catch anything from my kiss." He consoled.

His words eased my mind.

"Ok Tony I will kiss you." I said.

Tony came over later that night. He called me when he was outside. I was so nervous. I walked to the door and cracked it. He still was sitting inside of his car. I opened the door and walked outside. He opened his door and got out. This man was so handsome and maybe an inch taller than me. As I was leaning my body in for a hug, I could feel his erected penis poke me. I jumped and backed away.

"Are you ok?" I wondered.

"Yeah, I more than ok now that I finally get to see you in person and touch you." He declared.

"Ok cool but why are you hard?" I asked.

"You did this." He explained.

"How exactly did I do this?" I wondered.

"The first night talking to you on the phone, your voice and conversation turned me on." He stated.

"Wow!" I said.

"Come here Andre." Tony begged.

I took Tony by the hand. I walked him and his hard dick to the park that was across the street from my home. Soon as we sat down, he gave me the money. We talked for about 25 minutes. His dick remained hard the entire time because I kept looking down at it. One or two times, I may have touched it to see if it was still hard. I mean after all it was dark outside. That had to be one of the weirdest moments of my life. Tony was harmless though. I revealed to him that I didn't want to kiss him at the park and that I had rather done it inside of his car. We walked back to his car. I asked him if he could drive away from my home. Once he reached a spot that I was comfortable at, I asked him to stop the car. He leaned in for a kiss. I thought it was going to be just a kiss on the lips however, it was more than what I had intended. Tony kissed me like he was in loved with me. I had to stop and get out the car. It was too much and I liked it a lot.

"Tony, thank you so much but I have to go." I gushed.

I jogged back to my home and called him soon as I got in. It all felt like a scene from a romantic comedy movie.

84: American Idol

June 20th, 2013

Tony had called me.

"Hello?" I answered.

"Hey, how are you?" Tony responded.

"I'm good." I replied.

"Are you writing?" He questioned.

"Yes." I said.

"Ok good. I've noticed you're not writing like you used to. I don't want to distract you from writing your book Andre, and I still think you should cut your beard." Tony comforted.

"Tony you're not a distraction by any means. I'm not cutting my beard. I've told you that before. Just let it go already." I said and giggled.

"What are your plans for tomorrow?" Tony asked.

"I'm meeting up with Aaron tomorrow afternoon. We're attending a church function." I revealed.

"Oh, you mean your boyfriend." Tony said.

"Yes, my best friend." I responded.

"Ok. I'm going to check on you a little later then." Tony said.

"Ok cool. Talk to you later Tony." I responded.

Truth is, I wasn't writing. I was distracted however, for good reason. I was happy again to have someone in my life that not only cared about me but Jamari and J'Adora as well. What more could I have asked for? I got up off the couch and went to the bathroom. I was looking at myself. "Should I, or shouldn't I?" I thought. I took the scissors from underneath the cabinet and started cutting away. The clippers did the rest of the job. Wow! I investigated the mirror. My face hadn't been that clean since I worked at Walter Reed. I hopped in the shower. I got into my Jeep and headed over to Tony's. I called him.

"Hello?" He answered.

"Come outside really quick." I said excitedly.

About a couple of minutes later Tony reemerged from his home. As he was walking over to my Jeep, I stepped out. His face lit up.

"Awwww you look handsome." Tony admired.

"Thank you, Tony. I'm glad you approve. I did this for you and just so you know, I'm not cutting it again. Now give me a hug so I can go back home." I said.

Tony and I hugged each other. I got back in my Jeep and headed back home.

June 21st, 2013

Aaron met me at my home. He mentioned that he was
happy that I had cut my beard as well. I drove us to
Ebenezer AME Church. The line to the church was crazy.

"Aaron what's going on? Who's here?" I asked.

"Fantasia." He said.

"Aaron you're fucking lying! Quit playing who's here?" I
repeated.

"Andre, Fantasia." He said and laughed hysterically.

"Oh my God. I don't believe you, Aaron." I snapped.

We parked and walked to the front entrance of the church.
Once we entered inside, reality had finally begun to set in,
that was in fact who we were about to see. I couldn't
believe it. I was finally seeing the only American Idol that
I've voted for live. Fantasia was like the family member
who overcame so much in their life, despite all obstacles,
and you just wanted to see win. Fantasia shut it down in the
house of the lord, I could only imagine seeing her again in
the future, on a bigger stage, where she truly belonged.

85: **Mommy's Home**

Flashback:

Friday, July 26th, 2013

I was in the living-room working on my book and Paula walked in the kitchen.

"Andre Can I have a word with you please?" Paula requested.

"Yes, Paula go ahead." I replied.

"I'm just letting you know that I have found other work. Andre, I want to thank you for allowing me to watch you children over the past year and a half. I know your mother is coming back next month." Paula said.

"Yes, she is. You're welcome Paula. Thank you for being there for us." I reassured her.

"I will be out before they come back on Sunday. I don't want it to be too hard on them once I leave." Paula said.

"I'm sure they will miss you however we will be fine. Thank you again Paula." I responded.

I proceeded to email my mother to let her know. She didn't respond back until she woke up Egypt time. Her email read: *"Andre it's going to be ok. I'm coming back in a month."*

Fast Forward:

August 23rd, 2013

When the day of my mother's return finally arrived Jamari
and J'Adora had no idea. My mother notified me that she
was at Addison Road Center *(WMATA)*. We drove to Largo
Town Center *(WMATA)* and waited inside of my Jeep. I
must admit I was getting kind of anxious myself. This time
she wasn't going back. When the train pulled up, the
children and I got out of my Jeep. I still didn't say a word. I
had wanted them to spot her for themselves. It was still
early in the day, so it wasn't that many people getting off
the train. As the people were making their way out. Jamari
and J'Adora's attention turned towards the crowd. I had
spotted my mother first. As soon as Jamari spotted her, he
shouted "Grandma!"

"Grandma!" J'Adora did repeated.

"Heeyyy, my Grandma babies." My mother said, as she
warmly embraced her grandchildren.

86: Jack'd

Flashback:

A friend of mine that lived in Detroit from Twitter by the name of Justice Delore would always send me photos of men from the app called Jack'd. I simply wasn't interested, for one I didn't live and Detroit and two I was over the dating scene especially, after Tony pushed me away and told me that I should find someone who wasn't HIV-positive. Ever since him and I jerk off together back in June, and I used the same towel as he did, he freaked out. Things were never the same. I wanted to show him I wasn't afraid of him being positive. I had also revealed to Tony that we didn't have to have full intercourse sex, even that wasn't enough. He felt like I was cheating myself out of fully being loved. That shit stung like a bee when he told me that however, I had to move on and accept that Tony and I would be nothing more than just good friends.

Fast Forward:

September 1st, 2013

Justice Delore called me.

"Hello." I answered.

"Hello honey-bun. What are you up to? Are you writing?" She inquired.

"I am." I replied.

I received an iMessage.

"Hold on." I then said.

I looked down at my phone. Once again Justice sent me a photo of a man.

"Girl what did I tell you?" I snapped.

"Look you need to get over Tony. Andre this man is from your area." She said.

"He's handsome however, I'm not looking for a quick fuck." I said.

"I know the type of man you're searching for. Let me set-up an account for you. I promise I won't show your face." She reassured.

"It's not even that. I just... I don't know. I'm tired boo." I consoled.

"Awwww baby." She said.

"Ugh! Fine I'll do it myself." I replied.

After hanging up the phone. I had set-up my account around 4:00PM that afternoon. I was instantly addicted. I finally called it a night sometime around 11:00PM. Lord Jesus, the asses and dicks that I had come across would last me a lifetime.

87: **20 Something** *(Part One)*

I was starting to think that my only purpose of joining Jack'd was connecting with the guy who designed my book cover for **'Butterflies Hitting Home Runs.'** I was invited over to his place in Annapolis, Maryland to discuss the book cover and possibly other future projects. Well he wanted to fuck too, since it wasn't possible for a business relationship only, I left. You know what? I honestly wasn't sexually attracted to him, because I did have fun with a couple of guys on there in the beginning of September. Basically, my short experience on Jack'd with men were only wanting to fuck or I was being laughed at for promoting my new upcoming book on the dating app. That was until I met Diego who was the only guy from my Jack'd experience that wanted to go on a real date. He asked about my book and we also bonded over the movie list that I had on my profile. The only thing that bothered me though was his age. You see Diego was only 20 years old.

Friday, October 25th, 2013

Diego had iMessaged me, to let me know how far he was away from Largo Town Center *(WMATA)*. I had already told him the type of vehicle that I would be driving and the color. I hopped in the Jeep and headed his way. As I was pulling up, I saw a guy walking towards my Jeep. "OMG it's him." I thought to myself. I unlocked the door and he got in.

"Hello sir." Diego said.

"Hi Diego, it's nice to meet you in person." I responded and we hugged each other.

"Yes, I would fuck this boy." I immediately thought to myself. I rarely go by a person's photo because most of the time people don't look like their photos when I first see them. Diego was very handsome with beautiful smooth skin. His smile was adorable. He had a low haircut; however, the texture was soft, He reminded me of an African and Indian mixed Trinidadian, subcontinent descent, *Dougla (or Dugla)*. We headed to Arundel Mills to see Carrie. Even though it was just the movies I still enjoyed myself a great deal. Due to how late it was I had offered to drop him off at home in D.C. On the way leaving the movies before hopping onto the Baltimore parkway Diego told me to get some gas. As I pulled up to the Exxon gas station, Diego hopped out the Jeep, slid is credit card and started pumping the gas. I was floored. Never, ever in all my 29 years of living had someone ever did that for me. He got back inside of my Jeep.

"That was unexpected." I gushed and couldn't stop smiling.

Andre you're not fucking this boy tonight, I kept trying to convince myself.

"No problem." He stated as he stared with prolonged eye contact.

"Are you hungry?" I asked.

"Yeah." He said and giggled.

"You ever had Mario's Pizza? It's located in Arlington, Virginia. My mother introduced it to me when I was a little boy. It used to be black owned." I explained.

"I don't think I had it before." He responded.

"Alright. Mario's pizza it is." I stated.

Once we arrived it was stupid packed as usual. I didn't mind, I was enjoying this moment with Diego. We had ordered a large supreme and crushed the entire pizza in my Jeep. Afterwards I dropped him off at home. The evening was perfect. I think we both wanted to have sex, but we didn't. We hugged and I went home. Why did he have to be so young? He seemed so mature for his age too. If Stella Payne was 40 and Winston Shakespeare was 20 from the movie How Stella Got Her Groove Back then I was safe, right?

Tuesday, October 29th, 2013

Diego and I made plans to see each other again. Another night of fun, plus drinking was involved. This time he wasn't going back home. I wanted him. My ass hole was pulsating for his dick. By the time we arrived back to my home, everyone was asleep. We started off kissing. Never had I tasted someone who smoked cigarettes. It wasn't the most pleasant taste, nor was he the greatest dick sucker however, the boy could eat some ass. Every time I would fake run away, he would bring me right back and his tongue would go deeper and deeper inside of my hole with each resist. Diego was gentle with me. I must admit he was good. After the heated and sweaty encounter, we laid next to each other. He opened up to me about private things from his past which put things into perspective why he didn't care to bottom but wasn't totally against it. As he dug deeper in his colorful past, he broke down. He said he felt like he could trust me and didn't normally open up to people so quickly. I consoled Diego in the best way that I knew how. Then it hit me, the more guys that I had gotten to know beyond sex all had a past very similar to one another. This lifestyle wasn't what it's all cracked up to be. How many of these men were born gay or forced into a lifestyle due to their unfortunate beginnings? Diego and I continued to see each other frequently after that.

Thursday, November 28th, 2013

I invited Diego over for Thanksgiving dinner. This was my first time ever having someone over for a family gathering, that I was dating. I had officially introduced him to my mother and the rest of my family members as my quote on quote *"Friend."* We went to go sit down and we caught my cousin Kanika peeping around the corner of the kitchen with a plate of food. We had both laughed later about the situation when my mother requested me to go pick up something for Black Friday from Target. Diego was doing everything right not to mentioned he loaned Jamari and J'Adora his PlayStation 3 two weeks prior. Even though the game system was a little too advanced for them, I was grateful for the nice gesture.

Friday, November 29th, 2013

The following day, on my 30th birthday Diego surprised me by having 30 roses delivered to my home. Again, never had someone bought me flowers before. My birthday was amazing Jamari and J'Adora treated me to a movie called Frozen that I never heard of however, I was in awe by the time the movie ended. When I had reached back home there was a cake waiting for me. My cousin Audrekia said 2 guys had dropped it off. I eventually found out that it was Aaron and Tarantino trying to surprise me. I was even more shocked to hear Tarantino was a part of it, since him and I haven't seen each other in person since March. Later that evening Red and Diego treated me to my birthday dinner at my favorite Chinese restaurant in Chinatown, Washington D.C. My birthday outfit was the show stopper for the evening. I had ordered some all black leggings from Guess. They fitted like a glove. Very comfortable and yet sexy. I loved the attention that I was getting from the looks to the giggles. Hell, I was 30, feeling sexy, and getting dicked down by a 20-year-old on the regular, who seemed to be head over heels for my ass, and treated my children good too. I couldn't ask for more.

December 23rd, 2013

Some family members from North Carolina decided to spend Christmas in Maryland. Aunt Dollie along with her eldest daughter Tamara, uncle Allan, his girlfriend Tina, friend of the family Kent, and another gentleman. Aunt Dollie's other two children, son Brian and daughter Delvin didn't want their mother traveling such a long distance due to her cancer however, once aunt Dollie had her mind made up, she's unstoppable. I've always admired that about all the sisters in the family, very strong-willed women. Aunt Janelle hosted a family welcoming dinner at her home.

What an event it was. The highlight of the evening was my mother, aunt Dollie, aunt Celestine, and aunt Janelle singing "Silent Night", and they were all off key, of course it was filmed and uploaded to YouTube. Aunt Patricia didn't join, she's always been the party pooper of the bunch. You would have assumed that they all were extremely intoxicated however, that wasn't the case. It was so much fun. Lasagna night was at my mother's home December 24th that I made. We celebrated Christmas dinner at aunt Patricia's home on December 25th.

Friday, December 27th

My sister needed me to take her to the bus station at Union Station in Washington D.C. so she could return back to work for her weekend shift. Red called me on the way back. The conversation was quick and short, he ended up getting mad at me, and hanging up the phone. It didn't bother me. That was the norm for him and me, even though he has been acting funny lately ever since I was wrote and submitted my book last month to Racquel, my co-editor. Everyone thought we were a couple anyway. He always calls me back.

Monday, December 30th

I couldn't wait to see Diego again. It was still kind of early so him and I went for a drive. I didn't have much to offer him however, I had a bottle of his favorite alcohol waiting for him wrapped up as a Christmas gift. Also, I was looking forward to bringing in the New Year with him. I still couldn't believe all this was actually happening to me. Even though him and I weren't official, yet I convinced myself that this could work. Plus, Aaron and Red approved as long as I was happy. Diego and I were talking about everything and then we started talking about my book and some of the things that I had did in my past. I had sniffed and wiped my nose. He asked me did I snort any coke.

"No Diego I didn't. I have nose hairs. I'm a very hairy man just like yourself. It's been over 2 years now. Besides I wasn't a coke head it was fun for me until it wasn't. It's all in *'Butterflies Hitting Home Runs.'*" I stated.

My response wasn't received well at all. I don't know what had gotten into him in that very moment however, he requested to go home. The metro was closed for the night.

"Well if you want to go home, would you like to take your Play Station with you as well?" I wondered.

"No, it's for the kids." He stated.

I just wanted to get him back to my home. I felt like once we got back there, everything would be ok, and we could talk about what I said that triggered him so much. Diego still wanted to go home, so I took him. Of course, I ran a stop light worth $150.00. Up until then his age wasn't showing. *"Happy fucking New Year's Andre."*

88: *Butterflies Hitting Home Runs (1ˢᵗ Book)*

Flashback:

May 2014

Aaron had wanted to get me out of Maryland due to me overstressing my book. He gifted me a quick trip to New York to see Fantasia on Broadway, for the show After Midnight. She was amazing. That was my first time seeing a Broadway play in New York and one of the highlights was getting a chance to meet and take photos with her after the show.

I couldn't believe I put out a release date of my book and still no book publisher. I began to become nervous at that point, that was until I had a conversation with Aaron about not being published as of yet. Aaron recommended that I look into CreateSpace.com. The website provided all the tools needed to publish a book.

I wanted someone from my family to read my book first, just not my mother. The next person that came to mind was my favorite aunt, aunt Janelle. I was so excited that I had made a public announcement via social media *(Facebook and Instagram)* implying that I would be emailing her the book. The following Sunday I had confronted aunt Janelle if she started the process to reading my book. Her reply was simply "No" I didn't think nothing of it other than her being a busy woman and that she would begun to read it when she had the time. The following Sunday I had asked her again and it was the same response. I was a little concern however, I left it alone.

Fast Forward:

June 9th, 2014

The day that I submitted my book for review, about 12
hours later I received an email saying that my book had
been cleared to be sold online around the world, was a
feeling that I would never forget. It felt like I was officially
released from my past. I just knew I would receive copies
of my books first since I uploaded the link for my book the
following day to all my social media platforms. I was
deadass wrong. Two names that I would never forget are
Shannon Derby and Kemin Richardson, who I met through
social media, Instagram whom became my friends. They
received their books before me. Each day more and more
people were receiving their books and I had yet to received
mines. The response and the demand were truly
overwhelming however, I was a tad bit jealous due to my
books had yet to arrive.

June 16th, 2014

The package of my books had finally arrived. I ran upstairs
to my bathroom. I felt like a little kid on Christmas
morning tearing the UPS package open. I immediately
made a video to upload to Instagram to share with
everyone.

"Whoa these books are big." I said aloud.

My mother came upstairs too. She could see the excitement
on my face, she grabbed one of the books, and raced off to
her bedroom.

"No!" I yelled and chased her to her room.

"My right eye just started twitching Andre." She stated.

"Maybe I shouldn't read this book then." She continued.

"It's not that I don't want you to read it. I just don't want to be around you when you do." I stated and laughed.

I sat down on her bed and just started flipping through the pages of my work, and then suddenly I spotted one. A damn error.

"Oh my God, mom no!" I shouted.

"What is it?" She wondered.

"I see an error." I cried. "I'm going to have update my book asap on CreateSpace Mom. I just pray that was the only one." I continued.

Over the next few days more people from the likes of Iman of Chicago, Ronnie from New Jersey, and Mike from New York were tagging me with photos of themselves with my book, people were screenshotting their transactions letting me know that their book orders were on the way. I was receiving so many DMs with so many questions, I felt accomplished. People who wanted a signed copy I would simply tell them to go purchase it from the link in my bio on Instagram. I quickly learned my lesson with that, you see I was still learning how to be a business man and I should have taken it upon myself to order books for the people who wanted a signed copy.

The reviews on Amazon for my book were coming in and I was blown away from all the positive feedback, that was until I read a review by gifted writer Mark O. Estes from his blog. Mark let it be known that my story was a good read however, he noticed that there were quite a few errors. "Like why he couldn't tell me that in private?" I thought. My mind went back to Racquel. I submitted my book to her mid - November 2013 and didn't receive it back until mid - April. I wanted her to help me with the co-editing of the book. I paid her $500.00 to do the job, and I never took it upon myself to go over my book for myself. At one point she and I didn't talk for a whole week due to the stress and it was affecting our friendship. I valued our friendship more so I knew in the future I wouldn't work with friends again and furthermore it's always the author/writer's responsibility to go over his/her work.

Friday, July 11th, 2014

My mother, Jamari, J'Adora, my sister's daughter Saniah, and I headed down to North Carolina for a quick getaway. I hadn't been down there since my grandmother's funeral. I was finally getting the chance to meet Racquel in person later that evening. She was traveling from Beaufort, South Carolina. I met her at the outskirts of Shallotte, North Carolina which was only 8 minutes from my grandmother's mother's home. When we arrived back at my grandmother's home, I was finally able to see her in the light. Racquel was pretty in person, her photos from Instagram did her no justice and what a beautiful smile she wore, and that's the first thing my mother said to her when I had awaken her out her sleep to let her know that Racquel had arrived safely. Kids say the darndest things like how Jamari and J'Adora kept insisting that Racquel was my girlfriend. She did get the chance to meet a few characters from the book. When I had introduced her the Sandra Massey, we both died, it had got back to me that Sandra wasn't a fan of what I wrote about her character which was the truth.

My overall trip was one for the books. Aaron landed me my first ever radio interview which I had to call into Baltimore, Maryland. 5 out of the 3 days that we were there, we went to Holden beach 3 of those days. The last beach day aunt Dollie and Tamara came as well. It was good to see aunt Dollie out of the house being proactive. It didn't cost a thing to go to the beach nothing but hot sunny heat, and cool ocean breeze. On July 17th, J'Adora celebrated her 6th birthday. Spending time with family was always priceless to me and something that I cherished. Special thank you to aunt Dollie and aunt Julie for supporting my books by each paying for one. I had gifted my aunt Iris and my cousin Tamera one of each for free.

Friday, July 18th, 2014

On our way back up to Maryland, I had received a phone call and it was Tony.

"Oh, my word." I gushed.

"Haha, how are you?" He giggled and said.

"I'm doing well. My mother and her grands are on our way back up from North Carolina, after visiting family. How are you Tony?" I wondered.

"I'm good. Just so you know I have a bone to pick with you." He explained.

"Alright you want to talk about it now or later?" I asked.

"It can wait until later Andre." He replied.

"Come over around 8:00PM." I said.

"Alright bet." He said.

Later that evening Tony had came over and believe it or not he finally met my mother. He missed Jamari and J'Adora due to their mother picking them up for the weekend. He wanted to take me out to dinner to celebrate the release of my book. We ended up going to Copper Canyon Grill located in Woodmore Towne Center. Once we sat down for dinner that's when our talked began.

"I'm hurt by you Andre." He expressed.

My mood went from happy to sad in an instant.

"What did I do?" I wondered.

"Why did I have to find out that your book was released through social media?" He wondered.

"It wasn't nothing personal against you. It just happened and it kind of been non-stop ever since. I do apologize." I assured.

"I hope you're not letting all your success go to head and still keeping Jamari and J'Adora a priority." He stated.

"Well for one I'm proud and grateful for everything that's happening in my life. I took a risk with this book Tony and I didn't know what the outcome was going to be. I went from working on a security contract for 5 years, to unemployment, to a published author. I'm enjoying this moment as you used to say. Jamari and J'Adora was and will always be my number 1 priority. That won't change." I stated.

"Well I'm just saying Andre." He said.

"I hear you Tony." I responded.

"So, who are you fucking?" He wondered.

"No one, well not any more. He lied to me once and that's all it took. The person was someone popular from Instagram. An Instagram crush I shall say. Before him the only person worth mentioning is Diego. We follow each other on social media now however, I haven't linked up with him since last year. I really liked him; he was young Tony." I explained.

"Yeah I remember you telling me about him. I liked him for you Andre." He said.

"Yeah. So, what about you?" I wondered.

"Yeah, I'm having sex." He explained.

"Wait! What! Are you serious?" I asked in shocked.

"Andre I already know what you're going to say." Tony suggested.

"Is it serious? I mean if it is, I'm happy for you." I explained.

"No, it's just sex and besides he's HIV-positive too Andre." He explained.

"Is that supposed to make me feel better Tony? This has been an interesting dinner. It went from you grilling me to you fucking someone that you're not even serious about. Just wow!" I stated.

Tony didn't respond and we both just sat there for a few seconds staring back and one another. Tony's eyes began to water up. So, I decided to change the subject, after dinner Tony dropped me off back at home.

"You want me to stay the night so you can cook me breakfast in the morning like you used to?" He asked.

"Sure, Tony come on in. You get on my nerves." I gushed.

"Andre, Keshia doesn't want me having the book party at my house. She feels like you stole her dream. It was Dollie who convinced me to have it at my house. She said do it for Andre, don't let Keshia run you Tricia." - Aunt Patricia

89: Book Party

Flashback:

The idea for me to have a book party came about during my 2nd radio interview in Baltimore, Maryland back in July. My cousin Delvin had called in and requested that I should. My friend Kemin also revealed to me that he was listening in along with fellow author/writer Mike Riggins.

Since joining Instagram back in December, Diego and I have always followed each other, even though the last time I seen him was back in December. He contacted me back in August, we went out to dinner at Carrabba's Italian Grill located in Bowie, Maryland. It was good to see him however, I wasn't a fan of how he was rocking his hair, it was a super long high-top. We stayed in contact and continued to see one another as friends.

Fast Forward:

Saturday, September 6th, 2014

Tony had a surprise for me and had advised me to come over his place where he now was living to collect it. When I arrived of course the question was always who I was fucking however, that was the least of my concern. I was wondering where he got that white Yo Quiero Taco Bell dog from. I always loathed Chihuahuas and it reminded me of my cousin's Delvin's dog, same color and everything.

"You think the kids will like him?" He wondered.

"Yeah. I mean they just want a dog period." I stated.

"When's a good day for me to bring them by to see him?" I continued.

"It's for them Andre. I got him for you guys." He explained.

"Shit!" I thought to myself as I could only just smile and look at him. The gesture was nice but why did he have to be so damn ugly.

"Awwww thank you Tony." I said.

I stayed for a few more minutes and took the new named dog Subzero home with me. I was so surprised that he stayed in my lap the entire ride home. He slept in my room in the laundry basket on the floor. I was awakened the following morning by my mother.

"Andre!" She yelled.

"Yeah?" I yelled back.

"Is this shit on my floor?" She yelled.

I immediately looked at Subzero and hopped out of bed.

"This isn't going to work." I said aloud as I stomped upstairs like a 2-year-old to clean the feces up.

I was informed by my cousin Delvin who lived in Greensboro, North Carolina a week prior to my book party that she wouldn't be able to attend. Mind you I chose that date due to her being busy on September 20th, which was the original date I wanted.

Sunday, September 7th, 2014

When I picked them up from Baltimore, Jamari and J'Adora were overjoyed more so J'Adora. I let them know that the dog was a gift from Tony. It was all our responsibility to help with Subzero and if we all couldn't, he was going right back to his previous owner.

Friday, September 12th, 2014

After constantly talking to Jamari and J'Adora repeatedly I had to return Subzero back to Tony, the day before my book party, Diego had come along with me. Tony refused to take the dog food that I had purchased. I asked him was he still attending my book party and he never responded back to me. When I had got back in my Jeep Diego claimed that Tony had gave him a not so pleasant look.

"Tony was #TeamDiego over the summer, he just doesn't know you're that guy." I said.

"Andre you know that boy likes you." Diego insisted.

"Ok, Tony and I are just friends. It was too much for me to keep that dog Diego." I explained.

Even though I haven't spoken to Red over 9 months I still decided to reach out to him to let him know that my book party was tomorrow. I called, texted, called him again, and no response.

Later, that evening Racquel had arrived and I told her that I didn't want her moving her car until she headed back to Beaufort, South Carolina. I treated her to Popeyes in Mitchellville, Maryland. Diego, Racquel and I went to my favorite Walmart in Severn, Maryland to pick up the food that Diego and I were going to prepare for the book party. From prepping to cooking late night into the following day, I was exhausted. Not to mention the books that I had ordered still haven't arrived. I only had a few copies at home, but the show was going to go on.

Saturday, September 13th, 2014

I didn't purchase and outfit for my book party. I ended up cutting up a jean jacket that belonged to my mother. We packed up the food in my Jeep and headed to my aunt's where my book party was being held. A car was already waiting outside of her home that I didn't recognize. It wasn't going to take me that long to set up everything anyways. My concern was my cousin Keshia, aunt Patricia's daughter, did she leave for work?

Flashback:

Remember my cousin Keshia, who's 2 years my senior used to live in Japan and was in a horrific car accident on New Year's Eve 1999. Which brought her and aunt Patricia to Maryland. Over the years Keshia used the car accident as a pity party. If it wasn't about her, she had an issue and majority of the family functions she was problematic. She treated aunt Patricia and her sister Tameka like shit. As soon as her paycheck would clear it was spent on drugs and alcohol.

Fast Forward:

We carried the food to the house and as soon as we opened the door Keshia was standing there. I spoke to her and kept it moving. Diego followed close behind carrying the pasta salad. Keshia bumped into him on purpose which caused him to drop the pasta salad. Thankfully it was covered and didn't cause a mess. It was later brought to my attention that Keshia called out from work. Keshia's sister Tameka had called me to wish me a very successful book party. By the time people were arriving, everything was officially set up. Torrence was stopping by with the cake that he had personally made for me. Other than Keshia bumping into Diego and throwing down keys on the table from the top of the steps that made a loud noise in the middle of me speaking, I was overall happy with my first book event; drained however, happy. The highlight of the evening was everyone eating and mingling together afterwards. The original time of my book event was 6:30PM - 8:30PM however, everyone stayed passed 11:00PM. I was so grateful for everyone that came through. From my best friend Aaron to Shana, to all the people that took the time to attend. The most unexpected guest popup of the evening was the moment Tarantino and his best friend walked through the door mid-speech. I was so tongue-tied. I haven't seen Tarantino since March of 2013. Thank you to all my family members that showed up from my mother, Jamari, J'Adora, aunt Celestine, my cousins; Kanika, Ayana, Djuan, Dayvon, Mark, along with aunt Janelle. Mark revealed to me that she didn't want to be there due to what I had revealed in *'Butterflies Hitting Home Runs'* about her son Gregory. At the time it didn't make sense to me why she didn't take advantage reading my book. My cousin Delvin revealed to me that my cousin Audrekia went through her mother's email, started reading the book, and had given her mother the inside scoop. That's what aunt Janelle was upset with me about. At the end of the day Gregory was my brother too and things were never the same after he was accused of that crime. Kendrell, Gregory's brother was still living in Maryland at the time and didn't show up to my 1st book party either. Last but certainly not least special thank you to aunt Patricia for allowing me to host my 1st book party in her gorgeous home. We never had a family event at aunt Patricia's again.

Sunday, September 14th, 2014

Sunday morning Diego was feeling a way and he wanted some ass. He followed me inside of my bathroom and basically took it in the dark. The entire situation was just weird. I had revealed to Racquel what we just did. We all got ready to start our day.

Racquel's family members that lived in the northern part of Maryland, attended my book party. She, Diego, and I went to go spend the entire day with them in Elkton, Maryland and we all had a blast. We didn't get back home until the early hours of Monday morning.

I didn't mind spending time with Diego however, I haven't had the chance to spend one on one quality time with Racquel.

Flashback:

IG Crush

By Diego and I only being strictly friends, I felt like the conversation exchange between Racquel and I didn't have to be restricted. Diego found out who my IG crush was. Diego knew of him, he was a popular guy on social media, brown skinned, bearded, and he was from the DMV area. He shouted me out twice on his Instagram account after my book was released. He first came across my Instagram account back in February, he followed me and sent me a DM. My IG crush and I didn't officially meet in person until April. Our first night together he instantly became the best fuck that I've ever had at the time. He fucked me like he was waiting his entire life to do my body right. Him and I went to the movies a couple times once to see Godzilla at Potomac Mills in Woodbridge, Virginia we both drove however, he had followed me back home. After the movies had ended, it was pouring down raining. The blue pants that I was wearing was a satin, thin material was stuck to my skin and you could see everything. Did I forget to mention that I wasn't wearing any underwear. We weren't even on the road 5 minutes and he called me.

"Pull over so we can fuck." He demanded.

"Where? This is your territory." I wondered.

"Follow me." He ordered.

We ended up in a large abandoned parking lot and it only rained harder. He got in my Jeep and went to work.

"This pussy is going to be the death of me." He declared.

Again, to see X-Men: Days of Future Past in Bowie, Maryland. Later I would regret being too honest with Diego about my past. My IG crush never met Jamari and J'Adora and a couple times he was in my home the same time as they were. There wasn't an interest there. I wasn't mad I already knew what it was. I knew he wasn't the one for me. A couple of people did find out that him and I had a past it wasn't through me though. That experience, I learned that the gay community is small, people are miserable and messy as hell. People aren't always what they post on social media. I was in and I got out safe and remained healthy before it was too late. Most importantly I didn't give my heart away. Him and I still follow each other on Instagram till this day.

Fast Forward:

Racquel didn't leave until Tuesday and that's when Diego decided to go home. The next event was celebrating Aaron's 30th birthday. I was hoping that Diego was going to attend it with me however, he got mad over a misunderstanding. I ended up going with Shana due to Diego blocking me, Aaron, Racquel, and Shana on Instagram, basically everyone that I was close to. Tarantino and his best friend were there as well. It was lit.

90: I'm A Masterpiece

Special thank you to you Chris who resides in the Caribbean island of Jamaica. Thank you for supporting my 1st book *'Butterflies Hitting Home Runs.'* Thank you for the artwork that you drew of myself: Instagram @NovemberTheDevil

Special thank you to you Alexander. Thank you for the personalized t-shirt that you made just for me. Thank you for coming all the way from Pennsylvania to support me at my 1st book party on September 13th, 2014. Thank you for the amazing artwork of myself. I still have the original frame and it remains hanging up on my wall. I'm forever grateful: Instagram @El_Alexander_World

Special thank you to you JerWayne Gunn. You were the 1st person to ever draw me. Matter of fact I no longer have the original photograph on my Instagram account, so this makes it even more special: Instagram @Boosieboo11

Thank you again JerWayne Gunn for the artwork of my family. This was J'Adora's 1st year at Lake Arbor Elementary and Jamari's 2nd. 'Bring Your Father To School Day' 2014 - 2015 school year: Instagram @Boosieboo11

Special thank you to you Dawyane James. You drew my
waist smaller than the actual photo, so I appreciate this
even more. Don't stop believing in your gift: Instagram
@Dawyane_Artistic

Aunt Dollie and my mother in their 20's.

91: **Aunt Dollie** *(1956 - 2014)*

November 21st, 2014

I had fallen asleep on the couch and I heard what sound like my mother coming downstairs. I looked at the time and it was after 4:00AM, in that moment I knew something was wrong. I didn't have in me to reach out to Delvin. I was never good dealing with death, and this one affected me deep. I took it upon myself to send out my condolences on my Instagram account. Delvin liked the post:

"Aunt Dollie you didn't play no games lol. You were loved and respected. I told you this, this past summer but thanks again for supporting me, my book **'Butterflies Hitting Home Runs'***, and accepting the real Andre before you passed. I enjoyed spending time with you on Holden Beach this past summer in Supply, North Carolina. It was great seeing you smile and letting go. You visited Maryland last month. I cherished every day you were here. You were so determined to attend church every night but the highlight for me was making you and I smoothies and watching Little House on the Prairie while Jamari and J'Adora were in school during the day. We will continue to stay strong as a family. Aunt Dollie I love you and now you can finally rest in peace. Tell grandma I said hello and tell her happy birthday since it's tomorrow Saturday, November 22nd, also tell grand-daddy I said hello too. Until we meet again."*

The last time I spoken to Delvin was October 13th, 2014.

Poetice Justice with **Simone Stewart**
Friday at 7:28 AM · 🌐

OUR BLACK MEN ARE WALKING AROUND HERE LOOKING LIKE THIS BECAUSE MOST OF OUR BLACK WOMEN APPROVES AND ENCOURAGES IT. STOP IT!!! We need our MEN to be MEN, STAND UP.. #enoughisenough #itswartime

 Milk Man
9 hours ago · 🌐

I Guess weight wasn't the only thing Rick Ross lost .. 😂😂😂😂😂😂

92: Viral

November 23rd, 2014

My friend Ronnie messaged me on Kik.

"My Andre." It said.

He sent me a photo of myself that I had uploaded to my Instagram account, earlier in the month on November 3rd.

"I found this on Facebook My Andre, and I went in on the person." He then explained.

"Are you serious My Ronnie?" I asked.

I honestly didn't know what to say, I read the messages from strangers and they were disgusting. Good thing I didn't have a Facebook account at the time. I eventually went to sleep.

November 24th, 2014

Thanksgiving Day

I woke up to even more Kik messages, DMs, and being tagged in the photo on Instagram. It got so bad I ended up removing Kik from my bio. It was the worst Thanksgiving of my life, losing my aunt Dollie three days prior, to my photo going viral from people of color leaving discourteous opinions. I had wanted to delete my Instagram account however, my story was helping a lot of people, especially men. My purpose of being on social media was much bigger than myself. However, I did thank everyone that defended me. I didn't celebrate my 31st, birthday on November 29th, that year. Aaron, Shana, and Tarantino all wanted to, but I wasn't feeling it.

93: *Watermelon Seeds Of Daddy* (2nd Book)

Flashback:

The following chapter was a post that I stole from my Instagram account, which was uploaded on October 9th, 2014. *'Watermelon Seeds Of Daddy'* was released on April 14th, 2015.

*"Reflecting: I don't know what it is about the hours of 12:00AM - 6:00AM, however those are the hours that I'm awaken by God's voice and I must start writing. Working on my 2nd book, a children's book: **'Watermelon Seeds Of Daddy'** has me thinking a lot because it's inspired by the great single fathers of the world. My son Jamari turned 8 Saturday, October 18th, 2014. 8 years in the game of being a daddy. Blessed? Yes. Bittersweet? Yes. The above picture is the only picture of my father, mother, and I together taken the early winter of 1984. Adron is his name, such a tall man he is. I wished I had his height and his hair still at that age he is in the photograph. I wonder have my father picked up a copy of my first book: **'Butterflies Hitting Home Runs'**? Does he even care? Even though my father wasn't a part of my life, I still didn't use that as an excuse, if one day I decided to become a dad to be like him. I made a choice that I would be the best dad ever. Being a parent is one of the most challenging, yet rewarding, it's literally a 24/7, 365 days a year responsibility. What I have learned about being a parent is the only thing that children desire is to be loved, they crave attention, they want their parent's approval, and above all they want to make their parents proud. You see? Love is free. I love looking at old photographs because I'm able to relive those special*

moments, the good old days. I still have a couple of pictures of me and my children's mother together before the children came. We were so childish, happy, innocent, naive, young, and the best of friends back then; however, that's the past too. The journey that I'm now on is exciting, scary, and unpredictable however, I'm blessed to have God. Well that's all for now. Thanks again to my family and friends who's still riding with the 30-year-old kid."

94: No Call. No Show.

Flashback:

Sunday, January 25th, 2015

Jai had moved back in with her mother, father, and two of her sisters in their apartment less than 5 minutes away from me, in the beginning of the year. She had texted me to let me know that's where I could pick up Jamari and J'Adora. I knew I wasn't getting out the Jeep, so I put on one of my mother's dashikis that passed well below my knees and I wore my black and yellow batman cap. I hopped in the Jeep and headed in that direction. I called her to let her know that I was outside. Jamari and J'Adora got inside the Jeep. I was heading back home.

"Daddy grandpa cut my hair." He said.

I turned around so fast to look at him, that I hurt my neck.

"Let me see you Jamari." I demanded. I turned on the lights inside of my Jeep. "Oh, they know better." I snapped.

I immediately called Jai. No answer. I called back and still no answer. Jai knew why I was calling. "Oh, she doesn't want to pick up. Well let me head right back fucking over there." I thought to myself. Once I got there I didn't even bother to park. I pushed the emergency flasher switch, hopped out the Jeep with Jamari and J'Adora. I knocked on the door and Jamie answered. I could see Jai sitting on the couch feeding her face and I seen her father as well.

"Jai you saw me calling you. Mr. Richards you don't have no right to put your hands-on Jamari's head. The shit looks horrible. What you could have done was call me and ask permission to take him to the barber shop or given me the money to do so. You all don't do shit for them financially." I snapped.

"My wife told me to do it." He cried.

"Your wife doesn't have the right either. I don't mess with that woman." I explained.

"You don't come up in here and disrespect my father, he's sick." Jai yelled.

"Sick or not, respect has to go both ways. He wasn't that sick when he violated Jamari's hair. It looks terrible. He literally cut off half his mohawk, no shapeup, or nothing. He has school in the morning. Now I must cut all his hair off. Do you not understand he's basically returning back to school bald. What if he's teased? You damn people don't think before acting." I yelled.

As Jai was getting up talking shit. I closed the damn door and left with Jamari and J'Adora. Once again this was another time of me wanting to beat her ass, her mother's ass for telling her husband to cut Jamari's hair, and her father's ass for doing it. Throw the whole damn family away.

On January 28th, 2015

I received a letter in the mail.

On Thursday, April 2nd, 2015 1:56PM, Brooks, Patricia

Community Mediation Prince Georges (CMPG)

April 2nd, 2015

Andre Simmons

152 Perth Amboy Ct.

Upper Marlboro, MD 20774

Re: CMG-15-01-0012

Dear Andre,

This letter is to confirm that your mediation session has been scheduled for:

Date: Monday, April 13th, 2015

Time: 10:30AM

Place: South Bowie Library

15301 Hall Road, Bowie, MD 20721

PLEASE NOTE Other mediators from our program may be present during the session to observe the mediation for quality assurance reasons. Any additional participants must be discussed with the office prior to your session. All participants must agree for the individual to attend for them to participate in the session.

We ask that you arrive to your scheduled location promptly for mediation. In order to be fair to all participants, mediators and staff, we request that cancellations not be made except in cases of emergency. If you will not be able to attend, please contact our office at least 24 hours in advance.

Please plan on the process lasting approximately 2 hours. If more time is necessary, you will have the opportunity to schedule more time immediately after the initial mediation. If you have any further questions or concerns regarding your mediation, please contact me at 301-XXX-XXXX.

Sincerely,

Patricia Brooks

Mediation Staff

Fast Forward:

I wrote Jai a letter.

April 28th, 2015

"Ms. Richards, On Monday, April 19th, 2015 you and I attended J'Adora Krismas Simmons's last I.E.P. meeting for the calendar school year. You didn't attend Jamari Ondrej Simmons's I.E.P. meeting so I was left to make all the final decisions. J'Adora's teacher Ms. Sternberg mentioned that after every weekend J'Adora had trouble retaining what she learned the previous week. Every weekend Jamari and J'Adora are with you, Ms. Richards. Long before Ms. Sternberg brought this to both of our attention. I, Andre L. Simmons have pleaded with you many times, for the past 2 school calendar years, how important it was for both Jamari and J'Adora to get the proper rest at night. By Jamari and J'Adora taking naps during the school day, it pushes their sleep schedule back. On many occasions when Jamari and J'Adora both have taken naps while they were in your care, I've witness on many occasions how restless they both became at night during their sleeping hours. By morning Jamari and J'Adora are extra groggy than usual because of their lack of sleep from

the previous night. Jamari and J'Adora are then affected during the school hours of learning, due to poor sleep from the night before. Ms. Richards you know this to be true.

During mid-January - February of the school calendar year of 2013 - 2014, for the 2nd time you attempted to keep Jamari and J'Adora for one week on and one week off again. I didn't challenge you because Ms. Richards you said it would be a way for you to spend more time with Jamari and J'Adora, and that their school learning hours wouldn't be affected by it. Jamari Ondrej Simmons and J'Adora Krismas Simmons both had upcoming I.E.P. meetings in the beginning of February, where all parties involved notice a dramatic change in both of Jamari and J'Adora's learning abilities and behavior. The one week on and one week off didn't work in their favor. Jamari and J'Adora were back to their regular 5 days a week with their father I, Andre L. Simmons.

On January 28th, 2015 my mother, Joyce Simmons and I, Andre L. Simmons received a notice by mail from the Community Mediation Prince George's (CMPG). This letter was initiated by you, Ms. Richards. My mother and I had no problem with this meeting if it were going to end conflict between you and I, when it came to Jamari and J'Adora. On April 2nd, 2015 I've received a 2nd letter from (CMPG) letting me know that the meeting would be held on Monday, April 13th, 2015 10:30AM, at South Bowie Library. On April 13th, 2015 my mother and I showed up to the meeting. We waited for about 30 minutes before we called to find out the status of the meeting. Then we founded out that you canceled the meeting due to your work schedule. I was never called nor notified by letter that you did this. The purpose of the meeting was to end all conflict between you and me. On April 19*th*, 2015 the same day as J'Adora's I.E.P. meeting, J'Adora said she took a nap by you that evening, the same day as the meeting. I called you by phone to express to you how important it was for Jamari and J'Adora not to take a nap during school evenings of Sunday - Thursday but you never responded back. Last night on April 27*th*, 2015 Jamari informed me that he had taken a nap that you granted. The past couple of weeks I have stated to Jamari and J'Adora in front of you, pleading to them not to take a nap. Ms. Richards you insist on doing things your way. I'm writing you this letter to inform you that Jamari and J'Adora both have delayed learning disabilities. It's very important for them to sleep at night, so that during the day, Jamari and J'Adora are both alert and aware during school learning hours. I hope my words are affective enough for you, Ms. Richards to comprehend, that I, Andre L. Simmons is a concerned father and I want the best for our children Jamari Ondrej Simmons and J'Adora Krismas Simmons. I will be doing everything in my power to do so from this day forth."

Andre L. Simmons

95: **Baltimore**

Summer 2015

The last time Jai asked me was I seeing anyone was back in 2012 and it wasn't none of her business back then or was it now. However, she made it her business to tell me that she was seeing someone who resided in Baltimore, Maryland. When Jamari and J'Adora were with their mother on the weekends, at Jai's mom's, they would sleep on the couch in the living room. Jamari and J'Adora said sometimes their mother wouldn't always be there with them and they would spend the entire weekend with Jai's mother. I thought that was cute for the person who claimed they wanted their children but was running to Baltimore.

I didn't have a problem with the situation until Jamari and J'Adora started going up there for the weekends and she expected me to drive 45 minutes up there to pick them up, That's dead. I ended up finding out that he was a father of 3 from previous relationships, around our age, worked as a correction officer. The other interesting fact was there was another woman living there already who wasn't a relative of his, let's call her The Other Woman. At the time Jamari and J'Adora didn't have anything bad to say about the way he treated them.

Jai wanted me to meet him and I knew that I would eventually. At first Jai would drive from Baltimore with him, along with his daughter, and son, to pick up Jamari and J'Adora for the weekends. Then suddenly Jai got so comfortable that he started driving down without Jai to pick up Jamari and J'Adora. That's when it was time for him and I to meet. Let's call him Zazu, yes like the character from The Lion King. He revealed to me that he had an 18-year-old son that he wasn't that close to, a daughter who was a few years older than Jamari, and a son who was a couple of years younger than J'Adora. I did confirm to him what I'm sure Jai already told him that I was gay. He confirmed that Jai did tell him. He had revealed to me that he had to get on Jai about sleeping all the time while Jamari and J'Adora were up there for the weekends. He wondered what the point was going to war with me if all she was going to do was sleep. I was shocked when he asked me was Jai slow. My reply was people used to make fun of us both when she and I worked at Shoppers however, that was why we clicked in the first place. My only advice to him was stick around and he would discover what type of woman she truly was. It was above me now. I also let him know that everything would remain cool between him and I if no boundaries were crossed when it came to my children.

96: **Uber**

Flashback:

On Thursday, July 9th, 2015 my mother celebrated her 61st birthday. I didn't have much to offer; however, I made sure she came home to a cooked meal and a clean home. Jamari and J'Adora gifted her each with their own creative home-made birthday cards. Little did I know, my mother had me a surprise as well. She purchased me an iPhone 6 Plus. I couldn't believe it. It's been a year since I had a phone. I also believed it was her own way of telling me, she was proud of me that I was a published author however, these bills weren't going to pay themselves.

When **'Butterflies Hitting Home Runs'** was released last June, I was able to live off my book sales for months. **'Watermelon Seeds Of Daddy'** was released in April and didn't perform as well. It was a children's story and most of my following were from the gay community. Men, preferably it was preachers, guys in relationships, or the ones who claimed to be single always DMed me about my body and wanting to see me naked. I was able to sell a few books by me DMing a nude here and there. Most of them wanted to see my ass and that's what they received, a video of me twerking butt ass naked. I wasn't proud of what I was doing however, I looked at it as a business opportunity. I always felt like I was an exotic dancer in my past life anyway. Furthermore, I wasn't fucking for cash or putting my health at risk. I started applying for night jobs. Something that wouldn't interfere with Jamari and J'Adora's school schedule. My mother would be home with them during the night. I became so desperate for cash, the first call back from anywhere I was taking that job.

July 31st, 2015

I came across the car driving service called Uber. I was skeptical at first. The potential money that could be made in a week was unbelievable. However, I applied anyway. The requirements: *You must be at least 21 years old. Licensed to drive in the U.S.A. for at least one year, or three years if you're under the age of 23. Have access to a 4-door vehicle that is 10 years old or newer. In-state auto insurance with your name on the policy. In-state driver license.* The entire process took about 30 days.

Fast Forward:

September 2nd, 2015

I was on my way to Costco in Lanham, Maryland when I received an email from Uber saying: *"Congratulations Andre. You are now free to take your first trip."* I immediately called my mother, aunt Janelle, and Aaron to share with them the great news. I downloaded the app to my phone. My first trip took me to Washington D.C. during rush hour. Oh, the agony. Not to mention how much I loathed D.C. traffic; however, I was blessed to be officially working again.

97: **Madonna** *(Rebel Heart Tour)*

September 12th, 2015

Aaron turned 31 three days ago, and it was time to celebrate him. Even though he was the one who purchased the tickets for us to see Madonna. The crazy part he was telling people I purchased them. Aaron's the type of person that will go far and beyond to support people that he loved, and never want the credit. So, if you're reading this Aaron and even though I tell you this often. Thank you, I appreciate you, I don't take you for granted, and I love you.

Me being a huge Janet Jackson fan, I was determined to put my bias feelings aside and judge Madonna live for myself. The show was postponed for about a half an hour. However, it was worth the wait, Madonna's show was something that I've never experience before at concert. People can say what they want about her, for me she's the queen of stage production. Janet would mop the floor with Madonna when it comes to the choreography though. I have a newfound respect for Madonna as an entertainer, after that night. Another legend was under my belt.

98: 20 Something *(Part Two)*

Flashback:

Over the summer Diego had came into some money. He told me where it came from even though it was sketchy sounding, it was still none of my business. We were spending so much time together and I was genuinely happy. Him and I went to the movies so much that summer and we were fucking any and everywhere. One of the sweetest gestures that Diego had ever done for me was allowing me to use his credit card to order books and mail out to my readers. I took it as a sign that he not only supported me but trusted me as well.

The Fourth of July

Jamari and J'Adora were with their mother for the weekend and my mother along with the rest of the family spent the day at the beach. Diego and I went to LongHorn Steakhouse located in Laurel, Maryland. Something was different about him that day. He seem kind of anxious and nervous. He ordered me my favorite, White Cheddar Stuffed Mushrooms, for an appetizer.

"So, Andre." He stated.

"Oh my god." I started thinking. What is he about to ask me?

"Yes Diego?" I said smiling back.

"I was wondering will you be my boyfriend?" He explained.

Part of me wanted to say I do however, I was afraid to tell him yes for the simple reason. I still wasn't working, and I knew that I should've been. I wanted to be with him however, I can't keep having him run in and out of my life every time there was a disagreement. I think that's why he was always allowed to come back in my life just because there wasn't a title involved or maybe it was because no one I've ever dated or was getting to know compared to Diego. Age aside I knew Diego was something special and I felt he was worth the wait.

"I want to say yeah. I just need more time; however, I'm telling you no Diego." I replied.

His demeanor changed. "I hope I didn't make a big mistake by not telling him yes." I had thought.

Fast Forward:

Friday, October 9th, 2015

October 1st - December 31st had always been my favorite time of year. The leaves changed colors and starts to fall. The weather became cooler, not to mentioned that's when we had our first born, plus I had been taking Jamari and J'Adora trick-or-treating since 2012. I was low-key excited that Diego and I was going to make it through the holiday season this time around.

Diego was coming over later that night. My mother gave me permission to use her car to pick him up. Diego and I were going to have a little cookout on Saturday since my mother weren't going to be home for the entire day. After I picked him up, we headed to the grocery store. Diego always said he slept better at my home than anywhere else and boy could he sleep.

Saturday, October 10th, 2015

My mother left around 6:00AM that morning. I didn't bother to wake him up and I went to my favorite place in my home which was my bathroom and just started scrolling Instagram. I had to be in the bathroom over 45 minutes. I could hear him coming up the stairs.

"What you are doing?" He asked.

"I'm in the bathroom." I responded. "I didn't want to disturb you because you were sleeping. You don't have to stay in the basement. We have the whole house to ourselves." I continued.

"When are we going to start grilling?" He questioned.

"Whenever, we don't have to rush." I explained.

I don't know what gotten into him, but he didn't care for my response too much. He had mentioned something about me being on social media talking to dudes.

"Diego go downstairs and start prepping the food!" I snapped.

Diego rushed back down the steps, I could hear the basement door open, then I could hear him stomping down those steps as well. Then it went silent. About a minute later, I heard Diego stomp back up the steps, hopefully it was to apologize to me. However, he left out the front door. I just sat there on the damn toilet in disbelief. I didn't move for about 10 minutes hoping he would have walked back through the front door so that we could spend the evening together like we had planned. I came to the realization that I was living in a fantasy. I had finally gone to my bedroom; he had taken all his things with him. However, I did find out that he had left a pair of jeans, his ID, and house keys which I put in a plastic bag. I spent the rest of my Saturday lying in bed thinking about him. I never heard from him for the rest of the weekend.

Monday, October 12th, 2015

Diego sent an iMessage asking me did he leave his keys over there. I replied back yes, and I had also let him know that he had left his ID as well. He said that he was on his way over there collect it. I replied that his items would be in a plastic bag hanging on the front doorknob. Part of me wanted to see him again however, I had to accept the fact that we were too toxic for one another. The worst part of it all and I don't know when the feeling took over me, but I had finally fallen in love with Diego.

99: Snickerdoodle *(Part One)*

Sunday, November 1st, 2015

As good as I like to claim my memory is, I'm not quite sure how I ended up on his page. The thing I do know is that we've been following each other for a while. From his photos I could clearly see he was all about family and loved to cook. What sparked another interest was a certain photograph with cookies and not just any old cookies, they were snickerdoodles. The ones from Iverson Mall, located in Maryland. So, he had to be from the DMV area. I left a comment under the photo which was dated March 10th, 2014. Yes, I know I'm a creep.

"Lmbo! I just knew it before I read the caption." I said.

"Lol bomb. I just might go get some today." He replied.

"Haha I should meet you up there. I haven't been up there in years." I explained.

"That would be awesome just let me know." He stated.

I had decided to do something that I rarely ever do. I slid into his DMs. I sent him the photo of himself holding two little babies. I was right he was from the DMV area. He was getting ready to attend a baby shower. After DMing back and forth I asked him if he had WhatsApp. He assured me if I wasn't crazy that we could exchange phone numbers. I did mention to him that I was a writer and that I published two books **'Butterflies Hitting Home Runs'** and **'Watermelon Seeds Of Daddy'**. He told me to bring them both so he could buy them to support me. The date was set for us to meet the following day at the 7-Eleven off of Harry S. Truman and we would proceed from there to Iverson Mall to have our snickerdoodle cookies.

Monday, November 2nd, 2015

We linked up a little after 6:00PM. From his photos I never really paid attention to his looks however, over the years he became more attractive in my opinion, especially with the little extra weight gain. When I had first laid eyes on him in person was a different story. This damn man was stacked, His face and dreads just added to everything else. We talked for a few and headed to the mall. It felt good. To know me is to know that I cherish the little things. The cookies were still good as ever. I didn't want to come off too thirsty because those D.C. natives always came off as hard. I guess I passed the test because he asked to see me for lunch the following day at the Chinese buffet called Teppanyaki Grill located in Lanham, Maryland. I knew of the one he was referring to because my aunt Celestine and Paula talked about how good the food was there. There was no kiss before we parted ways however, we did hug.

Tuesday, November 3rd, 2015

Makah picked me up from my home and we headed to our lunch outing. The food was good, and I never knew they did hibachi there either however, Makah was the highlight for me. After we left, we went back to his place. His home reminded me of the country and especially my grandmother's home. I asked him if it would be cool if I took a photo of him holding the books and he agreed. I was shocked when he asked if we could take a photo together. I hope that it wouldn't be a problem especially with him still being in love with his ex, even though they were no longer together. Makah had uploaded a 4-photo collage of us, and I had uploaded my favorite one of us. Of course, I lost a couple of followers and my DMs were lit with questions and congratulations. The funny part of it all Makah was questioned by his ex about what was going on between him and I. In the back of my mind I hoped that wasn't his motive, to make his ex jealous.

100: Freaky Friday

Flashback:

So about 3 weeks of driving with Uber, my Jeep had finally given out on me. I took Lady Gaga aka my Jeep to several places and the cost of repair wasn't worth it. Like every time I took one foot forward, I was faced with another dilemma. It was one thing not having a job, now I was without a working vehicle. The worst part of it all my Jeep was paid off. I slowly slipped into a depression. When I looked back on things with Diego, he walked away from me when I needed him most. However, meeting Makah became my light at the end of the tunnel, even if it was a temporary flame.

Fast Forward:

November 6th, 2015

"Andre lets go see what they're going to say about us getting approve for a car. We won't know unless we try." My mother explained.

I got myself together. I just threw on anything and put a black rubber band around the end of my beard. My mother and I headed to the Waldorf Ford: Ford Dealership in Waldorf, Maryland.

"Is there anything you want in particular?" My mother asked.

"A working car would be a blessing." I suggested.

Once we arrived, we walked around and looked at cars. We were approached by a car salesman. We eventually settled for a 2016 black Ford Fusion. Now my mother had to go get approved for it. When my mother and I were walking back inside I just had to say it.

"Mom he reminds me of my dad." I said and giggled.

"Andre, he sho shit don't." She replied in her heavy North Carolina accent.

I said no more. I needed my car. After about 20 minutes of doing paperwork, He said we were approved. I just wanted to scream and shout right there. I wasn't appropriately dressed to take photos with Freaky Friday however, I drove off the parking lot with a brand-new car and I couldn't wait to see the look on Jamari and J'Adora's faces. I couldn't wait to see Makah that evening. My family and friends wanted to know why I gave my car the name.

Freaky Friday: 6th day + 11th month + 15th year = 32 which was the age I was turning on November 29th, 2015.

101: **I Just Wanna Fuck**

Flashback:

I was looking forward to spending my birthday with Makah. He wanted to take me to San Antonio Bar & Grill located in D.C. I was so excited because I haven't celebrated my birthday since 2013 with Red and Diego. Last year was canceled due to my photo going viral and losing my aunt Dollie to cancer.

Well that was until he iMessaged me if we could reschedule due to him getting too fucked up the night before. I didn't know how to feel. My feelings were torn. On one hand maybe I was moving too fast and expected too much too soon. He wasn't my boyfriend and he was honest with the fact that he was still in love with his ex, even though it wasn't possible for a reconciliation between them, well that's what he revealed to me. Not to mentioned I was the one who slid in his DMs. Makah and I messed around however, we never had full intercourse sex. Another year of me working on my birthday. I did receive an iMessage from Tarantino wishing me a happy birthday.

December 1st, 2015

Getting in my car to meet up with Makah, to celebrate my belated birthday outing. I ripped my favorite black studded leggings. I was pissed and had to change my entire outfit. I was over the evening. The drinks and the calamari were delicious. Wishful thinking, I took an extra special shower due to it being my birthday and all. Did my Makah and I have birthday sex? The answer is no.

Fast Forward:

Sunday, December 6th, 2015

I was out Ubering in Silver Springs, Maryland and I was checking my emails and noticed Diego had sent me an email.

"Happy Birthday. I'm sorry that I'm late." He said.

"Thank you." I responded.

"What are you doing?" He wondered.

"Ubering." I responded.

"What are you doing after that?" He asked.

"I don't have anything planned." I declared.

"I get off at 11:00PM." He stated.

"Oh, you still work at the hotel?" I asked.

"Yea." He responded.

"Alright. I see you at 11:00PM." I said.

I already knew what was going to go down. I needed and wanted some dick. I wasn't looking for love, not from him not anymore. Besides when he walked away back in

October, I no longer had a vehicle. I couldn't wait to see the look on his face.

"Hello sir." He said once he got in and gave me a hug.

"Hi, Diego." I responded.

"When you get this?" He wondered.

"November 6th." I responded.

"Okay. Okay." He said.

"So where are we headed?" I wondered.

"I got us a room in D.C. near The Wharf." He informed.

My nerves were starting to get the best of me. Then I started thinking Andre enjoy the moment as Tony would always tell me, and that's what I did. When we arrived, I didn't think that the hotel would have been so upscale. Come to think about it, Diego and I had never stayed in a hotel together and this was my first time not paying for a room. He told me where to park so that I wouldn't get a ticket.

Once we entered the room I sat down on the bed. He took off his clothes and got butt ass naked as he walked to the bathroom to take a shower.

"Andre what are you doing here?" I said aloud.

When Diego came from out the bathroom, he was still partially moist. Even though I didn't have a change of clothes I got into the shower anyway. Soon as I was done, I didn't bother to dry off. I walked back to the King size bed dripping wet, pulled back the covers and sheets, and got in. Not even 5 seconds he brought his warm bare body closer to mine and I could feel his dick pressed against my ass growing and throbbing by the second. "Damn I miss this boy spooning me. But fuck it let me do what I came here to do so I can leave." I had thought. I turned my body to face his. I could only look into his eyes for only a second. I closed my eyes as we started kissing passionately. I forgot how great it was just kissing him. We kissed for what liked same forever before we fucked the night away. He slept holding me.

Monday, December 7th, 2015

5:00AM

My alarm went off and I got up to get dressed.

"Where are you going?" He wondered.

"I need to get ahead of the morning rush, so I can make it back in time to get Jamari and J'Adora ready for school." I replied.

"Ok, drive safe." He said.

"Thank you, Diego, for everything." I stated.

"You're welcome Big Head." He replied.

Makah Facetimed me a little after 7:00AM. He was at work. I was getting Jamari and J'Adora ready for school.

102: **Snickerdoodle** *(Part Two)*

December 25th, 2015

It's been 2 and a half weeks since I seen Diego. Between me Ubering to make as much money as I could for the holiday season, I tried to spend time with Makah as well. I invited Makah and his family which included his mother and younger brother Demetrius over for Christmas dinner to my mother's home. I was so happy that all three of them showed up.

I thought it would have been a great idea for us to spend New Year's together. It's not like we haven't seen each other naked. I already knew what he was working with. Makah was different when it came to that though. I've never came across someone who liked me and wasn't all over me sexually. When I had brought it to his attention, he didn't say no, but his response left me doubtful. Was he not feeling me or did his heart still belong to his ex?

New Year's didn't happen, we ended arguing about some dumb shit and I spent New Year's with my family yet again and I decided to just walk away from Makah.

January 29th, 2016

Exactly 30 days had passed, and I thought about Makah every day and that wasn't normal for me. I thought to myself if I call him and he didn't pick up I definitely wasn't going to call him ever again. Well he did pick up, we talked for a little bit. He claimed that he did call me once which I never received that call. I met up with Makah at his job the following Sunday morning. I had gone on a ride along with him. I didn't realize how much I missed that man until I was in his presence again. The following day I took Jamari and J'Adora over to his house and his mother offered to do J'Adora's hair.

103: I Can't Compete With A Baby

Sunday, February 28ᵗʰ, 2016

Jai had iMessaged me that she was unable to drop Jamari and J'Adora off due to her vehicle having a flat tire. I told her I would be up there around 2:00PM without any hesitation and all I needed was the address. This was my first time having to do that. At least I got the chance to see exactly where they were staying on the weekends. After arriving up there I noticed Zazu's black Dodge Charger's trunk was smashed in, such a pity. Anyway, I called her to let her know that I had arrived. "Let me call Tony back." I thought to myself, as Jamari and J'Adora were getting in the car.

"Hi daddy." Said J'Adora.

"Hi daddy." Said Jamari.

"Hello." I replied.

I called Tony back.

"Hello Tony, I'm back." I reassured.

"You picked my kids up?" He asked.

"Yes, I did. They're in the car now." I replied and giggled.

"Hi kids. How are you guys doing? Did you enjoy your weekend? I miss y'all." He soothed.

"Hi. Tony. Good. Yes. I miss you too." J'Adora said.

"Hi Tony. I'm good. It was ok. I miss you too." Jamari replied. "Daddy mommy is pregnant." He then revealed.

"Whoa! You hear that Tony? How do you know this to be true Jamari?" I questioned.

"She told us." Jamari replied.

"Do you know what she's having?" I asked.

"Mommy's having a boy daddy." J'Adora stated.

"Yeah. Mommy said her Zazu are going to get married, and he's going to become our dad too." Jamari replied.

"Well that's fine however, mommy and I would have to get a divorce before that all can happen if that were to actually happen, Zazu would become your step-father." I reassured.

"Be nice Andre." Tony stated.

"I am, just stating facts though." I cautioned.

Jamari Ondrej Simmons, J'Adora Krismas Simmons, and Andre LeDale Simmons. This photo was taken 2 days before Jamari was admitted to the hospital. *March 9th, 2016.*

"Nobody wins when the family feuds." - Shawn Corey Carter

104: **Blood Son**

Monday, March 7th, 2016

That morning getting Jamari and J'Adora ready for school. Jamari was a little sluggish.

"Jamari are you ok?" I wondered.

"Daddy I'm so tired." He stated as he just sat down on the closet floor looking for his school shoes.

"Tired from what? Did you stay up past your bedtime? I need to know why you're so tired." I questioned.

"No, I'm just so tired daddy." He whispered.

"When you return home from school, you can take a nap since you're so tired." I confirmed.

Later that afternoon, Makah treated me to drinks. My mother called me. She informed me that she took Jamari to the doctor due to how fatigued he was and that the doctor wanted to talk to me in private about what Jamari and J'Adora revealed to her. The call from my mother kind of put a damper on the mood so we left shortly afterwards.

Tuesday, March 8th, 2016

My mother didn't go to work on Tuesday and I walked into her room to discuss what was going on with Jamari.

"What did Jamari reveal to his doctor?" I questioned.

"They were doing a regular check up on him, she followed up with questions, and that's when Jamari revealed that Zazu had hit him before and J'Adora said it as well." She explained.

"Really mom?" I said. I started thinking about how Jai was never forthcoming with certain information, she would cover up for her family all the time. Was it possible that Jai was protecting her boyfriend? Was it ruff play or did he really put his hands on my kid and overstepped his boundaries? So many questions ran through my head. Jai knew I didn't play about my children. "I'm about to iMessage her right now." I continued.

"Did Zazu hit Jamari?" I iMessaged.

"What are you talking about?" Jai iMessaged.

"DID YOUR BOYFRIEND HIT MY SON?" I iMessaged.

"No, he has never put his hands-on Jamari. I wouldn't let him hurt my children or me." Jai iMessaged.

"That's not what Jamari revealed to his doctor yesterday and J'Adora backed up his statement. I'm going in the morning to see her and I highly recommend that you show up. I don't know what to believe now. Jamari and J'Adora said he did, and you said he didn't. This is serious." I iMessaged.

"Where's his doctor located?" Jai iMessaged.

"The same place that Jamari and J'Adora have been going to since they were born. They open at 9:00AM." I iMessaged.

Wednesday, March 9th, 2016

I sent Jamari and J'Adora off to school. Jai was outside my home around 8:50AM. When I walked outside. She rolled down her window and asked where Jamari was, and I told her that I sent him off to school. She followed me to the doctor's office. When Jai got out of the car you could tell that she was pregnant. We walked inside the doctor's office together and all eyes were on us. Those people probably thought the baby in her belly was mine. I rushed to the front, only for the receptionist to tell us that their primary care physician wasn't in and wouldn't be in until Thursday. I let her know that I would be back tomorrow. Jai and I left out. Before departing I wanted her to know while she was on the phone with Zazu that for all their sake, I was hoping that he didn't put his hands-on Jamari, which led us to have a huge argument in the parking lot. I called my mother and Makah to let them know what had just transpired.

Thursday, March 10th, 2016

Each day I was monitoring Jamari very closely and I decided to once again send him to school, since he didn't go on Tuesday. I went to their doctor's office yet again and this time I didn't see Jai. I wasn't calling her to remind her where she should've been. I walked into the office building exactly at 11:00AM, the time his physician should've been there. About 5 minutes of waiting I was called to the back.

His doctor was talking to me and was notified that Jai was on the phone and wanted to listen in on the conversation. His doctor asked did I mind and of course I didn't. After discussing Jamari's health that's when the alleged allegations were brought up. Jai was on speaker phone and you could hear that another person was on the phone with her. The doctor wanted to know about the living arrangements concerning Jamari and J'Adora. The doctor did ask questions concerning the boyfriend.

"He's a great man and he would never hurt my kids. He's just really stern." Jai said in Zazu's defense.

The room went silent. The doctor and I looked at each other after she made that statement.

The doctor informed us both that when a child construct those type of claims, it was their job to report the situation to social services so they could investigate the matter further. The doctor also suggested that Jamari and J'Adora temporarily shouldn't spend the weekends with their mother until the matter was finalize and we all agreed, shortly afterwards Jai hung up the phone.

"I've been a doctor for years now, mom seems like she's protecting the boyfriend. Dad it's your responsibility to protect both children." She stated.

Once I left the doctor's office I went back home. I wasn't even laying down for five minutes and my phone rung. It was Jamari and J'Adora's school calling. The school nurse informed me that Jamari had vomited and if I could come and pick him up for early dismissal. When I had arrived, he was pale. I received another call from Jamari's doctor informing me to pick up the documents from earlier at the office.

Friday, March 11th, 2016

My mother didn't work on Friday and informed me that she was going to take Jamari to LabCorp located in Laurel, Maryland. I told her that I would be at Just Tires getting my oil changed if she needed me. While at Just Tires my mother called me.

"Andre this boy is too weak to get his blood drawn; I'm going to take him Bowie Health Center." She stated.

"Ok mom I'll meet you there once I wrap things up." I said.

Once I had arrived, they had Jamari plugged up to an (IV) due to extreme dehydration. We were later notified around 12:00PM that Jamari was going to be transferred to Children's National located in Washington D.C. I updated Jai on what was going on. She said that she didn't get off work until 6:00PM so that meant Jai wasn't going to arrive until 7:30PM - 8:00PM. She did say her mother was going to come. I haven't heard a peep from Jai's mother since she left a bible verse for *'Butterflies Hitting Home Runs'* as a review on Amazon. How could I forget the one star that she rated the book as well?

A Psalm of David

March 6th, 2015

Format: Paperback

*"The Lord is my shephard I shall not want he maketh me
to lie down in gree pastures he leadeth me beside the still
waters. He restores my soul: he leadeth me in the paths of
righteousness for his names sake Yes thou I walk through
the valley of the shadow of death I will fear no evil; for
thouart with me ; thou rod and staff they comfort me;
Thou preparest a table beforeme in the presence of mine
enemies; thou anointest my head with oil; my cup
runneth over. Surely goodness and mercy shall follow me
all the days of my life: and I will dwell in the house of the
Lord foreve. Psalm 23."*

It was going to be interesting to see her lovely face once
again. I had to leave to go pick J'Adora up from her bus
stop. I FaceTimed Makah to update him on what was going
on.

"You look handsome." He said.

"Whaaa… You never said that to me before." I gushed.

Now back to Jamari. Once I had arrived back with J'Adora,
we were informed that an ambulance would be moving
Jamari to Children's National. It was going to be either my
mother or myself. When Jai had finally arrived, she
couldn't stay too long, she had to report back to Baltimore.
I chose to stay with J'Adora, and my mother went with
Jamari.

Later that evening when I had arrived to Children's
National, Jamari was once again plugged up to an (IV). The
doctors diagnosed Jamari with Inflammatory Bowel's
Disease. Jamari was bleeding from his bowels. That's why
I was unaware what was causing him to be fatigued and
vomit. Jamari was most likely bleeding for weeks and we
were all clueless because he wasn't telling anyone about it

due to it being painless. I'm assuming his body had finally reached its limit. Jamari's mother has had Crohn's Disease since a child. A blood transfusion was highly recommended due to how much blood he loss, if I didn't consent Jamari wasn't going to live. I read over the side effects and I also asked many questions. I signed the dotted line. Jamari received the blood transfusion. I uploaded a video to my Instagram account Saturday, March 12th, 2016 after his energy, color to his face, lips, and hands had all returned.

Friday, March 18th, 2016

My friend Shana was hosting her birthday dinner at Bistro Bis located at Union Station, Washington D.C. I didn't want to go due to where Jamari was; however, she supported me at my book party, and she was one of the sweetest people ever.

Monday, March 21st, 2016

Even though I had communicated with Jamari's teacher on what was going on. I still needed to go up there and pick up work that he had missed over the past week not to mentioned Easter break was approaching. When I walked in one of my favorite staff members was there.

"Hi Dad." She said.

"Hello, Ms. A." I replied.

"How are you doing?" She asked.

"I'm doing good just ready for Jamari to come home." I said.

"I know you are. How's he doing?" She wondered.

"He's doing much better. They're looking to release him this week." I stated.

"Dad what's going on between you and mom?" She wondered.

Jai never stops. I wished she would go and sit her pregnant ass down somewhere.

"Why are you asking that?" I asked confused.

"Well mom called up here inquiring about the process of withdrawing Jamari and J'Adora from school." She explained.

"That's not going to happen." I stated.

"Who registered the kids in school?" She wondered.

"I registered Jamari by myself. She and I registered J'Adora together the following school year, due to me asking her to do so, to make her feel like she was involved in something." I explained.

"Well mom can withdraw J'Adora." She explained.

"Again, that's not going to happen." I snapped.

"Dad calm down and this is what you need to do to protect your children. I'm going to give you a new registration form for J'Adora. You also will need to get your lease agreement notarized." She explained.

I then asked Ms. A could she step outside for a second so that I could explain to her everything since Jai made it known to the school that all wasn't well between, she and I.

Soon as I left the school, I went to Upper Marlboro courthouse and finally filed for divorce and custody over Jamari and J'Adora. I also spoke to someone about what my rights were as a parent. When I confided in them about the situation and the fact that it was a pending social services case, the individual told me to stand my ground because I had the right to protect my children.

Tuesday, March 22nd, 2016

"Hey, they're releasing Jamari on Wednesday. I can pick up the kids on Thursday or Easter Sunday for spring break." Jai iMessaged.

What's wrong with her? He wasn't even out the hospital yet. I didn't respond to that for the simple reason we had agreed that Jamari and J'Adora wouldn't be going to Baltimore until the matter was resolved with social services.

Wednesday, March 23rd, 2016

Makah was having a cookout at his home and we went over there, even though we didn't stay long. I received the same iMessage from Jai yet again.

"Hey, they're releasing Jamari on Wednesday. I can pick up the kids on Thursday or Easter Sunday for spring break." Jai iMessaged.

"Listen, we agreed that they wouldn't go up there due to the case pending. You're more than welcome to come and visit them. I would leave my home." I iMessaged.

"Im not coming inside that house. They're doctor isn't the police an you cant keep me from my children." Jai iMessaged.

You could tell Jai was mad due to the errors she just sent in the iMessage.

"I'm trying to save you a 45-minute trip because you would be wasting your time." I iMessaged.

Jai didn't reply.

Sunday, March 27th, 2016

Easter Sunday

Early Sunday morning Jai iMessaged me.

"This is a reminder that I will be picking up my kids today." Jai iMessaged.

I didn't reply.

The morning had gone by and I wanted to go Uber. The family was coming over for Easter dinner later in the afternoon. I felt like soon as I leave Jai was going to pop up however, I was hoping she had come to her senses. When The family had arrived, they assured me that everything was going to be ok and that I could go to work. My cousin Kanika had said that Jai changed her profile picture on her Facebook account, to a photo of Jamari in bed connected to an (IV) with a message that said: *"Help Me Get My Kids Back"* and that she also made a GoFundMe account to help her raise money. I didn't care because the people on the inside knew the truth on what was going on. Besides I no longer had a Facebook account at the time and all her family members that I knew of were blocked on Instagram.

My first trip took me to the Washington National Cathedral, in Washington D.C., which was going to take me 37 minutes to drop off my rider. Soon as my rider got out my car, I was on my way to pick up another rider and my mother called.

"Jai is here with her father and sisters to pick up Jamari and J'Adora." My mother said.

"What did you say?" I wondered.

"I told her that they weren't going. She said was going to call the cops if I don't hand them over." She said.

"Ok I'm on my way back now." I stated.

"The dark-skinned sister that Jai fought, was in the backseat filming the whole thing." My mother also said.

I knew it was going to take me over 30 minutes to reach back home. Hopefully I would arrive back before the cops reached there. About 15 minutes later my mother called me again.

"Where are you? The cops are here and they're looking for you." My mother stated.

"I'm on route 50 now speeding. Let me talk to the officer." I told my mother.

My mother handed the phone over the officer and he identified himself.

"I'm Andre Simmons. I'm Jamari and J'Adora's dad. There's a current pending investigation going on concerning our son Jamari. Allegedly their mother's boyfriend had hit Jamari. His primary physician had advised our children not go to Baltimore until the investigation was over. Their mother and I both agreed on this March 10th. I have the documents. Not only that our son was diagnosed with Inflammatory Bowel's Disease on March 11th and was in the hospital from March 11th - March 23rd." I explained.

"Wow! Say no more Mr. Simmons." The officer said.

The officer handed my mother back the home phone. A couple of minutes later my mother called me once again.

"Where are you now?" She wondered.

I'm pulling up. What happen?" I wondered.

"He told them all to leave. The police officer didn't leave until Jai and her family left." She explained.

When I pulled up and walked inside. Jamari and J'Adora were in the living room playing video games like nothing happened. The twins Dayvon and Djuan had seen Zazu at the smaller park across the street. I'm assuming Zazu had parked his car on the other side so he wouldn't be seen, clearly, he was the smart one and he knew what the agreement was between Jai and I, that's why he laid low.

Easter dinner was delicious that year.

April 1st, 2016

8:05AM

"Jamari's doctor closed up the case. Give me my children."
Jai iMessaged.

I didn't reply.

My first thoughts were, was she lying because it was too
early. I attempted to go back to sleep however, my mind
wouldn't let me and clearly the devil was busy that AM.
Jamari, J'Adora and I all got dressed. It was time for their
mother to get served. I drove to the Upper Marlboro police
station. I was told that they are unable to serve someone in
Baltimore because it was out of their jurisdiction. Off to
Baltimore I went. I had googled the Baltimore social
services office which was in the city. Once I had arrived
and spoke to someone about Jamari's case, the nice lady
informed me that I needed to go to the Baltimore county
location. She apologized for the mix up, held the
paperwork on file just in case, and she wished me the best.

I arrived at the Baltimore county location, walked in, we
were the only ones there. The place was full of toys and
Jamari and J'Adora didn't waste no time playing. I greeted
the receptionist, signed in and waited. I waited and waited.
"Maybe she had someone in the back." I thought. Then
finally my name was called. I introduced myself and then I
inquired about Jamari's case. The vibe with this lady was
completely different, her aura was almost sinister. I was
waiting for her to hand me the paperwork like the previous
location, she never did. Then she asked me to step back
outside. About 5 minutes later I was called to the back yet
again.

"Listen is the case closed, because something isn't right
with you?" I expressed.

"Yes. The case was closed this morning." She stated.

"And was it you that closed up the case?" I wondered.

"Yes, it was." She stated.

"Why was that? Jamari wasn't present for an investigation to take place." I explained.

"There was no need to. Their mother said the boyfriend never got physical with the boy." She explained.

"I don't know what's going on however, my son is sitting out there right now, if only you would speak with him." I pleaded.

She refused. So just like that the case was closed because their mother said nothing didn't happened. Was my fight in vain? I didn't know what to do. Family and friends were so quick to tell me what they would've did if they were in my shoes. I didn't want anyone to think I was a pussy because I chose to fight them the legal way. On that April Fool's Day, the hate that I had for Jai had reached another level.

I made it to Baltimore county police department. I paid for a $40.00 money order and I had 120 days for Jai to get served before it returned to Upper Marlboro courthouse.

105: **911**

Friday, April 8th, 2016

My mother wouldn't stop pressing the issue on how important she felt for us to get a lawyer. We decided to meet up with one that was highly recommended by a colleague of hers. It was a white man. I liked his vibe, hopefully he was a beast in the courtroom. After leaving his office my mother and I went our separate ways. I drove myself to the Dutch Village Farmer's Market located in Upper Marlboro, Maryland. I was only few feet from the chocolate covered strawberries and my fried breaded mushrooms, my phone rung. It was the kid's school calling.

"Hello dad?" Ms. A said.

"Hey, how are you?" I responded.

"Dad mom is here to pick up Jamari and J'Adora and your daughter is crying and screaming refusing to go with her." She stated.

"OMG!! Noooo!! Please don't let her take my babies." I cried out loud as I raced back out to my car.

"Dad I can't hold them. She can no longer withdraw them from school, but I can't stop her from picking them up sweetie. Where are you? How far are you away? I'll do my best to stall Jamari." She suggested.

"Ok please do. I'm on the way." I said.

I was more than 15 minutes away from their school. I tried calling my mother, no answer. I tried calling Makah, no answer. I then called 911; they dispatched an officer to the location. I was recommended not to enter inside of the building due to their mother already being inside.

When I arrived, the officer was seen getting out of the car. I drove up behind the cop's car.

"Are you dad?" The officer questioned.

"Yes I am." I stated.

Then suddenly Zazu's black Dodge Charger speeded around to where the officer and I were. Zazu hopped out the car.

"Everything alright? My girl alright?" He shouted.

"Sir please get back in your car." The officer demanded.

Zazu sat back inside of his car. The officer entered the inside of the school building.

Zazu hopped back outside as we were just staring at each other.

"I would never hurt your kids. This is fucked up of you!" He yelled.

"That's not what Jamari and J'Adora said. I'm doing what any parent is supposed to do and that's protect their children by any means necessary." I said.

"You don't deserve them living the life that you do." He confessed.

"Where's your oldest son at and how's that relationship going Zazu? You need to put this energy in your own damn children and my soon to be ex-wife's baby that she's pregnant with by you. Let me worry about mine." I responded.

"Imma catch you by yourself and when I do…" He stated.

"Hey, say what you want… I bet yall not leaving with Andre's kids today." I said.

Ms. A walked back outside.

"Dad! Dad! Dad! Please get back in your car!" Ms. A shouted waving her hands. "Please dad." She continued.

Ms. A followed me to my car. I started the ignition to my car and rolled the window down.

"Dad I need for you to calm down. Trust me everything is going to work out." She consoled me.

I didn't say a word. My body was shaking, and I was on the verge of breaking down.

A few minutes had passed, and Jai was seen walking back outside with the officer. Zazu met her at the door. A couple of minutes of conversing with the officer, Zazu and Jai got in the car and drove off.

Minutes later Jamari and J'Adora was seen walking outside to my car.

"Andre don't cry. Andre don't cry." I said aloud.

I rolled my window back down.

"Dad, the principal and the officer asked who they wanted to stay with, and they chose you." Ms. A stated.

I got out the car and hugged Ms. A. We drove to Watkins Regional Park. When Jamari and J'Adora walked off to the park I FaceTimed Makah and balled my eyes out. That was the first time he ever seen my tears.

After updating my mother, we soon left the park. I met her back at the lawyer's office. I no longer wanted to wait for the courts to send the paperwork, something needed to happen immediately. I was shown favor that day, but I knew this wouldn't go on forever. The lawyer recommended that we should have an emergency hearing. The lawyer also warned us about a black female judge in particular that had a mood by the flip of a coin when it came down to her decisions. I was no longer sold on following through due to what he just confessed. Hell, I wanted to rep myself at that point. No one knew my story better than I. My mother still wanted me to be rep by the white man, so she dropped $1,000.00. I informed Jai where she needed to be on Monday morning.

Monday, April 11th, 2016

On my way to court solo I didn't know how to feel. My
mother felt like she didn't have to be there due to my
lawyer being by myside. I pointed out to my lawyer who
Jai was. She was there accompanied by her sister Ava.
When we were called to enter the courtroom other people
and their cases were ongoing. The judge that he warned us
about was there. By the disrespectful way she was
addressing the people, I just felt like all hope was lost. Ava
had walked out by the time Jai and I were called to the
stand. My lawyer spoke for me. Which I didn't like
however, that's what my mother paid for. The judge
wanted to know why we were there. The lawyer explained
the situation from Jamari's illness, the alleged hit that took
place, Easter Sunday, and the school incident that took
place on Friday.

"Your honor Andre has been keeping my kids from me. I
haven't had them for weeks and I want them living with
me." Jai stated and she started to break down and cry.

I looked over at her and the Oscar goes to… I couldn't help
but smile to myself because she suddenly had a case of
amnesia and became an actress.

"Why is Mr. Simmons keeping the children from their
mother Counselor?" The judge wondered.

"He's protecting them your honor and it was doctor orders
which Mr. Simmons and their mother agreed on." My
lawyer explained.

"What was the outcome of the case?" The judge asked.

"It was closed your honor. I just want my children. Andre is also gay!" Jai blurted out.

I could hear other people giggle behind me. I loved how the only thing they could all say about me was that I was gay like if I had a second-degree felony.

"Mr. Simmons's sexuality is irrelevant." The judged declared.

The judge wanted to know what the relationship was like between her boyfriend and the children. Jai insisted that he was loving, caring, and that he had been a huge support system to her since meeting him. When Jai acknowledged Zazu as her fiancée the judge quickly corrected her.

"He's not your fiancée while you're still married to Mr. Simmons." The judge said. "Are you currently working?" The judge then asked Jai.

Jai said she wasn't currently working and that she soon would be after the baby was born. I remember Jai saying the same thing when she was pregnant with J'Adora.

"If you are granted today to see your children, your boyfriend isn't allowed to be with them by himself. Is that understood?" The judge said.

Jai nodded her head in agreement.

"The children will continue to stay with dad during the weekdays, plus dad will be granted an additional weekend. Mom you will have them every 3 weekends of each month." The judge said.

"I want them for the summer too!" Jai blurted out.

"This isn't divorce court. This is only a temporary court order. Mom you need to get yourself a lawyer." The judge said. "Who else do you have to help you?" The judge continued.

"My mother and my sisters." She explained.

"You will pick up the children on Fridays at 6:00PM and dad you will pick them up on Sundays at a location spot that you and mom will agree on at 6:00PM." The judge stated.

I couldn't fucking believe what had just happened. How was that even possible? I was fucking convinced black children didn't matter. If something were to happen to Jamari and J'Adora in the future I was suing Baltimore county social services department and Upper Marlboro courthouse. My mother just wasted $1,000.00. I knew I wasn't going to use him in the future. I was going to rep myself. The only good that came out of that mess was the schedule of the children that we've been following since 2012 was official by law. I did my best to look at it from that standpoint and not that I failed. I just needed Jamari and J'Adora to know that I was fighting for them, the best that I could.

Tuesday, April 12th, 2016

I went to Jamari and J'Adora's school to update them with everything. I spoke with the principal and Ms. A. I confirmed to them about my sexuality since it was always brought up. Ms. A stated that Jai was pissed about someone notifying me about her being up there last Friday to pick up Jamari and J'Adora for early dismissal. The gag was due to her outburst by law they couldn't have released J'Adora anyway.

"In all of my years in the school I've never seen a child behave that way especially towards their mother." The principal confessed.

"I have to hand them over on Friday and I yet to tell them." I cried.

"Dad don't cry. We have your back." Ms. A confirmed.

Friday, April 15th, 2016

That Friday morning sending Jamari and J'Adora off to school was hard for me because I knew they wasn't returning home until Sunday. That afternoon as I got ready for work, I waited around for the phone call that I knew I was going to receive. Then the phone rung.

"Dad mom is here to pick up Jamari and J'Adora and they are both extremely emotional and refusing to go with her. Dad I need for you to talk to them." The principal said.

"I don't want to, but I will." I replied.

"Hello." An emotional J'Adora answered the phone.

"J'Adora I need for you and your brother to go with your mother. I will be picking you up on Sunday. I promise." I confirmed.

J'Adora passed the phone to Jamari.

"Jamari go with your mother and don't be afraid to call me. I mean it. I will come up there if you need me." I stated.

"Ok daddy." He responded.

Jamari handed the phone back to the principal.

"Thank you, dad." She said.

I received and email from their principal.

Friday, April 15th, 2016, at 3:06PM, Tonya Riggins

"Hi Mr. Simmons,

Thanks for your support today in helping us to get the children to go home with their mom. They were very reluctant, crying and refusing to go home with her. I called you to calm the kids and reassure them that you authorized them to go home on Friday with their mom. Even after speaking with you, they were still hesitant but after a while and much coaching, they got into the car.

This is a very disheartening situation for all involved. Mom was calm, pleasant and patient while me and another staff member talked to the children. However, this is the second time that the children have cried, clung to our sides and been unwilling to go with their mom. I hope that this matter gets better as they get use to going home with her on Friday."

Tonya Y. Riggins, Principal Lake Arbor Elementary

I emailed her back.

"Let me first start off saying thank you for the support. I know everyone wants what's best for Jamari and J'Adora and so do I. I'm glad that I was able to meet with you on Tuesday. You made me feel comfortable, and I love the fact you let me speak and tell my side of the story. Ms. A is a gem. I can't thank her enough. Thank you once again to you, and the entire staff at Lake Arbor Elementary."

Sunday, April 17th, 2016

My mother drove her car to pick up Jamari and J'Adora. Paula had come along for the ride. We met Jai at the train station. We would later change the pickup location to the Baltimore County Police, Precinct 4 Pikeville. She dropped Jamari and J'Adora off in Zazu's black Dodge Charger.

They revealed that their mother and Ava were the ones who picked them up from school Friday. Due to how upset they were Jai and the kids stayed at Ava's Friday night. On Saturday night they stayed at Zazu's house. Jamari revealed that Zazu was extra friendly with him and gave him $5.00. They said they had a good weekend. I was curious though. Did J'Adora receive money as well and the answer was no and that was all I needed to know.

"The stories of 'Little Kinky Kiki', are based on true events, inspired by my daughter J'Adora, and her natural curly hair. Dear little colored girls, you're beautiful inside and out. Dear little colored girls, your hair is your crown." - Andre L. Simmons

106: *Little Kinky Kiki (3rd Book)*

Flashback:

Between Jamari's health, the drama between their mother and I, and J'Adora's outburst at school on Friday, April 8th back when their mother attempted to pick them up from school early without my knowledge. I never knew how bad things were for J'Adora. Since the eruption J'Adora's eating habits had changed drastically. She was starting to hold her spit in her mouth and not swallow it. I would often find spit on the floor and wet marks on the couch. At first, I would yell at her because that wasn't like J'Adora until I realized it was much deeper and something was wrong with my daughter. It had gotten so bad at one point I had to take her to the emergency room. I went into detail with the doctor about the last few months of her life. He applauded me for being a concerned father and looking into the situation sooner than later.

Fast Forward:

One day when I decided to do J'Adora's hair.

"J'Adora what happened to your hair?" I shouted.

She didn't respond. I turned her around to look her in her face. I did my best to remain calm after I just yelled at her.

"Why did you cut hair? At least 20% is missing from the back." I asked.

"Because my hair is ugly daddy." She whispered as her eyes filled up with water.

"J'Adora your hair is far from ugly. It's a soft texture, just like your mother's hair." I confirmed. "When did you cut it?" I wondered.

"In school today, in the bathroom." She confirmed.

I said nothing after that. I just put hair up in her famous *"Dora Balls"* aka to puff balls as my eyes filled up with water. I just didn't know anymore what I should do.

June 21st, 2016

From the events that had taken place with my children I was now inspired to write again. I wanted to do something very special for J'Adora since so much attention was going to Jamari. I decided to write a book based on our father and daughter relationship however, I kept it a children's level of understanding and hopefully other girls, especially ones of color could relate. J'Adora's character name was Kiki for the book due it being one of her favorite movies called Kiki's Delivery Service.

107: **Snickerdoodle** *(Part Three)*

Flashback:

There was such a lesson to be learned when dealing with someone who was still in love with their ex. Every time I attempted to fade away something would always pull me back in.

Friday June 17th, 2016

I was driving on White House Rd. I was on my way to pick up an Uber rider as I was waiting at the stoplight, I could hear someone honking their horn beside me. I looked out of the corner of my left eye and someone could be seen waving at me. I turned my head and it was Makah's best friend Nikki. "What the hell did she want?" I had thought. I will never forget her telling me that "I was here before you and I will be here after you." Now there she was flagging me down. I rolled my window down.

"What's up?" I said.

"Hey! You know Makah in the hospital?" She stated.

"Ok he didn't tell me that so I'm assuming he didn't want me to know Nikki." I explained.

"I know how stubborn my best friend can be, but he needs us." She stated.

"Where is he located?" I asked.

"He's at Prince George's." She stated. "I'm going to tell him you're going to show up." She then continued.

Father's Day

Sunday, June 19th, 2016

The twins Djuan and Dayvon went along with me to go pick up Jamari and J'Adora in Baltimore. When they had got in the car, I had informed them that Makah was in the hospital and if they wanted to go and see him and they both said yes. I stopped at a Walgreens to pick up a beverage for him and a get-well card. When we entered the room his mother and brother was there as well. He looked like he was in a lot of pain. The room wasn't in the best condition, it was hot, plus he shared the room with another individual. He was ready to go. I made sure that I purchased fresh pillows and linen for his bed. I picked Makah up the following day to take him home.

Fast Forward:

Saturday, August 6th, 2016

Things were going smoothly between Makah and me. I wanted to plan something for him and I. To make sure I wasn't jumping the gun. I spoke with him about my plans.

"I want to do something for us. We barley get any alone time, especially due to Jamari's illness. The kids will be returning back to school soon and it's also a way for me to say thank you for being there for me and the kids over the months, even when we weren't on the best of terms." I explained.

He agreed and I was too excited. I couldn't believe he said yes.

Friday, August 19th, 2016

I had Jamari and J'Adora's back to school shopping out the way. School started on Tuesday, August 23rd, and Saturday, August 20th, was the big day. Hotel and dinner reservations were all set in Arlington, Virginia. One problem I wasn't hearing from Makah. I had called him that afternoon and he said he was going to call me back when he had free time. I Ubered late that Friday night. I ended up stopping at a Thai restaurant off of U St. It was horrible. I posted it on my InstaStory. Makah viewed it however, he had still yet to contact me back. Nothing bothered me more than being ignored by someone. I left D.C. and headed straight to his house. When I arrived, his car was parked in the driveway. I called and I didn't get an answer. I knocked on the door and his brother Demetrius answered.

"Where's your brother?" I asked.

"He in his room." He responded.

"Can you go get him please?" I asked.

Demetrius went to go get Makah as I waited outside. About a minute had passed and Demetrius came back to the door.

"He said he going to call you later." He said.

"No. Excuse me Demetrius." I said as I walked to Makah's room.

I knocked on the door and opened it. Makah was laying in bed.

"What's going on with you? You're ignoring me but you can view my InstaStories? Are you ok?" I asked.

"I will call you tomorrow." He responded.

"No let's talk now. Are we still on for tomorrow?" I asked.

"Nah." He said.

Un-fucking-believable! I rushed out the house and went home.

Saturday August 20th, 2016

I waited the rest of last night and that morning for Makah to call me because I was hopeful that he would change his mind. The early part of that afternoon I took a shower and shaved my head bald. I got dressed to go nowhere. I ended up taking a photo and uploading it to my Instagram account. I got undressed and hopped back in bed. I watched the late 80's version of Beauty and the Beast season 1 episode 1, my favorite TV series of all time on my iPhone as the likes to my recent Instagram post grew. If only I was loved and appreciated like I was on Instagram, in real life by the men that I would had given the skin off my back for.

108: **Blame Daddy**

Flashback:

Friday, March 11th - Wednesday March 23rd

Tuesday, May 31st - Monday, June 6th

Tuesday, August 23rd - September 1st

Sunday, October 30th - Tuesday, November 9th

Fast Forward:

Jamari was released from the hospital on November 9th. That was then his fourth time and prayed to God his last. Jamari spent a total of 41 days in the hospital. Over the past 9 months I had educated myself on Jamari's Inflammatory Bowels Disease. I've always searched for the signs of extreme fatigue, vomiting, and I had to constantly remind him to notify me if his stools were bleeding or not. Even though I could never feel his pain I always did my best to do my part as his parent. However, with each visit, the doctors would always try different treatments, you have to understand no child was alike.

I was in the bathroom getting ready to go Uber.

"Joyce it's due to Andre's lifestyle that Jamari keeps getting sick." A voice that could be heard from my mother's phone.

I just sat there and listened. I finally made out the female's voice and it was Rosa. She was a person that worked with my mother, who also came over for prayer some Sundays. Not only that she purchased *'Butterflies Hitting Home Runs'* after my mother got off the phone with her my heart wouldn't let me remain silent.

"So, it's my fault that Jamari is sick?!" I snapped.

I couldn't hear her reply due to me turning up the music on my iPhone. Yoo! those judgmental Christian folks killed me with their hateful opinions about shit they had no clue about. Listen I love my mother like no other. At the end of the day she's still a southern black woman stuck in her ways and that will never change. I just wished she would accept all of me. It went from Zazu's alleged child abuse to my son, to blaming his illness on me due to my sexuality. I wondered what it would be next. I lived my truth proudly. I have yet to officially come out to my son and daughter only because I learned my lesson in the past. Timing meant everything when it came to sensitive situations like that furthermore they were still very young.

109: **20 Something** *(Part Three)*

I had lost all hope for love. Nothing was more hurtful than when someone would pop up in my DMs and asked was, I single, and my reply was always yes. They couldn't believe someone like me was single. I started questioning everything about myself. I never felt so alone or insecure in all my life. The only two men I didn't mind being around that wouldn't hurt me were my best friends Aaron and Prince; however, as much as I love them, even they couldn't fill the void of a love/romance that I longed for.

Just like a new season would come, so would Diego. I was grateful for him showing up to visit Jamari during the months of October and November. Out of all of my friends he was the only one who visited Jamari. Not to mentioned he had bought Jamari a Mario Brother's theme birthday cake which he had never done before simply because he was never around for his birthday.

Diego requested to have all of my close friends Aaron, Darryl, Racquel, Le'Trell, and Shana's contact numbers because he wanted to surprise me for my birthday, I was in awe with the thought of him trying. Even though the gesture was nice it wasn't successful. I ended up spending my 33rd birthday with Aaron and him though.

That Christmas, Diego was part of our family's Secret Santa list. However, leading up to it he had got into a financial bind which left me having to buy two Christmas's gifts for people that year.

December 24th, 2016

Diego was coming over for Christmas dinner and I was on the phone talking to Prince when Diego called me.

"Prince. Be quite Diego is calling me." I clicked over and merged the call.

"Hello?" I said.

"Rite Aid keeps calling my phone in regard to Jamari's medicine." He snapped.

"Hello to you too Diego." I giggled.

"Do you want their number or not?" He stated.

"Diego what is your problem?" I snapped.

He hung up the phone.

"Prince?" I said.

"Yeah Pa I'm here." Prince said.

"What was that about?" I wondered.

"Pa I have not a clue." He said.

December 25th, 2016

My cousin Kanika loved her gift that Diego had got her. The family asked where he was.

"He's spending time with his family. He wanted to be here though." I explained.

That Christmas wasn't one of my favorites however, it was Jamari an J'Adora's favorite one. I had to get out of there, so I went to Uber and for the first time I had threaten to put this damn black lady out of my car. I don't know what took place in the house that I picked her up from, but I wasn't in the mood for her disrespect, even her adult children sided with me and apologized on the behalf of their mother. I didn't hear from or see Diego for the rest of 2016.

110: **20 Snickerdoodle** *(Part Four)*

Flashback:

When you learn to accept things for what they are and disconnect from certain attachments then you are truly free.

September 2016

Makah called me a couple of weeks later inquiring about Jamari and J'Adora. I didn't feel a way. I took them over there to see him. That was the thing he was such a family man so when the 5 of us; me, Jamari, J'Adora, him, and his brother Demetrius were all together it made me feel like we were a family, blended but yet still a family. Jai had it in Baltimore why couldn't I? I had purchased this black stylish jacket from Burlington Coat Factory. I wore that over there and when he seen it, he gave me a shirt to wear in return. I wouldn't have mind my boyfriend or husband wearing my clothes, but this guy wasn't even claiming me and never apologized to me. The funny thing was I had thought about buying him the same one as well. However, after what didn't take place and how everything went down between him and I last month I didn't bother. At first, I thought he was trying it on however, he kept it on. I never got my jacket back. I did see photos on his Instagram account of his mother, along with his brother all wearing it.

A Night In September

One-night Makah, his brother and I were together, and he wanted to stop by his best friend's Nikki's house. Once he got out my car someone was FaceTiming him. That was something that I didn't do in the past or was I about to start doing then, and that was answer someone else's phone without their permission. However, I did look down at the name which read: *"Futuro Marido."* I knew futuro was translated to future in English but what did marido mean? I went to google and typed the two words into the search bar. *"Futuro Marido"* was translated to *"Future Husband"* from Spanish to English. My mood instantly changed, and it wasn't due to my feelings for Makah I had pushed that to the back of my mind, but it shifted due to the fact that if he was talking to someone, why bother to call me? Children aside he knew how I felt about him. When I had brought it up to him, he claimed the person was just a friend. I thought it was odd for a friend to have that title when my name in his iPhone was *"Behind Time"* which made sense since I was always late. I didn't have proof and I had to believe what he said.

Fast Forward:

Over the next couple of months Makah was faced with life changing news. I tried to be there for him as much as I could, but I was beginning to lose myself and neglected certain parts of my life. I no longer knew if he wanted me or just needed me. My best friend, Prince's mom Chantel would always tell him and I that we gave people too many chances to hurt us again and again. I was able to talk to her about the men in my life, something that I couldn't do with my own mother. As much as we would express how tired we were, we always went back for more disappointment, hurt, and pain. Sometimes it felt like Prince and I were competing about who could get hurt the worst. There was never an official goodbye we just didn't stay in contact. He had a lot on his plate as did I. Jamari and J'Adora would often ask about Makah, especially when we were driving by his house. My last time seeing Makah was March of 2017.

111: You've Been Served

I was on Georgia Ave. in NW, Washington D.C. Ubering on the phone with Aaron, heading to my next pickup.

"Andre, Ava is going to meet you at the police station with the kids." Jai iMessaged.

"Ok cool." I iMessaged.

I didn't mind that. I didn't have an issue with Ava. Furthermore, Jamari and J'Adora had never given me a bad report on her besides promoting them to eat healthier especially, with her being a vegetarian.

Upon my arrival I was looking for a car with people inside.

"Jai, I don't see Ava." I iMessaged.

"She's inside of the police station." Jai iMessaged.

In that very moment something was off. I looked inside what appeared to be them. I parked and got out my car. As I was approaching the police headquarters, I could see Jamari and J'Adora sleep. I opened the door.

"Hello." I said as I was walking towards Jamari and J'Adora to wake them up.

Ava and The Other Woman that lived with Jai and Zazu was walking towards me. I looked at Ava.

"Here you go." She said as she handed me some papers, headed to the door, as The Other Woman followed her.

As I read over the papers. I felt a sigh of relief. Jai was immature in the way that it was handled, unlike her I was ready for this one year ago when she refused to get served. I guess #TeamJai was finally ready to go against me in court. As Prince would say "Let the games begin."

112: I Shit My Pants

April 22nd, 2017

My mother had gone grocery shopping. However, I was craving Alaskan Snow Crab legs.

"Mom you think you can run out and buy some Alaskan Snow Crab legs? Get anything you want. Take my card." I insisted.

"Andre, I don't feel like going there." She explained.

"You just said that you're going back out though. It's literally up the street. This is why I don't ask you do anything for me." I said.

"Give me your card then." She suggested.

My mother left and I started to get ready for work. By the time she arrived back, I was airdrying Sheba aka my beard. I went downstairs and started demolishing the crab legs. They were so damn tasty, and she didn't forget the butter sauce either. "Let me leave out for work, I can finish the rest later tonight." I thought to myself. I washed my hands and then I turned on the Uber app. I got in my car and headed to Largo Town Center *(WMATA)*. After about 5 minutes later I received an Uber request. It was a female rider and her destination was to the Walmart in Capital Plaza. Soon as I got on the I-495, my stomach started bubbling. "Noooo." I thought to myself. I turned up the radio volume from 8 to 11. I didn't want her to think that I was farting. Good thing I was 7 minutes away from dropping her off. By the time I arrived my stomach had gone back to normal.

"Thank you." She said.

"Have a goodnight, be safe." I replied.

As the customer closed the door, I received another Uber request, and it was 4 minutes away. 2 minutes from picking up the rider my stomach started bubbling again. "What should I do? I can cancel now, head home, and shit or take the chance and shit afterwards. However, what if the rider's destination is a long trip?" All these thoughts were running through my mind. I took the chance anyway. Soon as the rider got in my car, I started the trip. The destination was to District Heights, Maryland and the drop off time was in 23 minutes. "Fuck I should've canceled. What if I shit in my car with this woman inside?" I then thought. 10 minutes into the trip, as I was passing the exit to my home. I was so tempted to tell this woman "Please can I end your trip early and take you to my home so that I can take a shit?" However, I didn't want her to report me on some creep type of shit. After quenching my asshole tightly for the entire ride, 7 minutes remained on the trip. The storm that was going on in my stomach started to simmer down. "Thank you, God. I'm going to make it after all." I thought. Finally pulling up to the destination.

"I don't know why but Uber always have you all drop me off right here. I live in the back though if you don't mind." She explained.

"That's not a problem. Just direct me to your destination." I stated.

Saying that triggered my stomach yet again.

"Thank you, Andre." She said as she was getting out my car.

"Thank you. Have a goodnight." I responded.

She closed the door, I ended the trip and went off line. I hopped on Walker Mill Rd. and headed back home. On the way I was looking for places to pull over and poop. At that point I didn't even care. I can shower and put on clean clothes afterwards. I was so close but so far. As I was thinking about pulling over my poop started crowning.

"Nooo!" I yelled.

I unbuckled my seatbelt, took off the jacket that I was wearing to put under me. I released my clenched cheeks and just let it all out. It ran like water and the smell was the worst. However, what a relief.

"Well I won't be Ubering anymore this weekend." I said aloud.

When I arrived at home, I felt like shit, literally. I opened the door and went to the bathroom down stairs.

"Mom!" I shouted.

"Yeah, back so soon?" She replied.

"Yes. I shit my pants." I responded.

She came downstairs. Looked at me in disgust.

"I guess that's what I get for being mean to you earlier." I stated.

"You want some more crab legs?" She said and giggled.

I was speechless.

May 14th, 2017
"So J'Adora was crying like usual but I kept asking her what's wrong. She eventually said I want you and Daddy to get back together. I said we don't want you to feel hurt but me and dad are not getting back together, however if we all can do an activity together maybe she will feel better." - Jai iMessaged.

113: Janet Jackson's Back!

May 1st, 2017

I received a notification in a DM. OMG! It was a video of Janet Jackson from her Instagram account, remerging after months of hiding out in Europe, after just giving birth to her son Eissa, 5 months ago. The video was bitter-sweet, she was publicly announcing her separation from her husband Wissam; however, also announcing the continuation of her tour and released the dates. You never know with Janet Jackson. Rumors of a separation did leak a week prior, while I was in New Jersey visiting my bestie Prince. I didn't know what the outcome would be due to the upcoming trails; however, I ended up purchasing 3 tickets to see her on November 16th, 2017 with Jamari and J'Adora. This would be their first-time seeing Janet Jackson live.

J'Adora took this photo of me at Watkins Regional
Park. *May 10ᵗʰ, 2017.*

Come on feet start walking

Mouth stop talking

Arms let him go

114: **20 Something** *(Part Four)*

Flashback:

Saturday, February 5th, 2017

Even though the romance of Tarantino and Andre had burned out we remained friends. I would still bother him with Kelly Rowland news and vice versa when it came to Janet Jackson. We agreed to go to the movies together and I promised that I wouldn't cancel. I didn't know what to expect. I picked him up just like old times even though he offered to drive. Before the movies I wanted to go to the Cheesecake Factory at Tysons 2, Virginia, which was where him and I went on our first date 5 years ago. He paid for the movie, we seen The Comedian. Tarantino loved to laugh and as corny as I thought his movie choices were, they were for the most part entertaining. I had uploaded a photo of him and I to my Instagram account that following morning Sunday, February 6th. Diego had liked the post.

On February 13th right before midnight Diego sent me an iMessage.

"WYD?" He iMessaged.

"Ubering." I iMessaged.

"Ok cool, cool." He iMessaged.

February 14th, 2017

Before Valentine's Day was over, I had uploaded a photo of myself that I wasn't too sure if I should or not due to the amount of skin that I was showing. I wasn't showing my ass or dick but it kind of left little to the imagination. That time I wanted to do a picture video with a song playing but what? I ended up choosing Adele's song "All I Ask." I connected with those lyrics. Soon as I had uploaded the photo, he liked it and once again Diego iMessaged me.

"How was your day?" He iMessaged.

"Good and yours?" I iMessaged.

"It was cool." He iMessaged. "WYD?" He then continued.

"Ubering. Why?" I iMessaged.

"No reason." He iMessaged.

He was so random hitting me up before and after Valentine's Day. If he wanted to see me all he had to do was say so unless he was with someone and just wanted to keep tabs on me.

Fast Forward:

May 3rd, 2017

Just like the seasons come and so would Diego. He DMed me.

"What happened to your phone?" He DMed.

"I had to get another phone and number due to the water damage of my last one." I DMed.

After him bringing up the fact that Tarantino most likely had the new number. I iMessaged him because his number was still the same. We talked for a bit and I revealed to him that I had been served. We had made plans to meet the following day.

May 4th, 2017

After I Ubered I met him at his home.

"Hello sir." He said.

"What's going?" I replied.

He started to make a funny face and twitched his nose.

"What you been doing in here? It smells like booty." He wondered.

"Diego nooo OMG!" I shouted.

"What you been doing?" He asked.

"I shit my pants the Saturday before last. I could have sworn that I did a great job cleaning up my mess and letting my car air out. That means people was thinking I stunk." I declared.

He died laughing after I was telling him the story about what happened last month. We had gone out to dinner and surprisingly he asked how I was due to my upcoming trials. Before I went home, I had cleaned my car out yet again.

May 9th, 2017

I took Diego on a follow up job interview in Greenbelt, Maryland. I loaned him some dress shoes, dress shirt and a tie. He was nervous however, I comforted him letting him know that he had it in the bag. Once it was over, he came back outside, with a giant smile on his face.

Wednesday, May 24th, 2017

I had taken Diego to a follow up interview. While he was inside, I was catching up with Racquel on the phone. When Diego returned, he had confirmed to me that he got the job. I was so happy for him that things were finally looking up for him. Diego was a completely different person when he was working. Later that night Diego was on the phone with someone. From what I could hear I didn't like the conversation. Diego was showing me things on his phone. I just had the feeling the person on the other line was being flirty.

Thursday, May 25th, 2017

Diego and I were in my room smoking and once again he was talking to that person again.

"Diego are you kidding me right now?" I asked.

"What's wrong?" He wondered.

"Do that person on the phone you're talking to like you?" I asked.

His reaction gave me everything that I needed.

"How are you in my room, on my bed talking to another nigga? The fuck you were just inside of me. All that shit you had to say about me without any physical proof. However, I have never disrespected you to your face by entertaining someone right in your presence. I know now if I didn't know before you don't give a damn about me Diego." I snapped.

He just sat on the bed with a dumb ass look on his face faded. I just wanted to ride his face, but I was pissed. He didn't say a word at that moment. I had gone upstairs. A couple of minutes later I had received an iMessage from him.

"Can you unlock your trunk so I can get my stuff? I'm going to head home." He iMessaged.

He had to walked out the back. I unlocked my car for him to get his things. I didn't hear from Diego that night. Friday night he was out partying with his best friend because he had uploaded a video to his Instagram account.

Saturday, May 27th, 2017

As I was getting ready to go Uber, Diego DMed me.

"So, you used to talk to DeAndre?" He DMed.

"Who the fuck was DeAndre?" I had thought. That was it. That nigga was out during D.C. Pride and he had the nerve to ask me about someone else. I had the court shit to worry about. I immediately blocked Diego from my Instagram and Facebook accounts. I called Prince and had him do the same because Diego had a slick way getting info about me, out of Prince, without Prince even knowing it which at one time was cute but no longer. The breaks in between didn't help our cause. We both allowed new people to come in our lives, so it always felt like we were cheating on each other without a title. The way we were headed if we didn't stop him or I were going to end up catching something that we couldn't get rid of. I used to think Diego kept running back because deep down he knew I was the shit and it was nothing better out there for him however, every time I would allow him to return the disrespect went to a new level. He was a hurt soul and as much as I tried to help him it always backed fired on me and I was left mending the pieces to my broken heart. People will treat you by the level of respect that you have for yourself. It was long overdue, but I was finally done. The many chapters of us had ended. I started to focus and work on myself. It was time I chose me for once.

115: **Custody** *(Plaintiff VS Defendant)*

July 7th, 2017

11:18AM

"Hey court was yesterday you missed it. The next court date is August 4th 1:00PM." Jai iMessaged

"No, it wasn't. They changed it." I screen shot her my letter Then I replied to her and said, "I didn't miss anything." I imessaged.

"The mediator called you on July 6th to set up the mediation. Did you call back or not?" Jai iMessaged.

"Again, if you look at the copy above it says July 13th 8:30AM. When I go up there on July 13th, 8:30AM I will find out then." I iMessaged.

"Okay. I think they consolidated the cases and canceled that appointment. Did you get the notice for July 6th? You should call someone and make sure." Jai iMessaged.

"I received two notices for the exact same thing *(Order and Notice of Scheduling Conference/Hearing)* one for the 6th and then a couple of weeks later I received one for 13th. I assumed the date was pushed back. When I go up there on the 13th I'm bringing both letters with me to show them it's their screw up for mailing out the same letter for 2 different dates." I iMessaged.

Jai didn't respond back.

July 21st, 2017

7:02AM

"Dear Andre, good morning, I'm not mad this has been a journey I've grown from who I use to be that's important to me because some people never self-reflect but me, I see a better Jai, a better mommy, a better friend. I only have the best intentions for Jamari and J'Adora when I left, I was only thinking of them. Why would I ever take from their dad? It would never make sense to me but all I know now I definitely wouldn't do it again. Growing is about growth and what I learned is to be kind but cautious and I didn't do that with you. The betrayal I feel was you never verbalizing hey Jai I'm gay that hurt but I know it hurt you a lot more my pain doesn't really matter. Today I'm only concerned about Jamari and J'Adora we need counseling as a family or we need to sit down like adults and work through it. Andre I could never really hate you I'm proud of you for coming out and facing your truths. I'm not homophobic I think it's awesome that you're being honest to yourself. This is my forum to open communication because it's best for Jamari and J'Adora. I love you have a good day. God is strength." Jai iMessaged.

"Now that was random. I didn't know what to say or if I should've responded back to Jai. However, knowing her, Jai's true intentions will be exposed like always." I thought to myself.

August 4th, 2017

I woke up feeling good. I wasn't stressed or worried about a thing. My mother was off work that day. I didn't ask her to be by my side. I think she would've if I had asked her to.

I played my music. I shaved my head. After all of that I washed the night before off my body and headed to court. When I had arrived, I seen that she was sitting with The Other Woman that stayed with her and Zazu. Jai got up and handed me a stack of papers.

"What is this?" I asked as I took the papers.

She didn't reply just smiled slightly and walked away. I looked down at them and they were past tax documents. About 5 minutes later our names were called.

IN THE CIRCUIT COURT FOR PRINCE GEORGE'S COUNTY, MARYLAND

Andre Simmons Plaintiff,

Case No:

CADXX-XXXXX

VS,

Jai Richards Defendant,

Case No:

CADXX-XXXXX

ORDER OF COURT

The above-captioned matter was scheduled for a hearing before the Family Magistrate on AUGUST 04, 2017, on the Issue of Pendente Lite. Plaintiff and Defendant were present. Accordingly, by the Circuit Court for Prince George's County, Maryland, it is hereby,

ORDERED, that CADXX-XXXXX and CADXX-XXXXX be consolidated and that CADXX-XXXXX shall be the lead case; and it is further,

ORDERED, that Pendente Lite, the Plaintiff, (father), Andre Simmons, shall have custody of the minor children and the (mother), Jai Richards, shall have access with the minor children three consecutive weekends out of every four weekends. Father shall have one weekend out of four (his next weekend starting August 25, 2017); and it is further,

ORDERED, that this is the schedule that the parties have been following for the past year; and it is further,

ORDERED, that the Plaintiff pay the costs of these proceedings as taxed by the Clerk of the Court; and it is further,

ORDERED, that the pendente lite relief granted herein shall remain in full force and effect until this Oder is superseded by a further Order of Court.

Thomas J. Rogers Jr., Family Magistrate

After court was over, I couldn't help but think again how my mother and I wasted $1,000.00 on the lawyer from last year. Representing myself in court gave me such a confidence that I never knew existed. I always knew I was a good dad and who could've recited my truth to a judge better than myself, after all I was a published author that wrote the story of my life. I was going to be doing the exact same thing in November as well. I had called my mother to let her know about the outcome. She was extremely relieved, as was I. I headed straight home. My phone rung and it was Jai. I was cool, calm, and collected until Jai decided to become disrespectful. I said my peace and hung up the phone.

August 4th, 2017

2:08PM

"You're so hostile. I want to keep the kids a month the judge said nothing about Jamari and J'Adora not staying with me for the rest of August until they go back to school." Jai iMessaged.

"I'm picking Jamari and J'Adora up on Sunday." I iMessaged.

"We originally agreed that the kids would live with me even if you don't agree you have no reasonable excuse why you think they should not be with me for the school year. There are no restrictions in the court order that stops me from seeing my kids more than a week. I have always had them in the summer months. These are the dates I'll have the kids August 11th - 25th." Jai iMessaged.

"You're talking to the wrong person about the decision that the judge made today in the court room. The judge said what he said. If you break the law that's on you. You can't decide what you're going to do if I don't agree. You keep saying I can't keep you from your kids when in fact you wanted full custody and child support from me. Re-read the statement again we both have the same copy. I have custody and you have your 3 weekends. I was willing to reason with you getting them for a week until you shouted, "I want them for a full month!" I will see Jamari and J'Adora on Sunday and I will be picking them up the following 2 Sundays. Break the law if you want." I iMessaged.

"You are a sad excuse for a man. You are going through all this because you are afraid of child support. I don't want your money. I don't need your money. I want my children. Reason with me! I have not had my kids but for 3 consecutive days for months. Your mother has had you every day all your life. But you think it's unreasonable that I spend the last month of this summer with my kids. There is no law against a mother seeing her children. But since you think a month is unreasonable for a child who has lived with his mother for 33 consecutive years. I will play this childish game until you are ready to grow up and stop trying to make me seem like a dead-beat parent. I will have my children for two weeks. That is fair and reasonable being as they live with you. I will have my children! Keep your little coins. Even when the kids live with me, I don't want them coins. I have lived fine without your money for 6 years. Boy bye!" Jai iMessaged.

No need for a reply. I said what needed to be said. This was the main reason I didn't reply back to her iMessage from last month. Jai's snake ass truth always revealed its head one way or another. It burnt me up to hear her say that I lived with my mother all my life. She was forgetful of the 1 year that we had a place together 2008 - 2009. She was forgetful of the 4 months that my mother spent in Dushanbe, Tajikistan 2010. She was forgetful of the 2 years and 2 months that my mother spent in Egypt 2011 - 2013. Sorry Jai that my mother was a mother to me when times were good and bad. Just like my mother didn't give up on me, I wasn't giving up on my children. Me living with my mother didn't make me less of a man just like her having another baby and living with Zazu didn't make her his wife, while we were still legally married.

August 11th, 2017

7:02PM

"I'm outside." Jai iMessaged.

I didn't reply. I kissed Jamari and J'Adora goodbye and sent them on their way.

August 11th, 2017

9:07PM

"I see Jamari didn't go to his appointment on Thursday I'll email the lady and reschedule. Can I get a copy of their insurance cards? I put Jamari and J'Adora in tutoring while they're saying with me through the 25th." Jai iMessaged.

"Ms. Richards, I did not agree to you keeping them for 2 weeks. The court order said keep everything the same as we've been following for the past year. Please re-read what was typed on August 4th, in court. I've already got in contact with his doctor. If you don't meet me at our regular spot between the hours of 5:45PM - 6:30PM I will show up at your door with the police to collect Jamari and J'Adora. - Andre Simmons August 11th, 2017 9:40PM." I iMessaged.

"You did agree in front of the Judge, but you got mad because I wanted them longer than two weeks. The Judge said he can't get involved with any arrangements we make outside the courts. You agreed now you are acting like you didn't because you don't want me to spend time with my kids for no good reason at all." Jai iMessaged.

"I asked the judge could you get a week after the case was done. He said that we both would have to agree. You said a month and got in your feelings. We didn't come to an agreement! I'm sure the female you were with know I was the one who said that you could get a week first. FYI: You were the one who called me after court and sent all those iMessages. I didn't disrespect you in nothing I said in an iMessage. Why would I be mad when I have custody over Jamari and J'Adora? Either way I will be in Baltimore on Sunday." I iMessaged.

"Ok I agree with the week now we have an agreement." Jai iMessaged.

"Agreed. I Andre L. Simmons agree, and I will pick up Jamari and J'Adora up Sunday, August 20th." I replied.

No reply from Jai. She agreed to what I had originally suggested in the courtroom 7 days prior. It could've all been so simple.

116: **Book Trip** *(ATL: Guest Author)*

Flashback:

May 2017

I had noticed a familiar face always popping up in my InstaStory. I was unsure if I was following the person or not, so I decided to click on their profile. He was following me, and I wasn't following him back. I went through a couple of my post and he was also a liker. I definitely had to follow him back. Instagram has a following back limit which is 7,500. Once he accepted my request, he DMed me.

"Hi Andre, Question. Are you ever in ATL during Labor Day weekend? The reason I ask is I host a brunch every year that has about 60 - 80 people in attendance. I usually feature an LGBTQ author to feature their work and sell copies of their product to the group. They read excerpts from their work etc. I see you're a published author and if you're interested perhaps could feature your *'Butterflies Hitting Home Runs'* work. Hope you are well otherwise."

I was so honored; however, I didn't have nothing new to promote and I wasn't as active on social media as I once was. Things were never the same after Jamari's illness and dealing with court stuff which only my mother, Aaron, Prince, Diego, Makah, and Tyrell truly knew. I reached out to Aaron and Prince to see if they would be willing to come with me. Due to them both being booked that holiday weekend they were unable to commit which meant if I was going to go it would have been solo. In that very moment, I asked myself how bad did I want a career in writing. I told him yes, I would be able to commit.

Fast Forward:

August 26th, 2017

"Hey Andre, just checking in. I spoke with the venue and they will have a table set up for you so that you can bring any books that you want to put out for sale etc. Hit me back and let me know if you're still good for Saturday and I look forward to meeting you." DG DMed.

Friday, September 1st, 2017

My books: *'Butterflies Hitting Home Runs', 'Watermelon Seeds Of Daddy', and 'Little Kinky Kiki'* all arrived on Wednesday, August 30th. I called my cousin Audrekia the day before I had to be there, who had connections to the Hilton hotel chain. Due to it being pride weekend and other special events going on, the nearest hotel to downtown Atlanta that she was able to book for me was located in Macon, Georgia, which was an hour away. I had no choice. I left Maryland around 6:00PM that evening. I had talked to Audrekia within the first hour of my trip, she has grown and accomplished so much. I couldn't thank her enough because this trip wouldn't have been possible if it wasn't for her. As exhausted as I already was Tyrell stayed on the phone with me for over 10 hours until I arrived at the hotel the following morning.

Saturday, September 2nd, 2017

The Place Where Men Brunch

I was extremely exhausted after only getting maybe 2 hours of sleep. I wanted to cancel my appearance. Once again Tyrell was on the phone with me while I was en route. I pulled up.

"Tyrell I'm here. I see about 20 black people sitting all around the table. That's the largest crowd from what I could see; however, I don't see DG." I said.

I pulled up to the front and pressed the emergency flasher. I dropped off the books at the front. An employee said that it wouldn't be a problem. I then proceeded to go find parking. I walked around to the front. It was so hot in Atlanta, granted me wearing a black hoodie, jean jacket, and all black leggings didn't help the situation. Not to mentioned Sheba aka my beard.

"Hi I'm Andre Simmons. I'm here for The Place Where Men Brunch." I explained.

He just gazed at me with confusion written all over his face. Come to find out I was at the wrong location plus I was already late and hot.

"Tyrell this isn't the right location. I'm going to go back to the hotel." I suggested.

"Dre you're already there, just go to it." He insisted.

I notified DG to let him know that I was at the wrong location, he assured me that it was ok, and for me to still come. About 20 minutes later I had arrived. When I walked inside carrying the box of books I looked up and saw sea of men. Men, men, and men just everywhere, all different types that came in small, medium, large, extra-large, and extra extra-large. "Ok Atlanta. I see you." I thought to myself. DG greeted me and told me that I could start setting up in the corner. I saw a couple of familiar faces. The first person that I remembered greeting me besides DG was Terry that I had knew from Instagram. He had offered to buy me a beer. After a while I just couldn't remember everyone as much as I tried. I was able to talk about my books and what motivated me to write, I even brought up Jamari and J'Adora in my speech. I also was happy to meet Devin who had purchased my first book a couple of years prior and the king of Big Boy Pride himself Jay who also bought a book at the event. My overall experience at Big Boy Pride wasn't what I expected it to be at all. It was a learning experience. It taught me that I didn't always need Aaron and Prince to hold my hand and that I can stand on my own two feet. It was great that men, especially men of color came out and supported such a great cause. I will be forever grateful for DG having me as the: *"Guest Author of 2017"* at his event. I looked forward to attending more Big Boy Pride events in the near future. Special thank you to my cousin Audrekia for coming through for her big brother and finding me a hotel at the last minute. Special thank you to my friend Tyrell for staying on the phone with me the majority of the drive down to Atlanta and encouraging me to still go to the right location. I wouldn't have gone if it wasn't for him.

117: **Mr. 3000**

Let others know how awesome you are

ANDRE, thanks for putting in an amazing amount of time giving rides to people who rely on you to get them where they need to go.

Share this and earn a referral reward for anyone who signs up to drive using your link.

Happy earning!

Congratulations, Andre

You've completed 3000 trips.

3000

That's awesome!

On my 2nd, anniversary of Ubering, I also completed my 3,000th trip. Look at God. Won't he do it.

118: **Lonely Tony** *(Part Three)*

Flashback:

On Sunday November 12th, 2016 I had just finished dropping off my last rider of the night and Tony called me.

"Well hello stranger." I answered and said.

"Hey, how are you? You busy?" Tony wondered and giggled.

"I just finished my last ride of the night." I stated.

"Oh ok. Where are you?" He asked.

"I'm in D.C. at the moment." I responded.

"I wanted to come over so you could massage my body, it's sore, and for you to lay next to me." He explained.

"Ok Tony. Meet me at my home." I suggested.

"Ok then, see you there." He agreed.

When I pulled up Tony was sitting inside of his black Honda. As I was parking, I looked in my rear-view mirror and Tony was getting out of his car.

"You wore that to work?" He wondered.

"Yes, what's wrong with it?" I asked and giggled.

"It's too tight Andre." He responded.

"Boy hush and give me my damn hug." I demanded.

We both laughed, hugged, and headed to the door.

"Are you hungry or thirsty? My mother cooked today." I stated.

"Yeah please fix me a plate of food. Can I eat it downstairs?" He asked.

"Yes of course you can." I explained.

Tony headed downstairs. I washed my hands, fixed him a plate of food, and something to drink. When I got downstairs Tony was undressed laying across my bed.

"Here you go Tony." I comforted.

Tony sat up and leaned his back against the bed board. I took a pillow from my bed, laid it across his lap, and placed the plate of food on top. We looked at each other and smiled.

"Thank you. I always said that you were a good joint." He gushed.

"I know that." I explained.

I laid across the bed and watched him eat.

"So, tell me Tony. How are you doing? Where have you been hiding?" I wondered.

"I'm still in Anacostia." He said.

"Ok… You said that over the summer Tony. Where at in Anacostia? Like I stated before I won't just show up unannounced. Just in case if I call you and don't get an answer, I would know where to go to see how you were. You know how Jamari, J'Adora, and I feel about you Tony." I declared.

"Andre if something were to happen to me my cousin would notify every person in my phone." Tony said.

"That makes no sense to me. People's numbers change Tony but whatever I guess." I hissed.

"Are you done?" He suggested.

"I am." I stated.

After Tony finished eating, I did what he wanted me to do. I massaged his body and laid next to him until he fell asleep. Tony didn't leave until the following day around noon. Jamari and J'Adora never got the chance to see him. The last time they seen Tony was during the summer, he came over, treated us to lunch at Sonic, and we all went to the park afterwards. I would often call and text Tony however, no reply. On Sunday, April 12th, 2017 leaving Prince's home I had a sensor issue with my iPhone. It wasn't until the following day on April 13th, 2017 I had to get another phone and a new number. I went from an iPhone 6 Plus to a damn iPhone SE. I called and texted Tony to let him know that, and still no reply.

Fast Forward:

Thursday, November 2nd, 2017

"When's the last time you spoke to Tony?" Aaron would often wonder.

Even though Aaron and Tony never officially met in person, Aaron knew Tony meant a lot to me and vice versa. I was on my phone scrolling through old photos on Instagram and I came across a photo: *(May 25th, 2016)* that Tony approved of me uploading, only because I was fully clothed and not revealing too much. As I was reading the comments from my Instagram family I came across Tony's comment: *"You are such a handsome man."* He stated. I clicked on his photo which sent me directly to his page. I was searching to see when the last time he was active. I clicked on the first post and it was dated September 5th, 2017.

"I'm going to fuck you up Tony!" I yelled.

As I kept scrolling, I came across a photo from his favorite photo shoot. I started to smile. Then suddenly my heart dropped as I read the words that was printed on the photo: *"Anthony's Celebration of Life"* My body went numb. I couldn't believe what I was reading. There wasn't a family member or close friend of his that I could reach out to. My mind went back to last November of me telling him that I needed to know where he was just in case. I hated to find out that way. I left a comment under the photo. A family member reached out to me the following day. I called Aaron.

"Guess what?" I said.

"What?" Aaron responded.

"Tony did pass away Aaron." I confirmed.

"Andre nooo!" He cried.

"Yes Aaron, I hated that I found out through social media. I went to his Instagram page." I revealed.

"That's crazy Andre. You kept saying he passed away for the past year and now look. At least he can now rest-in-peace." Aaron comforted.

"That's true Aaron. I remember the first night we talked on the phone, one of his favorite songs were "Just The Lonely Talking Again" by Whitey Houston. I made that the soundtrack to our story together." I said.

We will always love you Tony.

"I should hate you. I want to hate you; however, I could never hate the woman who gave birth to Jamari and J'Adora." - Andre L. Simmons

119: **DIVORCED** *(Plaintiff VS Defendant)*

Flashback:

October 27th, 2014

Prince and I had always showed each other love on Instagram. *"Thank you Pa for the love"* were his first words to me in a DM. I couldn't believe how gorgeous this man was. I will admit I ended up falling for Prince. Even though a romantic relationship wasn't meant to be for us. Not only did I gain a best friend but a brother as well. I love his mother Chantel, father Darryl Sr., and baby brother Darius like my own family. Jamari and J'Adora loves them too, especially J'Adora she was always begging me to go up there, so she and Darius can play together. Prince's favorite color is white, mine's black. He's always on time, and I'm always late, most of the time. We argue like an old married couple. However, the important thing that Prince and I have in common are our love for family and friends. I traveled to New Jersey when he graduated from the police academy on October 7th, 2016.

Jai and I attended 2 mediation sessions together.

September 14th, 2017

Mr. Simmons, your Parenting Plan mediation is confirmed for Friday, September 15th at 10:00AM Location: Key Bridge - 9301 Largo Drive West, Suite 205. Largo, MD 20774 http://www.kbfcenter.org

September 28th, 2017

Mr. Simmons, your Parenting Plan mediation is confirmed for Friday, September 29th at 10:00AM Location: Key Bridge - 9301 Largo Drive West, Suite 205. Largo, MD 20774 http://www.kbfcenter.org

Fast Forward:

Prince traveled to Maryland to support me at my upcoming trail, and of course he came around 9:00AM Sunday, November 5th that morning after pleading with him to come that afternoon so that I could sleep in, since I Ubered earlier that morning.

Monday, November 6th, 2017

Judgement Day

12:00AM

"I've been up for 15 hours and still couldn't fall asleep. 7 more hours and I must wake up Jamari and J'Adora for school. The person who never sleep was knocked out on the other couch. Let me go get in my bed." I thought to myself. I watched episode after episode of Justice League the animated series. I don't know when I had finally dozed off however, the only thing I remember was my alarm going off.

"This can't be real" I said aloud.

My body never felt so heavy. By the time I had reached upstairs, my mother was already up, Jamari and J'Adora were too. I woke Prince up. My eyes were bloodshot red. I grabbed the clippers and proceeded to shave my head. Pressed for time, I hopped in the shower and got ready.

"Bye Daddy." Jamari and J'Adora both said.

My mother dropped Jamari and J'Adora off at school. By the time my mother had arrived back, I was downstairs in the guest bathroom with the door open, just sitting down on the toilet looking at myself in the mirror. With a million thoughts running through my mind.

"Andre are you ok?" My mother wondered.

I didn't say a word but closed the door shut. I felt I was about to burst. Once I got myself together, I had re-opened the door.

"Andre are you ok?" Prince repeated.

My eyes filled with water. As I blinked, the tears started to fall over my cheeks.

"Let it all out. Release it Andre." My mother cried out as she started praying.

After getting myself together again, I was officially ready. My mother mentioned that aunt Janelle and aunt Patricia took off work to support me. I knew aunt Celestine would have been there as well if she didn't have to work. The 2 other people that were missing that I've known would have been by my side were Aaron however, he had class. Diego which I haven't spoken to since I blocked him Saturday, May 27th, Memorial Day weekend.

When my mother, Prince, and I arrived inside the courthouse location, Jai was already there sitting down on the bench. I was surprised that she was the only one there unless her support system was running late. Aunt Patricia later came. Prince and I had walked to the other end of the hallway.

"Pa, J'Adora looks just like her mother." Prince said.

"I told you all that she did." I said and laughed.

"How are you feeling Pa?" He asked.

"Look this day has finally arrived and whatever the outcome is I'm sure it will be for Jamari and J'Adora's best interest." I explained. "You peeped the way she was staring at you when we walked up? She probably thinks you're my new lawyer." I continued.

"Yeah I saw that too." He said.

Jai and I were called to come inside the courtroom. After sitting down inside aunt Janelle walked inside and still no one was there to support Jai. I kind of felt bad for her. Jai and I were called to come forth. The judge asked were our children present and I responded with they're currently in school. Then the judge asked did Jai and I come to an agreement. My mind went back to when she and I had mediation back in September.

"Well we attended 2 emotional but yet therapeutic mediation sessions on September 15th and 29th, 2 hours each. She and I were able to put everything on the table about our past. We look forward to working together in the future when it comes to Jamari and J'Adora. Not only that she and I went trick-or-treating together as a family last Tuesday." I stated.

"That's great to hear. Did you two come to an agreement about the children?" She asked.

"No unfortunately we didn't." I confirmed.

"Ok thank you Mr. Simmons, you two may take your seats." The judge ordered.

A few minutes later the judge announced that our case would be transferred to another room in which she gave us the courtroom number. We all got up and proceeded there. When we entered the courtroom, the atmosphere wasn't like the last one, I was nervous. The judge was an older white man with a head full of white hair and wore eyeglasses. As matter of fact he favored Santa Claus.

As the judge was looking over our case. He had asked me to please stand up to say what I wanted to happen.

"Well your honor basically Ms. Richards and I have already come to agreement except for when it comes to Jamari and J'Adora. I choose that things remain the same as is. I have Jamari and J'Adora 5 days a week plus my additional weekend after every 3 weekends." I stated.

"Thank you, Mr. Simmons you may sit." The judge stated. "Ms. Richards what about yourself?" He then asked her.

"I'm not agreeing to those terms. I want my children living with me full time. I also want my children spending the entire summer with me as well." She suggested.

As Jai was talking, I think I blacked out. All I could hear was my family whispering however, my mother wasn't whispering at one point she was so loud I turned around to tell her to shut the fuck up. In that moment everyone got silent. I knew what I had to do at that point. I wanted to play nice and be fair. I then knew she was acting during those mediation sessions, and that it was all an act when she went trick-or-treating with us as a family. She almost had me.

"Your honor that's not what we discussed." I said.

"Ok here's what we're going to do. I going to give you a note pad to write down exactly what you two want to happen, if you can't come to an agreement, I will make the final decision." He explained.

Jai and I got up and headed to a room, just us two. As we were sitting inside the room my mother left out the courtroom. I knew she was upset; however, she wasn't helping the situation and I promised myself to apologize to her later.

"Now Jai what are you doing?" I asked her.

"I want my children. I deserve them. I'm their mother." She explained.

"Yes, you are their mother. You act like you wasn't going to see them any longer. I preferred keeping things the way it is. I'm not asking for full custody, child support, and passports like you're requesting. You know if we don't come to an agreement just be prepared for the other side of me to show up in the courtroom." I warned.

"I'm ready." She said.

"Let's go." I replied.

We both headed back inside. I purposely held the notepad in a way that when I was walking my family could see that nothing was written on it.

"He wrote nothing on it." I could hear Prince saying.

"Did you two come to an agreement?" The judge asked.

"No, your honor we didn't." I stated.

The judge asked me what type of person and father I was to Jamari and J'Adora. The judge then asked me if I had anyone that would testify on my behalf. The first person that I called was my aunt Janelle, then aunt Patricia, and finally Prince. My mother never returned inside the courtroom. Everyone was fair with their words about my character, no one bashed Jai, even Jai couldn't deny the man I was to my children. Jai had no one testify on her behalf.

Minutes passed away and when the judge read the outcome aloud, I felt a ton of bricks being lifted off my shoulders. Jai wasn't happy with the outcome.

"Why is it that he gets to make the final decisions." Jai wondered.

The judge slowly tilted his head down and looked Jai dead in her face.

"The children have been living with Mr. Simmons for almost 6 years. He has proven to be dedicated and wants what's best for all parties involved." He stated firmly.

My family all got up to leave out the courtroom. As Jai was gathering her belongings, I thought she and I was going to talk however, she just got up and walked out. When I walked out my mother, aunt Janelle, and Prince were all waiting for me. My mother said aunt Patricia had to leave.

"Congratulations son." My mother cried.

"Thank you, mom." I said as I embraced her. "Did Jai say anything to you all?" I wondered.

"Not a word." Prince said.

I walked in the courtroom on November 6ᵗʰ, 2017 as a married man and walked out divorced, newly single by law with primary custody over Jamari Ondrej Simmons and J'Adora Krismas Simmons.

I treated my mother, aunt Janelle, Jamari, J'Adora, and Prince to dinner at Cheedar's in Brandywine, Maryland to celebrate.

IN THE CIRCUIT COURT FOR PRINCE GEORGE'S COUNTY, MARYLAND

Andre Simmons Plaintiff,

Case No:

CADXX-XXXXX

VS,

Jai Richards Defendant,

Case No:

CADXX-XXXXX

JUDGMENT OF ABSOLUTE DIVORCE

This matter, having come before the Court on Plaintiff, Andre Simmons' Complaint for Absolute Divorce, it is hereby this 6th day of November 2017,

ORDERED, in Case No. CADXX-XXXXX, that Plaintiff, Andre Simmons' Complaint for Absolute Divorce from Defendant, Jai Richards is hereby **GRANTED**; is further

ORDERED, in Case No. CADXX-XXXX be dismissed and case is closed statistically; it is further

ORDERED, that Plaintiff, Andre Simmons is granted custody of the parties minor children, Jamari Simmons and J'Adora Simmons, subject to the right of visitation; it is further

ORDERED, in accordance with the parties prior agreement that the Plaintiff will be the primary custodial parent and the defendant, Jai Richards will have visitation three weekends per month, starting Friday at 6:00PM and ending Sunday at 6:00PM. In addition, thereto, the parties will divide the Thanksgiving, Christmas, and Spring Vacations pursuant to the school calendar such that the Thanksgiving holiday in even years will be with the Plaintiff and odd years with the Defendant. The Christmas and Spring Vacation will be divided the first half with the Plaintiff in even years and the first half with the Defendant in odd years. Defendant will be entitled to two weeks summer vacation with both children and will advise Plaintiff which two weeks no later than May 15th of each year. The minor children will spend each Mother's Day with Defendant and each Father's Day with Plaintiff. Each parent will have the minor children on the respective parent's birthday. The children's birthday will be with the Plaintiff in even years and Defendant in odd years; it is further.

ORDERED, that the issue of child support was not raised, and all other property issues were resolved prior this hearing; and it is further

ORDERED, that this case is closed statistically.

C. Philip Nichols, Jr., Judge

Jamari and J'Adora at the State Of The World Tour.
2017.

120: **Janet Jackson** *(State Of The World Tour)*

November 16th, 2017

10 days later after the verdict. The day had finally arrived. Jamari and J'Adora were going to witness Janet Jackson live for themselves. They went to school and I wanted to make as much money as I could Ubering because I knew how much Jamari and J'Adora loved magically getting huge appetites in those type of settings.

The time was getting near. I had to head back home and get ready. I wanted us to catch the metro to downtown Washington D.C. however, I didn't want to be late. It was so important for me that Jamari and J'Adora see the opening of the show, especially J'Adora. She loved Janet's song from her Unbreakable album "Burn It Up" and the lyrics "Whooo, I'ma shut this down Kitty kat, meow, meow, meow, meow, meow…"

My friend Lazain was attending the same show as well. He informed me the show had yet to start, as I was looking for parking, which gave me a sigh of relief. We eventually parked about 3 blocks from the Verizon Center which was now called Capital One Arena. Upon entering the building, I already had my phone unlocked and tickets ready to be scanned.

"Sir can you remove your hat?" An employee requested.

"Sure." As I rolled my eyes.

Talk about the embarrassment. You see I wasn't freshly shaved, and the back and the sides of my head were all growing back in.

"Sir you're going to have to go to the ticket booth so they can print out your tickets." She then stated.

"Why exactly is that? You can clearly see these are the tickets if only you take a look. I've never had to do this before." I snapped.

"New policy and security reasons." She replied.

As annoyed as I was, I totally understood. Soon as we stood in line. The crowd from the inside of the arena went ape shit. I knew what that meant. I had 10 minutes at most to catch Janet performing "Burn It Up" the first two songs were "The Knowledge" and then "State of the World". A quick wardrobe change then the third song "Burn It Up."

"Daddy is the show starting?" J'Adora wondered.

"Yes J'Adora." I answered.

We were next in line and then "Burn It Up" started playing I was officially over the night, even though Jamari and J'Adora was dancing in line. We entered on the fourth song which was "Nasty" our seats weren't the best however; it was a moment that I would never forget because I was sharing the moment with Jamari and J'Adora. Now from a fan perspective I expected more from an artist of Janet's caliber. The stage was so small, production was lack luster, and the screens was no better. If I wasn't mistaken it was the same stage from her Up Close and Personal tour back in 2011. However, Janet was only doing theaters which was totally understandable back then. If this was going to be the future of her shows, that would definitely be my last concert seeing Janet Jackson. Once Janet Jackson closed the show we waited until the arena was about empty and took a couple of pictures and videos. Prince had done J'Adora's hair the day before. He had drove back down from New Jersey after my trail to spend a couple of days with me.

Once we got back to the car I had wanted to talk to Jamari and J'Adora.

"Did you guys really enjoy the show? I do apologize that you all didn't get chance to see the opening of the show." I said.

"Yes, daddy I had fun." J'Adora assured.

"When are we going to see her again daddy?" Jamari wondered.

"Good and I don't know." I chuckled.

"Why you are laughing daddy?" J'Adora asked.

"I know you two are young. I was just disappointed with the show; she was lit during her prime. Like I said I'm just happy that you two finally got chance to see my favorite artist live. My first time seeing her live was with your mother the same year that you were born J'Adora. This is kind of like a full circle moment for me. I'm looking forward to sharing many more moments with you all in the future." I explained.

'When's our next adventure daddy?" Jamari asked.

"Aunt Janelle and the rest of the family are getting a beach house in North Carolina for Christmas. We haven't been down there since the summer of 2014. It should be fun. Plus, I'm finally getting my seafood platter from Calabash and if time permits, I want to see Racquel and I would love to see my friend Richard as well." I declared.

"Daddy going to see his girlfriend Jamari." J'Adora gushed.

"Yes, daddy's friend that's a girl and no school tomorrow since were getting home so late." I insisted.

"Yay!" Jamari and J'Adora shouted.

121: **Doll In The Basement**

Flashback:

Summer of 2017

My cousin Kanika sold items on eBay and over the summer Kanika put my mother onto it as well. My mother had a hard time adjusting, so she would often ask me to assist her. I had to let her know that I didn't mind helping from time to time; however, this wasn't something that I was going to devote all my time to. If my mother wanted to continue, she would have to learn it for herself. Well shortly after that conversation my mother became a pro. My mother and her sisters didn't miss too many Estate Sales and the basement was evident of that because it was slowly becoming her own personal boutique.

Fast Forward:

December 2017

One Sunday back in December my aunts and cousins were over like normal in the living room. I sent Jamari to collect something downstairs in the basement. Time had slipped away, and I had noticed that Jamari had never came back upstairs.

"Jamari?" I yelled.

"Yeah?" He replied.

"Do you see it?" I asked.

"Yeah!" He replied.

"Ok, bring it upstairs!" I demanded.

Another two minutes had passed and still no Jamari.

I walked back to the basement door and walked downstairs and as I reached halfway, I bent my head around the wall, and I could see Jamari standing still.

"Jamari?" I said.

"Yeah?" He responded.

"You ok?" I wondered.

I came down the rest of the steps and wondered what the holdup was. I stood next to him. He still wouldn't move, and he was faced looking forward. I followed his eyes and there it was, a damn doll that my mother had recently brought home. I forgot how afraid of dolls he was. Makah used to have a Chucky doll that Jamari was terrified of too. Plus, he still refused to watch the Chucky franchise. The doll gave me major Annabelle vibes.

"Mom this boy is creeped out over this doll you brought home!" I shouted.

Everyone laughed. I removed the doll from the table. It was funny and at the same time it wasn't. The situation reminded me of a scene from a horror film. Jamari was so dramatic and suddenly I could hear Makah saying, "He get it from his daddy" in the back of my mind.

122: **Misery & Co.**

January 1st, 2018

After just shaving my beard completely off. I felt so
exposed, venerable, and only came out when I absolutely
had to. I was waiting for Jamari and J'Adora at the usual
pick up spot, the police station. Jai wasn't normally late
meeting me unless she was plotting, and neither was I when
it came to me picking Jamari and J'Adora up from
Baltimore. With each passing minute seeming to be like
hours. I knew something was up. 6:07PM car lights could
be seen turning in. I was looking down at my phone as a
car pulled into the parking space, two over from mine. The
left passenger door opened up and the driver's door did as
well. Jamari and J'Adora walked towards my car and
another person as well whom I thought was Jai. I looked up
finally only to see who it was and unlocked my door for
Jamari and J'Adora. It was Jai's sister Ava with papers in
her hand knocking on my window.

"Hi Andre. I have something to give you." She explained.

"Jamari and J'Adora please get in and close my door." I
demanded.

"Andre, I have something to give you." She continued.

Once Jamari and J'Adora were in. I put my car in drive and
drove away. "It hasn't been 60 days yet and here Jai goes
again with the same shit in a New Year." I thought. I
looked in my rearview mirror I could see Ava still standing

up outside with the papers in her hand, the further I drove away the image of Ava became smaller and smaller.

January 29th. *2018.*

123: **Mind-Game**

Going into the New Year being officially divorced and single by law, I was hoping and praying that my life would take me in a new direction. I was ready to reveal my truth to my son and daughter, even though friends had always said that they knew that I was gay, it was still nothing like a confirmation from the horse's mouth.

People wondered why I decided to cut Sheba aka The Beard, truth is I just wanted change in my life. I was so attached to the beard, it was the new makeup for me, a new way for me to hide.

I wasn't aware of mental awareness/illness existed until I joined social media. In my family if you felt depressed, they would say "You're not depressed. Fight that demon." So that's what I had to do. The demon and I had been battling it out for almost 20 years. Between Jamari's illness, court, and my personal life, I felt like I was losing control. "Andre is everything ok?" My reply would always be "Yes I am." Truth was I was screaming on the inside. I was extremely irate, mean, and deeply sadden. I wanted to go seek help however, I didn't want to lose my children in the process. I still couldn't believe that I didn't abuse drugs and alcohol to escape from my reality during that period in my life. That was the main reason I had always been a social drinker. I didn't trust myself enough to drink by myself and be left with my thoughts. Throughout my many struggles, I've always wanted to help other people deal with their own issues. I felt like I was strong enough to bare everyone else's burdens along with my own.

I was alone, and I didn't feel lonely. All the tears that I had cried only lets me know that I was still alive, and a new day would always come tomorrow. The spiritual journey towards my healing, inner peace, and selflove was beginning to feel fantastic.

124: **S N O W** *(7 Years Later)*

February 5th, 2018

10:32PM

An individual by the name of @Goatfck left a comment under my photo that I had uploaded on Instagram January 29th, 2018.

"Figure out how to message me before I delete this."

The person then left another comment.

"Ummmm bite me."

I immediately went to the person's account. They had 0 post. 0 followers, and they were only following me. In their bio two words written in it that read; *"Officer Snow"* in that moment I knew the person knew me or either read **'Butterflies Hitting Home Runs'**, or both. Could it be Diego no way could this be Officer Snow from my old job, this man is anti-social media. I screenshotted everything and DMed Racquel. Her response was "No way." My thoughts exactly. Racquel encouraged me to find out who it was. I decided to DM the person.

10:41PM

"How can I help you?" I DMed.

"Long time my friend. I'm glad you're doing well." The person DMed.

"Ok who are you?" I DMed.

"Bite me." They DMed.

"Ok, I'm about to block you." I DMed.

"Strader, ass-wipe." Snow finally DMed.

"You're lying." I DMed.

"I don't lie. Dead serious. Officer OB called me a while back and told me you wrote a book. Haven't read it yet but I'm truly happy for you." He DMed.

"Interesting. I don't know what to say." I DMed.

"It's all gravy. That was a dark time. I know why you did what you did... I'm sorry I didn't see it that way. I'm sorry I treated you the way I did. Now fuck off." He DMed.

"I busted out laughing. You're still the same." I DMed.

"I have my moments. I'll buy you lunch in Crystal City one day." He DMed.

"Are you setting me up?" I DMed.

"Ummmm. Na. 202-XXX-XXX. I'm deleting this shit cock-breath." He DMed.

He deleted his page right afterwards. I texted after about an hour later. We talked on the phone for hours. I met up with him in Crystal City, Virginia that following Saturday and it was just like old times however, I didn't do cocaine, oh yeah Snow was happy that I had cut off my beard he told me to never grow that shit out that long ever again, and of course he wasn't going to get what he wanted.

125: Liar Liar B-More On Fire

Friday, February 16th, 2018

4:09PM

"I'm on my way to get the kids." Jai iMessaged.

That was Jai's first time ever being early to pick Jamari and J'Adora up. I didn't mind due to the fact she was the one picking them up and I knew how traffic can become commuting from Baltimore. I told Jamari and J'Adora that their mother was on the way.

"Daddy it's not 6:00PM. Court said 6:00PM." Jamari stated.

"I understand that and you're 100% correct, however how many times have your mother been on time picking you all up?" I asked.

"She's never on time daddy." He confirmed.

"Exactly, well today she is, so get ready." I explained.

I went upstairs to use the bathroom.

4:31PM

"Outside." Jai iMessaged.

4:32PM

"It's not 6:00PM but ok." I iMessaged.

"Jamari and J'Adora she's outside. I'll see yall on Sunday."
I yelled from the bathroom.

I heard the front door open. J'Adora told me bye before
closing the front door. I wrapped the towel around my body
and headed to the window and I saw J'Adora walking to
the van. The van parked away from my home, 3 houses
down, and faced in a way that I couldn't see who was
driving. There were 3 available parking spaces for Jai to
park in. "Damn she got issues." I thought. About a minute
later Jamari had left out.

"Bye daddy." Jamari yelled.

"Bye Jamari." I replied.

I went back inside the bathroom. Before I could even sit on
the toilet, I heard the front door open.

"Daddy! Daddy! That's not mommy, that's Zazu!" He
yelled.

"Jamari is J'Adora with you?!" I asked.

"No! She's still in the van." He replied.

"Jamari go get J'Adora!" I shouted.

That lying ass girl. Jai cannot be trusted, and she knew
good and damn well that man can't pick Jamari and
J'Adora up by himself. She says she wants her kids;
however, her actions never match up. Immediately I called
her phone the hell with iMessaging her. The phone rung
and rung. Of course, she didn't answer. She knew better.

Jamari returned with J'Adora. I addressed the situation with Jamari and J'Adora.

"Jamari I'm so proud of you for doing what was right. Not only did you protect your sister, you stood up to Zazu. No matter what your mother says, you were right in your actions." I confided in him.

"Thank you, daddy." He gushed.

I phoned my mother to let her know what had just transpired. Jai never returned my call. I didn't leave out for work until my mother was home. I told my mother do not let Jamari and J'Adora out the house until she seen Jai for herself. I'm sure she was coming down herself to collect them. My mother agreed.

8:33PM

"I'm on the way to get the kids." Jai iMessaged.

I called my mother to let her know that Jai was on her way.

8:47PM

"I'm outside." Jai iMessaged.

My mother called me to let me know that Jai did come herself. I wasn't relieved. I was frustrated. I was pissed. I couldn't help but think it was only a matter of time before she and I ended up in court yet again and this time I wasn't going to play with her ass.

Sunday, February 18th, 2018

3:29PM

"I'm in the area. I can drop the kids off." Jai iMessaged.

Oh, she's down here? Maybe her mother and father had a Superbowl party or something. I called my mother to make sure that she was home because I was out Ubering. By the time I had arrived home. Jamari had revealed to me that Zazu didn't want him staying in Baltimore since he refused to get in the van and that his mother was mad at him for refusing to do so as well.

"Jamari how do you feel about that?" I asked.

"Daddy I didn't care, I had fun staying with my other grandmother." He revealed.

My thing is this, as a blended family I would've respected Zazu more if he would have talked to Jamari like a man instead of having a bitch fit just because things didn't go the way that him and Jai had hoped for. I'm Jamari and J'Adora's father and like I said time and time again I will do anything and everything in my power to always and forever to protect them. It had saddened me though that Jai allowed Jamari to stay with his other grandmother and not J'Adora. The only other time Jamari and J'Adora were separated was due to Jamari being hospitalized not due to a grown ass boy being in his feelings. Just sad honestly.

126: Their Mother's Cry

Wednesday, April 4th, 2018

9:59AM

"Jamari got his Infusion today. I can drop him off when I get out the hospital." Jai iMessaged.

"What time will that be?" I iMessaged.

"1:30PM." Jai iMessaged.

Hallelujah!

I didn't have to make that drive up there. Not only that she took it upon herself to take Jamari to get his Remicade Infusion early. "My ex-wife is showing out I see." I thought to myself. The last time she took Jamari to his Remicade appointment was August of last year however, something was up. Around 1:00PM I had got myself together since they would be on their way soon.

1:47PM

My phone rung and it was Jai's mother.

"Hello." I answered.

"Hello Andre, are you home?" She asked.

"Yes I am." I responded.

"Ok, I'm about to drop the kids off." She said.

"Ok. I will be here." I responded.

"Why did Jai tell me that she was going to drop them off
and now her mother is? So, her mother is in Baltimore on a
Wednesday? Again, like initially thought something is off."
I had thought to myself. I had gone downstairs to unlock
the door for them and went back upstairs into my
bathroom. A few minutes had passed, and I could hear the
door open.

"Daddy?!" Jamari shouted.

"Yeah?!" I responded.

"You're not going to believe this. Mommy and Zazu broke
up." He stated as he was walking up the steps.

"Oh yeah?" I responded.

I wasn't completely sold if this was the truth or not. I was
careful not to show any excitement or joy because after all
Jai was still Jamari and J'Adora's mother. He began to tell
his story to back up his claim.

"So, on Saturday I was asleep, so I didn't hear anything.
J'Adora and Zazu's daughter heard everything. Mommy
and Zazu was downstairs arguing. They heard all this
moving and yelling. Mommy was crying and had a mark on
her face. Mommy called the cops. Zazu left before the cops
got there. Me, J'Adora, and our baby brother *(Zazu's son
by him and Jai)* went to go stay at aunt Ava's." He
explained.

"Wow! Are you and J'Adora ok?" I questioned.

"Yeah daddy I'm fine." Jamari assured.

"Yes daddy." J'Adora said as she quoted the exact same story.

"I didn't receive a call from your mother about this incident." I said. "Why did she iMessage me saying she was at the hospital today then?" I continued.

"Our baby brother *(Zazu's son by him and Jai)* was having breathing problems, that's why mommy had me get my Remicade Infusion while we were at the hospital. Mommy called grandma and grandpa today. Grandma also said mommy is never getting back with Zazu again. I told you daddy I was telling the truth about him." Jamari stated.

"Jamari, I stood by your side. I've always and forever will have your back. Reason being why I go so hard for you and your sister, especially after what you said about him back in March of 2016. No matter what happens in the future because I can't predict it. Always remember to tell the truth. No matter who gets upset. One question though, did your mother ever go back to his house after yall left there Saturday night?" I wondered.

"No daddy we've been at aunt Ava's the whole time. Mommy said we're getting our own house next year. Mommy also said Jamari don't hit girls when you get older." He explained.

What a sigh of relief. *"The Real Man"* that she painted him out to be wasn't so perfect anymore. Now her family knew the truth about him, and I hoped they knew that their daughter was covering up for him as well. I wasn't never expecting for Jai to call me. She's been the type to keep things from me in regards of our children. However, God had always found of way of bringing the things that needed to be exposed to the light. Was this the end of them as a couple, only time would tell. Again, I only wanted what was best for her. A man to come in her life and love her in ways that I struggled to, and most importantly accept our two children. May God bless them both.

Animal Kingdom. Tree of Life. *May 4th, 2018.*

127: **Disney World**

Flashback:

Getting to know guys that lived in different states I was always greeted with the same ole lines:

"Andre, I wished you lived closer."

"You have too many fans."

"Everybody wants Andre."

Like how are you truly interested in me if those were the excuses not to take it any further? At that point in my life I was truly optimistic about whatever or whoever God had in store for me and my children. When I reflect on the men of my past, I was truly grateful for all the experiences from the good, to the great, to the spectacular memorable moments, even to the guys that wasn't worth mentioning.

I had known Bo for a few years, and I had connected with him through Instagram. Bo was tall and dark skinned. He had the best smile and pair of teeth that I had ever came across. He worked in the dental field. Bo's passion was cooking and he hopeful to one day run the food industry world. He did show an interest in me at one point however, he ended up in a relationship with someone who at the time he claimed was the love of his life. For me not to have met him in person Bo always had a genuine love for Jamari and J'Adora.

Bo started messaging me more and more throughout the first quarter of 2018 on Facebook messenger. Of course, I had to give him a hard time about what happened to the love of his life and everything. I was no longer taking on anyone's words if their actions weren't adding up. I made it clear to everyone that I would rather be left alone, and we could remain just friends. Well Bo then offered to treat the kids and myself to Walt Disney World in Orlando, Florida to prove he was truly interested. I didn't take him seriously; however, he was dead ass serious. I couldn't believe it. This was something that I've always dreamt of doing with Jai. This was on the top of my bucket list as a family taking my children to Walt Disney World. I wanted to do for them what my mother did for me 21 years ago. I asked him what he wanted in return due to how much the tickets were. I knew from my past dealing with people everything eventually came with a price. He assured me that he wanted to bless me and the children with this. I did let him know that I would be responsible getting the three of us down to Florida. No, he didn't like the idea of us driving however, I love to drive, and it was a way to bond with Jamari and J'Adora. I started working a little bit harder due to the trip was happening in about 6 weeks.

Fast Forward:

I didn't tell Jamari and J'Adora about the trip until the day that we were driving to Florida which I captured the moment on video, and it was hilarious. Only my mother, Aaron, and Prince knew about the trip.

When I first laid eyes on Bo in person I immediately thought to myself what a manly man he was. Bo had purchased tickets for us to attend all 4 parks: Epcot, Magic Kingdom, Hollywood Studios, and Animal Kingdom however, we only made it to 3. Two of my favorite moments at Disney World were the 4 of us, all on the DINOSAUR ride at Animal Kingdom. Splash Mountain at

Magic Kingdom and seeing the fireworks as we were going down the slide, was such a magical moment. Prince said that we would need more than one day, and boy was he right.

I loved spending time with Bo and the trip was over in the blink of an eye. He didn't want us to leave however, we had to get back to Maryland. I packed up the car and left the car running while the kids were inside. I ran back in the house and closed the door behind me and gave Bo a kiss on the lips and he kissed me back.

"Thank you, Bo, for everything. I owe you. I have to be quick before J'Adora follow me in here." I explained and laughed.

"Thank you, Andre. This was one of the greatest weekends of my life." He confirmed.

"I'll call you once I get further down the road." I stated.

I kissed him once again and said goodbye. I turned around and looked at him once more before I walked back out the door.

128: **Forgiveness**

May 15th, 2018

April 2017, I had decided to make another Facebook account as another way to connect with people and hopefully gain some potential new readers. I pretty much took photos from Instagram and uploaded them to my Facebook page. However, I made a video to let everyone know that it was my page. Facebook lets people know when you're online, which I'm not the biggest fan of because my Messenger be lit. I feel like I have to respond back to everyone. Being ignored doesn't feel good and I didn't want people to think that I was too good to respond. Sometimes it was too much, and I would remove the app from my iPhone. That was until I told by Prince to go check my messages on Messenger. I stumbled upon the side of my messages where people weren't my Facebook friend. As I was going through the messages, I seen a very familiar face it was Jai. What on good mother earth could she have to say to me that she couldn't have iMessaged? I'm not going to lie I was nervous.

9:06PM

"Sorry I hurt you."

Those were her words which was sent on May 1st, 9:54PM. I just kept re-reading those 4 words repeatedly. I wanted to respond back however; I didn't know what to say. I wanted to be her friend and I believed that we were going to be however, after the stunt she pulled in the courtroom I gave up, not to mentioned what transpired between she and Zazu back in April. I knew it was going to be just a matter of time before she went running back.

I kept scrolling down. A few people I did recognize and then suddenly, I had got chills when I saw the photo of him with his dog. I was scare to open his message. A few minutes later I did. It was a missed video chat from him on February 3rd, 2018 at 9:18PM. I replayed the voicemail.

"What's going on Mr. Simmons? Happy New Year uhm, I called the babies' phone I guess they don't have their phone no more. Some dude answered I don't know uhm, but yeah I just wanted to talk to them see how everyone was doing... stuff like that."

He sound the same. I was torn about calling him. I wanted to tell Jamari and J'Adora and then again, I didn't. They both loved Makah and I did too. At the end of the day I wanted to try and build a future with him however, he wasn't ready for a relationship, according to him. So, it left me believing I wasn't enough or the right man for him. To be brutally honest, I was plagued with so much doubt because I just knew if we connected again those feelings would return. I told myself if he reached back out again, I would respond.

My mother in her late 20s.

129: **Queen Butterfly**

Friday, June 1st, 2018

If I were able to speak back then I would have told you,

"Don't you worry your pretty little self-lady. I'm here now, and you will never be alone again. I will always be by your side. You've got me, and I've got you."

If those were my first words, I believe that would have freaked you out. I know you've had many sleepless nights because of me, especially when I would kick while I was inside your belly. I'm sorry about that Queen. We've had had quite a journey, together haven't we? The best part is that it only keeps getting better. I'm going to take you down memory lane… Do you remember cleaning up on Friday nights, to wake up early Saturday mornings when you, aunt Janelle, Kendrell, Gregory and I would go to yard sales and the flea market? If it was a pay week, we would wind up at Golden Corral. Those were the days. I'll never forget the drive to North Carolina that we would all take together to go to grandmothers. That's still the best drive in the world. I still get butterflies to this very day. I remember the time when you and aunt Janelle left Kendrell, Gregory, and I at home while you two attended a Prime America meeting.

"No running in the house while we're gone." You stated.

When three boys are home alone by themselves trouble awaits them. I can't remember what game it was that we were playing but it required running. We were running around in circles in our home. The kitchen, living room, and the hallway all connected. As we were running, I hit my left baby toe on the bottom corner of the wall exiting the kitchen. I fell straight to the floor, but I quickly got back up to continue running. I knew something wasn't right. Something was terribly wrong. I was in so much pain; it hurt like hell. I couldn't even walk on my foot. Suddenly I went into panic mode. Instantly something became more important than the pain itself. I was terrified. My mind reverted back to what you said to us before leaving the house. I started thinking about how I was going to explain this incident to you. Later that evening when you and aunt Janelle came back, I was sitting down. I began telling you how I accidentally hit my baby toe and that it hurt.

"Were you running?" You wondered.

"No mom, I wasn't running." I replied.

"Well Andre, you're going to school tomorrow." You continued.

I don't remember falling asleep that night; and I don't remember taking a shower or bath that following morning either. Queen, you gave me a ride to school the next morning and when I got out of the car, I hopped onto the side walk. I continued hopping to my class. While I was sitting in that classroom, I felt it was the happiest time ever. I was such a little jokester back then. None of my classmates believed me when I told them that I hurt my baby toe; not even Ms. Walker. Every time I attempted to walk on my foot, I couldn't. On my way to lunch a classmate tried to race me to the cafeteria. The moment I placed my foot down and put pressure on it, I fell to the ground and began crying. The next thing I knew, I was being carried to the main office by a coach and they notified you of everything that happened. I was later picked up by you and taken to Andrew's Air Force base where we were told that I had broken my baby toe. Queen, do you remember the time when we were living in Trinidad and you enrolled me in swimming lessons? I was the only fat black kid, and I didn't feel comfortable enough to take my shirt off. I felt shamed, and I didn't want to go to the other end of the pool with the other kids.

"Andre you get down there." You said through clenched teeth, careful not to speak too loudly so other people wouldn't hear you.

I just stood in the pool and cried shaking my head. I refused to do so. It made me feel uneasy. I wasn't used to that type of environment. That was one of the worse days of my life at that time. Queen, I remember our trip to Barbados and we stayed at a friend's house. That was a big mistake, because the next morning we woke up to monkeys in the driveway. I knew I was afraid, and I think you were too. I don't know about you, but I was happy to return to Trinidad from that horrible vacation. Queen, I remember you giving away cars before Oprah Winfrey ever did. You gave your car to a married couple with children in Trinidad at Jesus Is The Answer *(J.I.T.A.)*. I remember everyone crying and clapping for their blessing. I was extremely proud of what you did, and the way you were able to bless that family. The best week of my life had to be in 1997, when you took me and Ambassador Donnelly's son Brian to Epcot, Magic Kingdom, SeaWorld, and Universal

Studios. That was best spring break I've ever had. I can't wait to experience that with Jamari and J'Adora. I want them to experience the same type of excitement and enjoyment I had when you took me. I'll never forget that moment because you fulfilled my ultimate childhood dream. I never thought it was possible; however, you made it happen. How about the time you enrolled me in Shotokan Karate; and the dojo was right behind The International School of Port-of-Spain. You were at every test and match I had cheering me on. It was unfortunate and too damn bad when they relocated to The Falls at West Mall; those bastards got money hungry and I was forced to leave. Thank God I at least made it to brown belt. Do you remember when you and I use to play hide-and-seek in Trinidad with Georgette and Materra? Oh man, it was just priceless to see your face light up like you were a kid again.

Then when we moved back to Maryland, we included the family, and had them playing as well. Those were some of the best times of my life. It warmed my heart to see you smile and laugh. I was 16 years old and you knew I wanted to work. However, I wasn't out looking or filling out any job applications. You made it possible for me to get the job at Shoppers. I want you to know that you are the reason I started working there; because I remember receiving a phone call from Ms. Kathy. I got the job and began working around Memorial Day weekend in the year of 2000. Do you remember that time we were coming from Andrews Air Force Base and I had an attitude about something, and I didn't feel like hearing what you had to say? You only tried to make me smile; however, I was too

busy being in my own funk. In that moment Shirley
Caesar's song, "No Charge" started playing on the radio.
That was my first time ever hearing that song. Sitting there
listening, it felt like God was telling me something. To this
day you and I always laugh about that moment. The most
unforgettable time was the night you made me feel like a
prince. You rented out a limousine for me, so I could take
Jai to the prom. I originally didn't want to go because I was
unsure if I would have a prom date. Besides, I was sick that
night with a cold and I wasn't feeling well. Once I saw how
everything was coming to together, I quickly changed my
mind. I will always cherish that moment. God only knows
what you had to do to make all of that happen for me.
Thank you because you made it possible for not only me,
but for Jai too. To this day I still don't know how I
graduated high school. I hardly remember being there. I
spent more days at home in bed than I did attending school.
I've realized that I have always had God and a praying
mother in my corner. Therefore, nothing was impossible.
No matter the situation or the circumstance I always felt
secure, and I knew my needs and wants would be met with
the help of you and God.

When I was 19 years old, I recall you purchasing a pearl
colored 1993 E300 Lexus. My ungrateful ass didn't want it;
however, when you brought it home, I was determined to
get my driver's license. I was so spoiled back then. I
literally see how spoiled I was. It reminds me of the way
you never missed a year to write me a birthday letter. No
matter if we were living under the same roof or if were
continents away. I could always count on you to write me a
heartfelt letter, full of encouraging, reassuring words. You

would always let me know how proud of me you were. That always gave me the strength and the desire to keep pushing and to never give up.

Queen, I admire the fact that you never forgot where you came from; and you didn't let your past define the woman that you are today. Even though you didn't have a strong support system; you never played the victim, never pointed the finger, and you never gave up on your dreams. Queen, you have endured discrimination, racism, and being teased about your weight as a little girl. You know what it's like for a mother to show favoritism to your elder sister. Queen you didn't break, even upon hearing that your classmates never knew you two were sisters when she won best dressed in high school. You stood your ground and kept going. You may not have had a mother/daughter bond with my grandmother, but you were there by her side until the end. I have learned by studying you that a person's childhood experiences can make or break them. It's up to the person to make his/her choice.

"I'm your mother not your friend." You explained.

That six-word sentence used to hurt, but I later grew to understand what you meant by it when I became a dad. I'm almost 35 years old and you're still the first person I run to whenever I'm having a problem. You are the number 1 person that I can always count on. I couldn't replace you even if I tried. Queen you're more than a fearless woman. Queen you're more than my hero. You're more than my best friend. Queen you're my life. I can't thank God enough for choosing me to be a part of your world. No woman in this world holds a candle to you. Queen you're the Blueprint of what a woman should be. I loved you then, I love you now, and I will love you forever. You have been my cocoon for 34 years, 6 months, and 2 days which has given me a great platform to spread my wings and fly.

130: LEGACY: Dear Jamari & J'Adora

Friday, June 1st, 2018

Daddy can't promise you two that life is going to be a walk in the park, because it isn't going to be. Daddy can't cry your tears. Daddy can't fight your battles. Daddy can't take your footsteps for you two, if I could I would. You two have your own journey called life to experience. Daddy can promise you two this though; if you two believe and trust in God you two will be more than ok.

Do you two remember when I would sing the lyrics to Whitney Houston's song "Until You Come Back" every morning while getting you two dressed for school? Jamari you would ask me, "Who have your heart daddy?" I didn't know the answer back then to be quite honest. J'Adora would sing that song all throughout our home so many days and nights by yourself. Daddy finally realized that Jamari you have one half of my heart and J'Adora you have the other. Together you two complete me. You two are my purpose in life. I'm inspired by the both of you. You two taught me how to love unconditionally. Daddy just wants you both to be happy. I'm never walking away from you two no matter how challenging things may and will become. I will never stop fighting for you two. Jamari and J'Adora, even though your mother and I aren't together, that doesn't make neither one of us less of a parent to the both of you. No matter what happens your mother will always be your mother, and I will always be your father. Without her you two wouldn't exist, for that, I am eternally grateful.

Jamari you are my first born. I see so much of myself inside of you, reason being why I'm a little hard on you. Even though you are my son, I have learned a lot from you which pushes me to become a better man and father. You're giving, compassionate, and sensitive. Jamari it's ok for boys to be sensitive, no matter what society says about black men. Jamari you shy away from conflict but will hold your own when needed be. Like the time you stood up against the person you feared the most. I was so proud of my soldier that day protecting your little sister. Jamari my DNA runs through your veins and you're made from greatness. I love you forever and daddy will always have your back.

J'Adora you're my guardian angel and my kindred spirit. You love your daddy and will go to the end of the world to protect me. J'Adora you're one determined, special little girl, whom doesn't give up until you get what you want. For example, if I'm down you're not content until my frown is turned upside down, with your story telling. J'Adora you challenge me for the better. I'm a work in progress; however, I can work on being more affectionate, gentler, and more understanding when it comes to you. J'Adora you are my Leonardo Da Vinci. I love you and I will forever hold your hand, my Black Cover Girl.

Thank You. I Love You.

To my mother Joyce Simmons. To my son Jamari Ondrej Simmons. To my daughter J'Adora Krismas Simmons. To my aunts; Patricia Robinson, Dollie Gardner *(Rest-in-Heaven)*, Iris Simmons, Celestine Simmons, Janelle Simmons, and Julieta Simmons. To my uncles; Allan Simmons, Vonice Simmons, and Clarence Vereen. To my cousins; Kendrell Simmons, Gregory Simmons, Delvin Campbell, Kanika Simmons, Audrekia Simmons, Djuan Riggins, Dayvon Riggins, Ayana Allen, Amaya Ruth Simmons, Tamara Gardner, Keara Mcmillan, Tameka Robinson and LaRhonda Simmons Black *(Author)*. To my childhood friends that I attended school with at The International School, in Port-of-Spain of Trinidad and Tobago *(1994 - 1999)*; Arthur Baitz, Brandon Jamison, Callie Martin, Kelly Zollner, Chuck Rogers, and Materra Drafts. To Debbie Jacob an English teacher that taught at The International School, in Port-of-Spain of Trinidad and Tobago for believing in me many years ago and encouraging me to write. To my friends that I worked and connected with at Shoppers Food located in Largo, Maryland *(2000 - 2005)*; Yvonne Wilson, India Taylor, Torrence Miller, and Anthony Bivins. To my friend that I worked and connected with at Walter Reed Army Medical Center that was in NW, Washington D.C. *(2007 - 2012)*, Officer Tracie Tyler and Elvis Vasquez. To my friends that I met and connected with through social media Twitter @TheDimplePuppet *(2011 - 2015)*, Instagram @AndreTheAuthor *(2013 - Present)*, Facebook @AndreSimmons *(2017 - Present)*; Aaron Patterson *(Best friend)*, Le'Trell Oliver, Racquel Harris *(Singer and Dancer)*, Megan Ambers *(Blogger)*, Kevin Bradford, Kevin

Marshall, Anthony Peaks *(Rest-in-Heaven)*, Derrick
Thomas, I love you *(Special friend and Chef Diego)*, Iman
Moore, El Alexander Sr. *(Artist)*, Shana Greenwald,
Ronnie Groomes, Kemin Richardson *(Photographer)*,
Aubrey Lenyard, Steve S. Russ, Aly D. Williams II, Mark
O. Estes, Richard Johnson, Daniel Ottica, Raymond
Jahmel, DeMonte aka OhBoi, Timothy Simpson, Donnie
Don'vond, Kellz Mirrage, Joseph D. Barnwell Jr., Raphael
C., Mattixz Hastings *(Author)*, Jerry Weakly, Brandon
Hall, Michael T. Terrell Jr., Navi Wendell, Steven
Mitchell, Brendan Williams, Bernard Baker, Michael
Austin, William B., Marie Johnson, Creative Poetic Style,
Vanessa B. Jackson *(Author)*, Joseph D. Barnwell Jr.,
Sharp Mokeki, El-Rah, Quron Hicks, Walter H. Jones Jr.,
Enoch K. Taylor, Christopher Allen, Mike Hair Guru
(Hairstylist), Shavian Martin *(Makeup Artist)*, Kaiya Clark,
Justice Delore, Josh Blake, Oscar Thomas, Charles Allen
(Chef), Raymond Lynn, Richard Johnson, Jimmy Jermaine
Ford, Brandon Lloyd, DeAngelo Marquis, J. R. Mack
(Author), Marcus J. King *(Author)*, Michael G. Riggins
(Author), Brandon Uzzle, Chad Morris, Daniel Holsey,
Terry Allen, Maurice Wright, Gregory Hunter, Richard
Brown, Todd Hammond *(My friend from Australia)*, Julian
Jackson, Daon Drisdom *(Singer)*, Anthony David, Greg
Schroeder *(Designer)*, Tony Bennett, Jamal Talley aka
Chef Talley *(Chef)*, McKenzie Moraven, Marlin Colyer Jr.,
Jivon Savoy, Brandon Shaw, Damian-Michael Williams,
Dom Dom, Tony Pippen, Complex Commodity
(Musician), Kristen Thomas, Justin Haynes, Sergio of Las
Vegas, Devonne Jadarius Vaughn *(Hairstylist)*, Dwayne
Davis, Jeff Monroe, Terrell Willis, Mar C. Williamson,
Daniel Navarro, Bryon Johnson, Roy Cummings, Willie L.
Golden, Jobe Jackson, Keith A. Simpson, Drew Deelyte,

Karlos Green, JerWayne Gunn *(Artist)*, Juice Sauvage, Maurice James, Maurice Laster *(Activist and Designer)*, Sebastian Wellons, Curly June, Andrae Brown, Jacob Steffen *(CNA)*, Jonathan Rogers, Darrius Brunson *(Hairstylist)*, Derek Terry *(Author)*, Louis Gaines, Roy Catlin, Donte Smith, Tavorres De'Shon Eskew, Lariq Hardy, Carlton Wesley, Devin Benjamin, Anwar Walker, G'Mario Charleston, Tyrell Presbury *(Hairstylist)*, Dawyane James *(Artist)*, Bovell Crews II *(Chef)*. To Paula John for assisting me with my children *(January 1st, 2012 - July 28th, 2013)*, thank you for everything that you've done for us when we needed you. Special thank you to J'Adora's hairstylist; Ashely. To my brother Adron Massey. To my sister Lyndyann Garcia. I can't wait to meet you in person Shannon Derby #TeamDerby. My 2nd family the Howards; Darryl Howard II *(Best friend)*, Chantel Howard *(2nd Mom)*, Darryl Howard, and Darius Howard. To Pastor Margret Lee of Trinidad and Tobago. To Pastor Tyson Rowe. To my late grandparents; my grandmother Katie Ruth Simmons and my grandfather James Simmons. To my number one favorite music artist Janet Jackson. To Winston Herbert for treating me like your own son and for making my mother feel beautiful on the inside and out. To wrap things up to Mr. Makah Beaty *(Chef)* I love you; Jamari loves you, and J'Adora loves you.